Farmhand to Chief Constable

by

Alexander A Rennie

Bound Biographies

Probationary Constable 967

Produced in association with

Bound Biographies

Heyford Park House, Heyford Park, Bicester, OX25 5HD

www.boundbiographies.com

ISBN: 978-1-905178-30-8

Foreword

Quite frequently we are invited 'To Take a Walk Down Memory Lane.' The ensuing article usually restricts itself to a particular theme, but in this case the author has produced a slice of social history, some war memoirs, thrills, mystery and perhaps daring-do.

When a man or woman writes from the heart and uses sincerity as a prime method of communication, the result is often striking and compelling. Such is the case in this book.

There is something in the book for everyone, and I therefore invite the reader to sit back in a comfortable armchair with their favourite slippers and enjoy this compelling, interesting piece of history. Students starting out in life, and those wishing to enhance their management and leadership skills, will benefit from the way Alex Rennie, the author, explains how he dealt with varied tricky situations. He left school, and home in North-East Scotland, at 14 years of age and progressed from working in the fields of Aberdeenshire to become Chief Constable of West Mercia Constabulary in England. This via War Service with the RAF, the USA Armed Forces and a Commission in the Army with the Northumberland Regiment, along the way being hand-picked for a Security Assignment by W.S. Churchill.

Barrie Florentine OBE, OStJ, QPM

Acknowledgements

I am most grateful to the many kind people, far too many to mention by name, who encouraged me to start writing and who helped in other ways. But without the positive and time-consuming work by Claire Arnold, my granddaughter, and Barbara Owen, a good friend, there would have been no book. Their husbands Philip and Derek also deserve special thanks for their forebearance.

Contents

Introduction 11
The Aberdonian Spirit 13
The Formative School Years 19
Working on a Scottish Farm 25
An Offer of Employment 37
Training to be a Policeman 45
The Rookie Probationer 51
A Declaration of Intent and War-time Policing 65
Policing the War 71
Policeman to Pilot 77
A Bump to Earth in a Khaki Suit 91
On Active Service 101
Back to the Beat 117
Promotion to Sergeant 131
Promoted Inspector 147
A Tough Assignment 161
College Life 181
Returning to Durham County 187
A Move to Shropshire 201
The Amalgamation Annoucement 211

Called to the Police College 215
Assistant Chief Constable, West Mercia 223
Attack on Building Workers 227
Appointed Chief Constable 233
A Crime of the Century 239
Increasing the Strength 245
Getting Out and About 253
Keeping the Peace 257
A Family Force 263
Preparation for Retirement 267
What Next? 273
Appendix - Family Album 277

Introduction

My family and friends have from time to time asked me to write an account of my life and career. Until recently I have been reluctant to do so as I thought it of little interest to third parties and over-indulgent to assume that it serves a wider purpose. However, in my ninetieth year and regarded as head of the tribe, which includes at the time of writing eleven great-grandchildren, I have been persuaded of their genuine interest in my story. This now being told is solely from memory so lapses and inaccuracies may be expected, which I trust will be forgiven.

During my lifetime, which I have found most rewarding, there have been good times and bad times, difficulties to be overcome and temptations to be brushed aside. My parents were good parents, very strict and hard-working. They did their best to instil in me high standards of honesty and integrity, not always appreciated at the time but much valued in later life.

Another reason was that I was alone after my wife's illness and needed a challenge to sustain me. Surprisingly the writing has been enjoyable and therapeutic, and I feel that others in a similar situation may well benefit from such a course.

The Aberdonian Spirit

I was born on 13th June 1917, at Goval Cottages, Parkhill, Aberdeenshire, not far from Dyce, now a busy airport. The row of cottages, two-up-two-down, with gardens are still occupied at the time of writing.

The author returns to his birthplace 90 years later.
Little Goval, Parkhill, Aberdeenshire

I was the first son and third in the family; my immediate older sister, Susan, died when she was quite young. Two more sisters and two more brothers came along later, effectively making a growing-up family of six.

We were of farming stock in Aberdeenshire in the North-East Lowlands of Scotland where the land has been farmed for generations. The coastal and flattish land comprises varied soils, from rich, good and easy to till, to too-heavy clay which demands intensive working, and there are wet areas where constant drainage is required. The climate can be unkind, more so around the coast in the District of Buchan where biting winds, driving snow and rain from the North Sea can make life unpleasant, especially when working in the fields. There are climate benefits in the summer with longer daylight and sunshine than in the south of the United Kingdom. The arable land is capable, with good husbandry, of producing fine quality crops, and splendid cattle, sheep and horses are reared. The tractor has now replaced the horse, which makes me completely out of date with modern farming. Success in creating the conditions and maintaining this land at its best is due to the ingenuity, hard work and determination of the men and women over the centuries for making it so. It is however the sort of land which if neglected will not produce good results.

The 1914-18 Great War disturbed the economy in addition to the tragic events which wars bring about, and in the 1920s there was a worldwide depression which stretched into the late thirties when further changes were brought about with another war looming. The conditions and hardships which prevailed throughout the depression years through poor trade and unemployment imposed poverty upon so many lives. The song from the United States of America, 'Buddy can you spare a dime' aptly sums up the world situation. In farming, workers were paid off: skeleton staff could not sustain the land at the required standard for good growth and fewer livestock were carried as they could not be fed adequately. There was little demand for stock and it was not unusual for sheep and cattle to be brought back from auction sales because there were no bidders or the prices offered were unacceptable.

Motor transport was in its infancy until well into the thirties so there was still a market for horses. They were used on farms and also in the towns and cities for delivery and movement of all kinds of merchandise. My grandfather, Charles Rennie, had a small farm but his main source of livelihood was buying and selling horses, very much as motor vehicles are now traded. The same jibes were about then as now in that a horse dealer was thought likely to be capable of sharp practice. In fact, most well-bred horses of high value were examined at the time of sale by veterinary surgeons and certified fit and free from blemishes or, of course, otherwise, very much a form of MOT with which we are familiar.

Hardship in rural areas where most people know each other can cause a form of blight in the district. One such incident when I was about nine years old remains in my memory. A neighbouring farmer committed suicide by shooting himself because he could not pay his way. The boys of the family were of my age and we were good friends, which made the sadness greater. Helping hands were quite generous when it was apparent that households were finding it difficult to pay their bills but people dislike charity and cans of milk, vegetables and suchlike were left at night to be found in the morning and no doubt appreciated.

In the summer we went to school in our bare feet, which probably sounds dreadful now but it was great fun: we could paddle in the burn for 'tiddlers' on the way home without being scolded for spoiling our footwear. Hardships were not new to the Aberdonians, as it appears our forefathers had a hard struggle before settling in this corner of Scotland. If the historians have got it right, we are neither Highlanders nor Celts and the suggestion is that we have more in common with the Flemish. Their argument may be plausible as trading with Scandinavia and Europe has been in operation for centuries, the Grampians to the west being more formidable than the North Sea, and trading south to England being as difficult in the absence of roads and bridges. Cattle and sheep were brought south using drove roads but it was a hazardous trade and not really financially viable as only a trickle of the herds arrived at their destination in reasonable shape; some died and others were stolen on the journeys.

Wherever Aberdonians came from originally, they are generally hard-working and cheerful, self-labelled as being mean. They do enjoy spirited parties, but usually have the wit to keep a penny or two for a rainy day: 'thrifty' would be applicable and acceptable. A fault, as with many Scots, is being too independent and beholden to no one. Scots had for many years emigrated either to escape poor conditions or to apply their engineering and many other skills in developing countries. For example, following the Jacobite Rebellions, large numbers left the country when driven out of their crofts and cottages in the highlands; death was not uncommon for those who resisted.

In the 1920s the government provided conditional assisted passages for young able-bodied men and women to emigrate to the Colonies, mainly Canada, New Zealand and Australia. The scheme laid down very strict rules of eligibility. They had to accept they were going as settlers to places where their skills were most needed. Engineering, building, farming, quarrying and forestry were indispensable skills for breaking new ground and were the key necessities in the main. Babies and very young children were either not allowed to go or their parents were discouraged from taking them. The reasons for their being left behind were probably a combination of things. The sea journeys could be rough, the ships were overcrowded and the food was said to be of poor quality.

Whatever the reasons for leaving the very young behind, much sadness and distress was caused. Those left behind were cared for by grandparents and other family members. There were understandings and promises that the children would join their parents when they were settled in their new homes. In a number of cases this never happened and in my knowledge it is still a bone of contention within families. There were probably good reasons for promises not being kept. The émigrés might not have expected a land flowing with milk and honey but some of the conditions were atrocious. There were long treks in rough virgin territory, and extreme weather conditions, while in some instances they had to clear ground and fell trees to build and provide shelter. Earning a living could be equally hard and there were times when there was little income and great hardships for many years after their arrival. It is perhaps understandable why families were not re-united throughout their lives but healing wounds and providing peace of mind for those involved is virtually impossible.

My earliest memories of these events are of when I was four to five years of age. Aunts, uncles and cousins came to Goval Cottages, where I was born, to say their goodbyes. They would come on a Sunday on a horse-drawn cart or gig and have lunch which Mother made. It always included a large dumpling containing silver thre'penny bits suitably wrapped. Irrespective of who won the thre'penny bits in the course of eating they were given to those going away as parting gifts with wishes of Good Luck. I suspect there was a touch of superstition in the giving. There were tears, sadness, and promises of writing. The men folk were usually quiet and wished each other Good Health with a dram or two. The net result of these departures was that the only members of Mother's family left in Scotland were her mother who died a few years later and a nephew whose parents had emigrated to Canada.

Mother kept her part of the bargain by writing and recycling news and photographs, mainly to Canada, Australia and New Zealand. As a family growing up we looked forward to the many letters and snapshots, not only learning of how our cousins were getting on but all about the countries involved. Mother kept a large-scale atlas and we all pored over it spread on the kitchen table when news arrived. Many years later grandchildren backpacking around the world would arrive at our parents' cottage at the Brig of Balgownie, Aberdeen and announce their relationship, sometimes somewhat tenuous; in time most of them called her Aunt Susie. The visits gave great pleasure to my parents who had always a bed for the travellers.

Regrettably, the important link which Mother had maintained for over 60 years was lost when she died at the age of 93. There was another bright spot for Mother when her elder brother who had left for Canada with his wife and young daughter in the 1920s paid his first return visit to his birthplace, as a widower aged over 70. He spent several weeks with my parents and made a return visit about five years later when a further reunion was enjoyed.

I spent a little time with him on his second visit and he told me some aspects of his early life as a settler. Initially he and his wife built a house with trees which he felled. In his early years he was a lumberjack and was employed in many other forms of heavy work until getting farm land of his own which was his objective. He spoke of the long winters, the low temperatures, heavy snow and icebound conditions when work was impossible and money was scarce. Eventually he retired to Vancouver to enjoy a better climate. He was cheerful and had no complaints about the earlier hardships encountered; in fact he was full of fun and enjoying himself. With other members of the family we saw him off at Prestwick Airport,

Glasgow. The flight was late so extra time was spent in the bar. The last I saw of him he was waving and weaving his way towards the aeroplane singing, "We are nae awa to bide awa."

The Formative School Years

There was great emphasis on education in my schooldays. On special occasions such as prize-giving those teachers with University degrees wore their gowns and caps. Various trusts were available to pupils for books and bursaries were awarded according to ability and qualification by examination. Parents were encouraged to send their children to school at an early age. The qualifications were that you could print your name, know your address and undertake a visit to the toilet without assistance. In those days belts were not available for keeping up boys' trousers: they were supported with shoulder braces. The buttoning and unbuttoning of the leather loops over the trouser buttons took a bit of mastering particularly when the braces were new and the leather hard. I recall practising the art of operating my braces for days before first attending school. Despite that, accidents were known to happen now and again and when they did and the matter was serious, an elder brother or sister or a neighbour's child would accompany the unfortunate child home safely. The printing of the name was easy compared with the toilet test.

I was four in the June and started a few weeks later at Parkhill School, which was only a short distance from Goval Cottages. I enjoyed school from the very first day and there was never a thought of rebellion at the school gates which occurred now and again with the new starters.

It was a small school with three teachers. There were no school dinners: children brought their own food and drinks. In winter children took flasks of warm and enjoyable cocoa which were placed on the hearths of the open schoolroom fires. When there were no fires in summer some brought milk in bottles, while others drank water. Thermos flasks were available but they were too fragile for school use.

Each child had a tin box which contained sandwiches, jam and bread and invariably home-made oatcakes and home-made cheese; it was like a daily picnic at lunchtime and was eaten in the classrooms under the supervision of the teachers.

We were taught reading by the phonetic method and the target for memorising numbers was 100. Those of us who had older brothers and or sisters at school had, with the help of parents, already practised the beginnings of the earlier lessons. We used framed slates and slate pencils for all our work and the cleaning off was with a damp rag and a spit or two if the teacher was not looking! We sang hymns in the morning and nursery rhymes at other times of the day. It was a simple but happy time.

I was at Parkhill School for barely a year because my family moved out of the district. Two never-to-be-forgotten events which occurred that year were the Annual Sunday School Picnic and the Annual School Picnic. We went to the seaside on both occasions but to different beaches. We travelled in lorries drawn by heavy draught horses yoked in pairs to each lorry. The horses and the lorries were highly decorated. It was a wonderful occasion on each journey with the sight of the horses dancing and prancing impatiently as the adults and children were ushered aboard. Adults knowledgeable about the behaviour of horses, especially in the summer season when the horses were full of fresh green grass, endeavoured to sit on the boxes at the rear of the lorries. Those sitting up front were treated to the horses farting and the accompanying aroma!

We ate the food we had taken with us and we had lemonade and ice-cream. We paddled in the sea, played games on the sands, and ran novelty races, prizes being awarded to the winners. There were also races for the mothers; the fathers were not there as they could not take time off work. When the end of the time on the sands came we scrambled back on the lorries, tired, sunburned, but very happy. The mighty 18-hands-high horses took us back in double quick time to school from where we had started. Horses always go faster when heading for home and these journeys were no exception. I have no idea of how many teams of horses were in the convoys but they were memorable sights never to be forgotten and never to be repeated in my lifetime.

We moved a distance of about 25 miles from the two-up-two-down at Parkhill to live in an old farmhouse where we had much more freedom. I will deal later with life at the farm and how it affected my life. My sister and I started at Muirtack Public School as soon as we moved. I have to explain to the non-Scots that this was an ordinary council school run by the Local Education Authority. In Scotland, council schools are called Public Schools and fee-paying schools are known as Private Schools, whereas in England, Public Schools are fee-paying. The distance to our new school was about two miles and in our early days it seemed we would never get there. I was five and my sister seven. There was no public transport and we walked both ways, summer and winter. It was a typical country school with one teacher, Miss Ross. She was ginger-haired, young and stamped her feet when there was the slightest inkling of indiscipline which immediately had the desired effect of delivering order. The number attending varied from about 25 to 30 of pupils of ages ranging from 4 to 12 years. There was one large classroom which became two when the partition was closed. At morning assembly it became one room where we said prayers and sang a hymn or two to the accompaniment of the piano.

Miss Ross did not spend too much time on the religious aspect of the assembly. She would start off each morning on similar lines, first involving the very young by asking if any one of them would care to tell anything which might be of interest. Most children being from farming backgrounds, the little ones would tell of the arrival of a new calf including its colour. It might be about pet lambs, new babies and christenings.

Most of us, though money was scarce, came from good homes and had hard-working parents. However, there was one very large family whose father was the local poacher, petty thief and general layabout who never had a real job. On this particular morning a very young member of that family was keen and excited to give his story and when the teacher allowed him to speak he said that his father was lying across the bed and his mother was picking peas out of his bottom with a fork. The teacher took the information in her stride: she was a country girl and could guess what happened, as did the older pupils, giving rise to laughter and knowing smiles which on this occasion went largely unchecked. The poacher, petty-thief father was known to raid the fields for vegetables during the night and when people of his sort got too greedy and too bold, traps were set. Harvested potatoes were a tempting target: the potatoes were stored in pits and covered with straw to be further protected from the frost with soil while the ends were left open overnight for the continuing work next day. Even when it was apparent that thefts were taking place, the police were not informed. The farmers and farm workers would remove the lead pellets from twelve-bore cartridges and replace them with hard dried peas and gun powder. They would conceal themselves in a suitable place and when the thief had filled his sack they would give a warning shout: the thief would drop the loot and turn his back on the watching gunmen, and at this moment a shot or two would be fired at his backside. There was never any intention of serious injury to the culprit and he was unlikely to report it to the police.

After dealing with the younger children's stories of events, the teacher would open the daily newspaper and read and discuss current affairs at home and abroad and questions were encouraged. The lessons made everyone in the school involved and stimulated our interest far beyond any formal lessons.

Although we regarded ourselves in classes for some subjects, most times we were guided along individual lines dependent upon our ability and progress. We were encouraged to read and by the time I was ten or eleven I had read most of Dickens' books which I still enjoy. We were given homework which Miss Ross marked and whatever the result she would move about the classroom and spend a moment or two explaining the answers and correcting mistakes, or if the work was of a good standard providing more difficult lessons. She was always encouraging children and helping them when needed.

The next step up was for pupils to go to the local secondary school until 14 years of age which was the normal leaving age. The other means of study was by examination to the High School/Academy. Financial help was available, the amounts depending on the examination results. The money was for travelling and some books, the top amount per annum being £12.00 which my sister was awarded two years before me. The girls got the top rate for using the service buses; the boys' top rate was £10.00 for the provision and the upkeep of a bicycle, which is what my parents were granted for me.

Miss Ross held regular evening meetings for parents to discuss her pupils' progress and also took a leading part in arranging social events in the school during the evenings. Concerts, film shows and outside speakers were regular events catering for the whole family. The picnics were just as jolly as the one earlier described when we were living at Parkhill but the getting there and back was less colourful. Instead of horse-drawn vehicles, motorised charabancs were hired. They were the forerunner of coaches. They were high and had light canvas tops which were collapsible. The problem with the ones hired for our picnics was that the engine power was incapable of taking us up and over some of the hills. The older boys and girls had to push it to the top of the rise when the charabanc became stuck, this being repeated a few times on the 15 mile journey to the points nearest the sea and sands. It was great fun!

The school was for me so good that despite heavy snow and blocked roads, I insisted in going and still proudly possess a Certificate of Perfect Attendance for the year ending June 1926. I would be nine years of age then. My continuing interest in new subjects and research which has been a feature of my life is I believe due to the stimulation provided at Muirtack Public School under the guidance of an exceptional teacher. One of the things which occurred frequently was when the local policeman rode up on his cycle in uniform and had a brief conversation on the steps outside. Policemen were held in awe in those days and the mystery was not solved until it was announced that Miss Ross was to marry him! Presents and parties were suitably arranged and she was given a wonderful send off. She was succeeded by a Mrs Bothwell who had two children and was said to be divorced. I was not under her for too long but found her method of teaching different and it took a little time to adapt to her style of working. In retrospect I believe I had a crush on her elder daughter who was more or less my age.

Working on a Scottish Farm

My father was brought up on a farm and on leaving school at the age of 14 worked on farms for several years. He then had a variety of occupations, I am not sure in which order, as a nurse, a policeman and a shore porter transporting goods to and from the docks. My first recollection of his work was his coming home with his clothes soiled with fertiliser dust caused by his working at a chemical factory.

Although I was probably not quite five years of age, I remember the excitement and pleasure felt in the home when Father obtained employment as a Farm Grieve at Mill of Kinmuck which was about 25 miles north of Goval Cottages and seven or eight miles from the market town of Ellon.

I had better explain to the non-Scots what the title 'Grieve' means and what it entails. In England the situation would probably be compared to a Farm Manager or Estate Overseer, but neither label quite fits. In England, the person so appointed wears a hat and would rarely be seen labouring alongside the staff of which he is in charge. His Scottish counterpart works and sweats on the farm in suitable attire unless he has to conduct farm business. On such occasions he will shave, clean up, put on a collar and tie but still wear a flat cap and go forth on a bicycle. Depending on the size of the farm and whether the employer is an absentee farmer, the extent of his responsibilities will vary. Either way he has to be decisive, take positive action and be capable of dealing with all aspects of farming. He has to have the skills to tutor and train staff, for example, in building hay and corn stacks, a specialist task. If not done properly, stacks will deteriorate and be valueless. He will hire and fire staff, issue daily orders and if he is going to be absent he will, if the farmer is not available, usually authorise the foreman to act on his behalf.

The Rennie Family at Mill of Kinmuck, Aberdeenshire 1928/29
Fanny, Father (Charles) with Ben, Jean, author, Mother (Susan) with Betty, Charles Jnr.

There is a militaristic element in managing a farm: animals have to be fed at regular intervals, and in the case of dairy cattle, milked at precise times as any deviation may result in a drop in the yield of milk with financial loss. Similarly the conditions for sowing and harvesting have to be correctly judged. Many other day-to-day decisions have to be varied at short notice because of unforeseen or changing circumstances, particularly arising from weather conditions. Farm servants do not remain idle when the rain stops one job; they are switched to another. Where there is an absentee farmer the grieve will to a greater or lesser extent deal with financial matters, buying and selling stock and produce grown on the farm in accordance with the farmer's policy.

Father was to be a grieve to a farmer who did not spend much time at the farm, although he lived only approximately 30 miles distant, but he did go overseas now and again on shooting trips. The farmer visited the farm at irregular intervals when he spent a few hours with my father and joined him in whatever jobs were being carried out. At harvest times he would stay a few days when he would live in the farmhouse and Mother would look after him. On such occasions he spent whole days shooting game and rabbits on the extensive acres of land, sometimes by himself and at other times with his friends; Father occasionally joined the party. The farmer had a telephone at his home but the telephone system had not yet reached the farm. The farmer would send a postcard if he intended to stay and in a rare farm emergency my father would cycle off to the nearest public telephone and speak to the farmer. The nearest doctor was some seven or eight miles distant and he was called by the same means.

There was a great variation in the jobs and job descriptions of those employed on farms in Aberdeenshire. In general terms they were referred to as farm servants, the title embracing foremen, horsemen, shepherds and baileys (cattlemen) indicating the skill and experience they possessed and for which posts they were suitable. In my time, farm servants were contracted to specific posts to run for a term of six months. If the farmer wished to engage servants for a further term, he had to ask the employee some two or so weeks before the end of term if he wished to renew his contract. Farmers were sometimes guilty of not acting promptly in asking employees if they wanted to be re-engaged in case it gave the employee the idea that he was worth more than he was being paid and would be tempted to ask for a rise in wages above which the farmer wanted to pay. Good employees did get small increases but hard bargaining was the order of the day. If an employer did not wish to retain an employee it was usually apparent long before the end of term that there would be a parting, but appropriate notice had to be given. There were also mutually-friendly exchanges when servants left farms and it was not unknown for re-engagements at a later date.

End of term could be a stressful time: the economic prospects were bad and to be out of work was a bleak outlook. About ten days or so before the end of term, feeing markets were held in the recognised market town applicable to that district. All employees were entitled to attend. The streets would be crowded with hundreds of men milling around and going to and fro asking questions and gathering information about the abilities of those seeking work and likewise about the farmers seeking employees.

The grieves were usually appointed beforehand and they or the farmer or both would select a foreman who would be given half a crown to seal the bargain and in addition sometimes a dram or two. The foreman would help in selecting a second horseman and so on until the posts were filled. It was essential that the staff chosen were compatible and the method of selection, which had evolved over the years, was found satisfactory. The lesser mortals on appointments would probably get two shillings and the juniors a shilling. By the end of a market day there was considerable evidence that the public houses, which were open all day, had done good business and it was great fun watching unsteady bodies trying to mount cycles or a farmer getting into his gig and relying on his horse to take him home. Some came away happy, while those without the prospect of work had to ask their employer for another day off to attend the next nearest feeing market; it was very much like horse trading. The moving of people from job to job took place on the last day of term which was 28th May or 28th November. The furniture and personal belongings were loaded on to a farm cart, alongside members of their families.

A week or so before we moved, Father was away quite a lot, attending roups (auction sales) buying implements, tools, horses and everything necessary to equip a farm. I think it was 1922 and I was barely five when we moved to Mill of Kinmuck where my parents remained until the farmer died and the farm was sold. I cannot remember the actual journey to our new home, with Father, Mother, my elder sister and younger brother and sister who was just a baby. I have a hazy recollection that the farmer conveyed us in his motorcar. There was great fun and excitement as my older sister, Jean, and I explored the big rambling farmhouse. We squabbled about where we should sleep but of course we slept where we were told and that settled the matter.

It was an old house with a large kitchen and wide open fireplace where an iron kettle hung from a crook and was constantly on the boil. Most cooking was done on the fireplace and in the built-in oven, but as there were occasions such as harvest time, lambing time and threshing when many hands had to be fed, Mother had a paraffin stove with a small oven which she used. The smell of the paraffin from the cooker and the lamps percolated through the house. There was no hot water system, gas or electricity and the water was obtained from a pump with a handle situated just outside the back door; it was slow and hard work. Occasionally it went dry and had to be primed so water was never wasted.

There were front stairs leading to the bedrooms where the family slept and a back stairs, presumably provided for accommodating domestic staff, which we used as a storeroom. There was a sitting room, a dining room, and another room on the ground floor at the front of the house which we used as a guest room or when people were ill or for the arrival of a baby. There was a long stone flagged passage leading from the kitchen to the front door with a large pantry and another storeroom leading off the passage. We would hide and try and frighten each other, using the nooks and crannies leading off the passage. Although the farmhouse was old and draughty we were fortunate that we had an absentee farmer and we had his quarters.

The alternative for married farm servants was a cottar house. I do not think my parents would have taken a job where the accommodation was a cottar house. The typical cottar house which was tied accommodation usually comprised a kitchen, with what was known as a box bed in a recess where a curtain was hung, the bed fitting the recess precisely. There was another downstairs room used as a bedroom and upstairs was probably an open space more in keeping with a loft and fitted with skylight windows, access being via a steep ladder fitted to the wall.

A few of the cottar houses were slightly better than described but not many. Each house had a garden where vegetables were grown and it was standard practice for the cottar to have one load of good farm muck from the farmer each year. The occupier normally got a daily ration of milk and there was a pen where a prescribed number of hens were allowed. Most farmers would allow small quantities of not very good corn but it was quite satisfactory for feeding hens, as it was free. Woe betide anyone sneaking off with corn, potatoes, turnips or any other item of farm produce without permission; dismissal might follow. Single men slept in a chamar (bed chamber), which was usually one big room with no privacy for the occupants. There was always a fireplace and a few pegs on the wall to hang clothing and some chairs. When farm servants left school and got their first job, they bought or had made by the local joiner a kist (chest) which lasted a lifetime and in which were kept, securely locked, their clothing and personal belongings. I wonder what happened to my kist which I had forgotten about until the moment of writing. The kist was also used for sitting upon in the chamar if chairs were scarce.

The chamar was normally situated above the cartshead which had arched open entrances and could be draughty, but where the chamar was above the stable, though warmer, wee beasties came out of the hay and were a nuisance. Access to the chamar was via an outside staircase or if above the stable a fixed ladder from within the building. A chamar is frequently quite erroneously referred to as a bothy, a place where people sleep, prepare food and eat. A chamar was a place without any facilities for cooking or doing laundry and when used the occupants ate elsewhere. Single men normally ate in the farm kitchen, food prepared by the farmer's wife, grieve's wife or whoever occupied the farmhouse. They went to the kitchen at the appointed times throughout the day where the table was already laid and they either helped themselves or were served.

In my time breakfast was simple to deal with and required little preparation. Oatmeal and a boiling kettle were already available and each person put the amount of oatmeal he required into a wooden bowl, added a pinch of salt, and poured on the boiling water stirring vigorously for a few moments; milk was added and that was what was known as brose, ready to eat. It was a simple but sustaining meal, a little less sophisticated than porridge. At the breakfast table there was sliced bread, butter and syrup or home-made marmalade or jam and, as with every meal, there were home-made oatcakes and frequently home-made cheese. Farm work is hard work, conducted largely in the open in sight of other people where the opportunities for skulking are rare; therefore men need to be well fed to work continuously for long hours.

The only times when food was given between meals was at harvest, haymaking and threshing. On such occasions the women folk would take jam sandwiches and large pots of tea to the fields to be consumed nearest to where work was taking place. If the weather was good the harvesting activities would go on from early morning to late at night; overtime was not given to full-time farm servants who would probably get an extra day off when things were not so busy. Casual workers employed by the hour had to be paid accordingly.

Charles Jnr, Father and the author enjoying a well-earned break in the hayfield.

So far I have dealt mainly with the duties and responsibilities of the farm servant but without the wife of the farmer or of the grieve, whichever occupied the farmhouse, the place would be at a standstill. I think my mother and people in similar situations were the backbone of farming in those now far-off days. Mother was brought up on a farm owned by her parents and on leaving home trained and became a fully-qualified nurse. She was therefore well aware of what being the wife of a grieve entailed: much was expected and the financial rewards were small. However, I know that Mother was happier in her new situation than she was when previously living in a small up-and-down.

The family was brought up in a warm and caring atmosphere despite the world depression, and many other obstacles which arose from time to time. Irrespective of age or sex the children worked as if the farm belonged to the family and there was never a mention of financial rewards. We may unknowingly and indirectly have contributed to our parents' savings but the subject was not discussed and pocket money was unheard of. One summer we gathered from the fences what was known as broken wool which was processed at the local wool mill and made into fine warm suits by the local tailor. A family photograph still to the fore shows my brother and me wearing such suits. Father was fully occupied with farm work, leaving the management of the farmhouse to Mother. In addition to tending a growing family for whom she knitted, altered and made clothes on her sewing machine, she cooked for the single men. The regimented approach to farm work ensured the domestic animals were fed at strictly fixed hours, as were the workers. Any deviation was frowned upon except for serious illness of man or beast. The family ate in the dining room and the single men in the kitchen.

At harvest and lambing times there would usually be extra hands to be housed and fed. In the autumn the lambs were weaned and sorted into flocks. They were lost without their mothers, bleating continuously: the noise was deafening and heart-breaking. I spent a few Saturdays herding flocks of them along the roads which meant scampering about, waving my arms and shouting to encourage the strays to stay with the flocks. It was hungry, tiring work with a long walk home at the end of the day. However, herding sheep was preferable to some of the tasks.

The coal store at Kinmuck was replenished every summer with 20 tons of coal brought from the railway station in farm carts. As I grew older it fell to me to keep full the large heavy scuttles, two for the kitchen fire, two for the chamar and one for the sitting room. I had also to chop firewood from old fence posts, which was heavy work. I was glad when summer came and only the kitchen fire required a daily supply!

There were more jobs to be done on a regular basis, the worst and most memorable being for a few weeks one winter. The farmer, ill-advisedly it was said, bought a large number of Canadian steers: they were wild, difficult to handle and had to be secured in the byre. They developed pneumonia and were dosed morning and night with gruel, a sort of porridge to which turpentine was added. Father poured it down their throats. The gruel was made in the kitchen and on many mornings and evenings I carried the buckets to the byre. When I was only half awake, it called for nifty footwork to escape from the end product, the stench of which lingered and was nauseating. There was never a thought of calling a veterinary surgeon as that would have cost money. Miraculously they all recovered. The experience put me off looking after cattle and thereafter I tried to get out of work connected with them. Looking after sheep suited me and I became quite competent at lambing time and in summer in dealing with maggots and foot-rot. I found horses easily manageable and long before I left school I was trusted to harness and yoke them to a variety of implements for cultivating the land.

People with little knowledge of farming have a tendency to underrate the abilities of farm servants and have no idea of the range of skills required on a mixed farm. The majority of young men I grew up with were intelligent, hard-working ambitious people endeavouring to improve their skills and prospects in a world suffering a depression.

As mentioned above, I was awarded a place at Ellon High School (now an Academy) by means of an examination and my parents were granted £10.00 per year for the purchase and upkeep of a bicycle and books. The school was about 8 miles distant and for two years I cycled there and back, rarely missing a day despite dreadful winters which brought frost, snow, rain and strong gales. The teaching methods were alien to my way of learning. Previously I had been encouraged to read, research and clarify subjects with the teacher. At the High School, note-taking was a must for some subjects, and then written up as homework. In an effort to have more time at home for the more complex subjects which I really wanted to master, my homework notes became a précis of the history and geography lessons. In course of time the teachers questioned me about the brevity of my work. I explained that I thought I was keeping pace with the lessons by reading the books from which the lectures were taken. One teacher accepted my pleadings and said he would test me from time to time which he did by springing verbal questions at me. I was usually capable of giving him convincing answers; it became a game which we both enjoyed! I had probably been spoiled by the freedom allowed me at the lower school. Throughout my life my best examination results have been from self-study, for which my thanks go to that brilliant teacher in sole charge of that country school.

The long days during which I was usually fully occupied were tiring and I found it hard to concentrate on the volume of homework required. I realised that if I stayed on at school, my examination results would be second rate, so I decided to leave at 14 years of age. I had an amicable interview with the Headmaster, a kind man, who advised me to maintain contact with the educational subjects and wished me well. I had learned much at the High School and it was an achievement getting a place there. The Scottish character is not at all sympathetic to losers and that was another very good reason for leaving early, as I did not wish to be so categorised. Most parents did the best for their children, as did mine, but like birds on reaching the fledging stage, they were expected to fly the nest and fend for themselves which is what I did. I think Mother was disappointed; Father was non-committal.

Learning a trade was out of the question as it was too far to travel to the towns and lodgings were unaffordable because apprentices received little or no wages. I therefore had to find work for which I was reasonably equipped. It meant leaving home which I knew I would miss. We made our own amusement, we played games and listened to the gramophone. One record I still remember was 'The Laughing Policeman'. There was no radio or television then. The occasional family outings and birthdays were great occasions, and eating together was enjoyable. An outstanding memory is of Sunday afternoons in the winter with the family squatting on the sitting room floor and Mother reading stories from the Bible.

A Sunday outing in the 1920s

An Offer of Employment

As mentioned earlier, the feeing market was where work was found, a great spectacle with hundreds of men and boys dressed in their Sunday best, milling around. The public houses were open all day and as deals were completed drams were dispensed: some were happy, others disappointed. An occasional fight broke out but there were sufficient hands about not to let things get out of order. There was only about a week between the feeing market and the start of a new job for those looking for work. The work contracts expired on Scottish Quarter Days, 28th May and 28th November. These are the dates when accounts were settled and farm servants were paid their wages six months in arrears.

My first experience of attending a feeing market was at Ellon when I was 14 years of age. The younger lads like me got together but as the day wore on we became included in the business of the day. It was a testing time and I was not at all confident about how to handle the situation if the offer of a job arose. Farming folk know a great deal about each other and they depend upon their local knowledge on such occasions. Farmers endeavour to avoid employing the less able and farm servants are equally selective, the single men being very much concerned to find a place where the quality and quantity of food was of a good standard. As already mentioned, farmers and grieves first appointed a foreman, or if he was in post he would attend the market and help to ferret out likely candidates for the lower jobs. The prime requirements were for good capable workers but considerable emphasis was placed on character and whether or not the persons appointed would be socially acceptable, as they had to work and live together in small units.

Two young men, both of whom had previously worked for my father, sought me out and one of them said he had accepted work as a foreman and he would be happy to have me as second horseman. I had never in my wildest dreams expected other than an odd job! However, they pointed out I had certain advantages over many boys of my age: I was tall, well-built and had the benefit of experience of farm work from an early age under the tutelage of my father. We then met the farmer, Sandy Gray, who knew my father and after lots of questions he offered me the job at £10.00 for six months. I sought out my father and with his approval I accepted the offer and was given one shilling to seal the contract. It was a small farm and I knew the work would not be as heavy as on a larger place, but I was also aware that it was a wonderful opportunity and a real challenge.

Within a week of the feeing market I was off to my first job as a farm servant; a wee bit apprehensive. There were three of us in the chamar, the usual sparse room for single men. The privy for the occupants was some distance away and for obvious reasons was not always used. We washed our hands and faces in the kitchen after supper with water heated on the kitchen fire; towels were provided. Single men had to make their own arrangements for washing their clothes. The hours of work depended upon the seasons, times for getting up varying from 5.00 am to 6.30 am. Horses needed two hours of feeding, watering and grooming in preparation for yoking time. When the horses were attended to and the stable cleaned out, the horsemen went to the kitchen for breakfast of brose, bread, butter and tea as described above. Lunch and supper were prepared by the housekeeper. The food was just about adequate but there were occasions when I could have eaten more.

Life to me has been a balance of obstacles and such an event of the latter occurred when I had been at the farm for about three months. The housekeeper was unmarried and had a lovely little girl then aged about two years. Her mother was fully occupied; the child was lonely and spent much of her time in the farmyard with the dog, a harmless animal. On this day I heard the child cry, the dog barked and I found her head down in the horse trough under the water. I ran to her mother with her and thankfully she was none the worse for her adventure. She had obviously climbed up the embankments above the trough and stumbled. Thereafter, I had the impression that the rations on my plate improved and occasionally the child would bring me snacks to eat between meals. This action would certainly not have had the approval of the farmer, a bachelor in his later years. He was kind enough but was thrifty to the point of meanness and there were hours spent mending and salvaging things which should have been discarded.

One of the pair of horses allocated to me was deaf which was a new experience and a challenge. She was a good-natured beast but a bit jumpy; she responded to a sort of deaf and dumb language of light or heavier pats on her rump. On the long days at sowing time and during harvest, I was ready to fall into bed after supper. The soil was heavy clay and depending upon the weather required more cultivation than lighter soils to produce a suitable tilth for sowing seeds. The fields had to be harrowed many times which was a light task for the horses so the pace was fast compared with ploughing. Although lightly clad we sweated a lot, and if you were chubby inflammation occurred between the buttocks. There were no medical cures in the middle of a field but the old hands knew the remedy, which was to put a pebble or marble in the appropriate place, thus parting the flesh; the cure was almost instant as I can testify.

The author, aged 14, employed as second horseman at Nether Mill, Birness, Aberdeenshire

I stayed on a further six months at that farm and for the next two years was similarly employed on other farms. Socially life was good: we attended dances; between dances the girls stayed on one side of the hall and the boys on the other but we escorted them home, all on bicycles. In the long summer evenings we played sports and in the winter evenings, classes were well attended by both sexes, there being a common desire to improve our situations. The prospects of bringing up a family in a small tied cottage and just scraping a living for years ahead did not appeal to me. By this time I was 17 years old and had made a firm decision to be a policeman when I was old enough.

I enrolled with The Bennet College, Sheffield for a correspondence course tailored for candidates taking police entrance examinations. The method of learning suited me and for the next two to three years I studied a wide variety of subjects. In the meantime the farmer who had employed my father had died and Father did what many farm servants aspired to. He rented a farm, Threepleton of Pitcaple, Aberdeenshire, extending to about 120 acres of good arable land. The farm buildings were in three parts on a hillside; the unmade road was about half a mile from the main road; the farmhouse was old but reasonably comfortable. The shortcomings so described were undoubtedly reflected in the rent and with the help of the local bank manager Father became a farmer. I was more or less ordered to go home and work, which I did: the days were endless and the remuneration negligible.

It was with considerable determination that I continued with the correspondence courses. However, Mother, always helpful, allowed me to use the sitting room and unless it was otherwise required my books and papers were undisturbed and I was able to snatch time for study as opportunities arose. My younger brother Charles was growing up and could undertake the heavier work normally done by me. I was 19 years of age and Father indicated I should find additional work but still live at home and give a hand with the farm work. I did a variety of work including forestry and being a driver's mate on a ten-ton Albion lorry: we moved everything including farm stock. We carted barley and wheat from the docks at Aberdeen to the distilleries for malting and occasionally got a drop of the best when offloading was completed. Finally, before joining the Police, I worked as a navvy with a pick and shovel digging a sewer trench for the township of Rothienorman.

By my 19th birthday I was sufficiently confident to start making applications to become a policeman. My father gave me good advice which was to apply to the larger Forces as the prospects of being accepted would be greater and the possibilities of advancement would be better than the smaller ones. The only large Force in Scotland was Glasgow City to which I applied and was put on a long waiting list. In the course of a year I applied to 15 Forces and completed seven educational tests at the local police station, eventually getting on to five waiting lists. In the summer of 1937, Durham County Constabulary advertised in the Aberdeen Press and Journal for recruits. I applied immediately and mentioned that I was on five waiting lists. Within days I was invited to Durham and exempted from the usual preliminary examinations.

The detailed correspondence included the train and the times to travel and said that a uniformed policeman would be waiting at Durham Railway Station to meet me. He was a young Scot obviously hand-picked for the task by Inspector James Short and it was typical of the welfare practised in Durham which I enjoyed for many years. The day started at 8.30 am with 85 candidates. We were split into small groups and rotated through the various tests of dictation, reading aloud, a short essay, mathematics and general knowledge. It was quite unnerving as by 10.00 am many candidates drifted away. After lunch there were interviews before a Board of Senior Officers and finally the Police Surgeon. Fortunately, I was one of 22 survivors and immediately offered an appointment to start training the following Monday which was 13th September 1937. Relief did not do justice to my feelings! When I got home the following day there were two firm offers from other Forces to join them but I had given my word to Durham and have never regretted doing so.

[87.]

DURHAM COUNTY CONSTABULARY.

Articles of Clothing to be brought by Candidates.

~~1 Clothes box.~~

1 Suit of plain clothes.

3 Shirts.

4 Pairs of Stockings or Socks.

1 Razor and Shaving Brush.

1 Hair Brush and Comb, Collars, Handkerchiefs, etc.

2 Pairs of Boots. Derby Pattern.

~~One Hard Felt Hat (black.)~~ Suitable headgear.

3 Body Shirts and
3 Pairs of Drawers. (If accustomed to wear such.)

1 Pair of Slippers.

13 SEPTEMBER 1937.

Clothing required when reporting to Durham County Constabulary HQ on 13th September 1937

The next few days were hectic. I knew I would miss my family and friends and many good memories still survive. One such event was a competition in a twelve-man team from The Drum of Wartle at the Braemar gathering, which is held in the autumn after the other local games have been completed. The best of the teams are expected to compete at Braemar, which included police forces, the Armed Services, industry and town and villages. There is caber-tossing, pillow-fighting, wrestling, cycling, foot races and tug-o-war. The field on which it takes place is a sort of large saucer with the mountains in the background. There are bagpipes and dancing competitions for all ages going on, almost all tartans being represented. The Royal Family always attended and their welcome is something never to be forgotten. Everyone on the field made a repetitive singing chorus of 'A Hundred Thousand Welcomes'.

We were the underdogs but we reached the final which was the tug-o-war to be performed close up to the King and Queen and the two young princesses. The judges expected us to wear kilts for the final event which we did not have but there were plenty of offers and I think most of us were turned out in the Gordon Highlanders' tartan, except for underclothes. We won the first pull, lost the second and the third pull seemed to never end, on top of which a strong breeze blew some of the kilts aside much to the amusement of the spectators. We won to a continuous chorus of, 'Never mind your arse!'

Training to be a Policeman

On reporting for training as a probationary constable on Monday 13th September, 1937, I joined a class of 24. We were allocated a collar number: mine was 967. Next it was uniform, a whistle, truncheon and a two-foot wooden folding ruler which was for taking measurements at scenes of road accidents. Somehow I have still got a Durham issue ruler which has come in very handy over the years. Handcuffs were issued at a later date when we had been trained to use them.

Probationary Constable 967

My colleagues were mainly from within the county, but there was also a Northumbrian and a Yorkshireman. Understanding the language was not the problem I had anticipated, but there were words and phrases which were new to me. For example, colliery workers, or pitmen as they were known, verbally and in writing used the words 'Up Bank' meaning they were going 'Uphill'. Some of the accents were equally puzzling. My Scottish accent did not appear to be an obstacle.

Most of the young men away from home for the first time found sleeping on bunk beds in a dormitory, without any privacy, an uneasy experience. However, quite soon any shyness wore off and with one exception we called each other by our preferred names and became good friends. The exception invented odd and not always complimentary names and announced he would always refer to me as 'Jock the Scottish B......d'. Initially I ignored his jibes; I tried reasoning with him explaining that I had been christened and that my parents were married. This approach caused him great amusement and eventually one evening I said to him quite quietly that if he did not change his ways I would punch him in the face. He immediately took up a boxing stance and faced me. I got up from my bunk without a word, hit him on the nose, and down he went with a bloody nose. He tried to rush out of the barrack room saying he was going to report me for assaulting him but the other occupants of the barrack room stopped him and threatened him with all sorts of dire consequences. His bullying stopped. However, he was sacked some months later for some sort of bad behaviour. Apparently fighting between recruits could result in dismissal from the Force in which case my police career might have been quite short!

We trained at Durham for twelve weeks, studying the criminal law which entailed learning definitions, some of which I still remember, powers of arrest and statement-taking. There was no radio or speedy means of communication in those days and officers on the beat had to make quick and accurate decisions, especially in executing powers of arrest. We visited Assize Courts, Quarter Sessions and Magistrates' Courts observing the procedures which were later discussed in class. The next twelve weeks were spent in barracks at Jarrow, which was a modern police station and the divisional headquarters. We studied for four hours each morning in the classroom on theory and practice. Actual case papers were discussed and report writing was given a high priority. We were taught to take fingerprints and plaster-casts as policemen in Durham were their own detectives except for the more complex and major crimes when the CID were involved. Four hours of the day, between 2.00 pm and 1.00 am, were on patrol with an experienced constable. His word was law and it was inadvisable to question his orders.

Soon I was nearly in trouble again. One of the duties at Jarrow was to spend a shift in the General Office learning how to take and record telephone messages and other clerical duties. On the afternoon shift, part of the duty was to take the mail to the General Post Office which was some considerable distance away. My specific instructions were to go straight there and back and to ignore whatever else was happening, added to which was the caution that it was dole day and there might be drunks about. This was the first occasion I had been in the streets in police uniform: I was self-conscious and I knew it must have showed.

I reached a point on the journey where there were a large number of men barracking me and I was obliged to walk around them as they were slow in giving me passage. On the return journey a man of about 40 and better dressed than most of the others confronted me and took up an aggressive stance with his fists. I assumed he was going to strike me so I punched him in the face in self-defence. He went down with one blow and his broken dentures were scattered on the ground. The instructions to ignore incidents were ringing around in my brain coupled with the advice and training which I had so far received which was 'Never bark unless you can bite and if you have to bite you must produce the evidence.' The man was drunk; he had attempted to assault me, so I arrested him amid general uproar with hands trying to release him while I was getting my shins kicked. Most timely, a petrol tanker from the nearby oil refinery stopped: the driver opened the passenger door of his cab and I dragged my prisoner inside and he drove us to the police station. The prisoner was immediately recognised and identified as the leader of a large section of the Communist Party who regularly held meetings at which he taunted police and was generally a thorn in their side. There was a hint of praise for arresting this man but I expected to be dealt with for not taking the advice given.

Court day arrived. The prisoner was charged with being drunk and disorderly. He pleaded not guilty and applied for summons against me for assault and for damage to his dentures, adding that he had ten men present in the court and more outside as his witnesses. It was agreed the case could be dealt with that day. The offence of assault was put to me and I pleaded not guilty. He and two or three of his supporters gave evidence on his behalf. My Superintendent asked him why he appeared to be wanting to box me, to which he replied that he often shadow-boxed police recruits but never hit them.

In the witness box I was asked the questions: one, "Did you hit this man?" to which I replied, "Yes," and secondly, "Why did you hit him?" I said, "In self defence." The cases against me were dismissed. I gave evidence of the drunk and disorderly behaviour for which a fine of £2.00 was imposed. As we left the court the Superintendent gave me a pat on the back and said, "Well done – always tell the truth and you will not go far wrong." I felt relieved at the outcome.

Parading for duty was a formal occasion: the Senior Officer present would order us to fall in, in one or two ranks depending on the numbers present. We were briefed on specific matters requiring attention and ordered to produce our appointments, truncheons and handcuffs presented in a regimental manner. On being ordered to take our beats the sergeant led the way into the street: he marched on the pavement, with the constables in single file on his right on the roadway. It was an impressive turnout and at the places where individual allocated beats were reached the officers fell out and when possible exchanged information with the constable on the beat they were relieving. The beats were patrolled in a clockwise direction and were so arranged that contact could easily be made by whistle or, during the hours of darkness, by flashing torches with at least one or more officers on adjoining beats.

Policemen were expected to have a comprehensive knowledge of all aspects of their beats and of the people living there. The photographs of known criminals and suspects were exhibited in the parade room and we soon came to recognise them. The modern expression 'zero tolerance' was unheard of then but that is how the place was policed. Our Supervising Officers at the conclusion of shifts would question us about what we had done and learned until it became second nature to notice anything unusual.

Police work was by no means all locking up and issuing summonses. We were taught to be friendly and helpful by which means we retained respect and trust from the majority and when crimes were committed we got valuable information from most sections of the public. There were occasions when trainee constables found themselves in embarrassing situations. One of our group was asked by his tutor to speak to a young lady who left a public convenience with her dress tucked into her knickers. The trainee objected not only because he was embarrassed but he did not think it was a matter for police attention. The sergeant was informed of the incident and the young policeman was given strong advice. A not-too-dissimilar incident happened to me on a fine sunny afternoon at the central bus station adjacent to the Ben Lomond Hotel. A fairly busty lady walked off a bus with one of her breasts bare. My tutor told me to have a word with her. I stuttered and spluttered as I approached the lady and I don't think I uttered one coherent word. She looked down, smiled and said in a lovely Geordie accent, "Why man, I've left the bairn on the bus!" and added, "Thank you, son!"

The police were very much closer to the people then than in current times. Apart from the fire brigade we were the only organisation available 24 hours a day. There was free help from the NSPCC and some other local voluntary bodies but the only ambulance service was St John and unless people were subscribers, a charge was made which many people could not afford. When accidents took place in the street, the injured remained there until the police arrived and called the ambulance. Each policeman was entitled to do so as we subscribed a small amount from our wages to St John. It was deemed to be a voluntary contribution, but it did hurt on our low wages.

Our six months' formal training was coming to an end and we considered ourselves fortunate in having been well-prepared to serve the public compared with many Forces. Even in the large Forces where formal training was provided, the courses were usually not more than twelve weeks and some of the smaller Forces limited instruction to accompanying an experienced officer on the beat. The members of our class speculated as to which of the 13 territorial divisions each would be posted. Some wanted to be near their homes, which was unlikely, others near their girlfriends, but we all knew there was no choice. In some respects it was immaterial to me where I went but I was hopeful it would be Jarrow as it was the only place in the county of which I had any knowledge and there was plenty work to do. I was therefore delighted when the list was posted and I was staying in the Jarrow Division.

We got six days' leave on completion of the course during which I went home to my parents on the farm. It was good to be back and to be with so many friends. I knew that with annual leave limited to 14 days per year and one Saturday and Sunday week-end duty off in seven, I would in time lose touch with the people and the life I had known. I enjoyed the holiday and made a firm decision that being a policeman was the life for me. On return to Jarrow I was placed in private lodgings, joining PC FC Charlie Davis who was a year or so senior to me. We became lifelong friends.

The Rookie Probationer

By regulation a police officer is on two years' probation during which time a detailed record of every aspect of his work and conduct is made. In Durham we were required to complete an educational paper every two weeks, in our own time. The subjects were arithmetic, English, general knowledge, geography and an occasional essay. Towards the end of probation-time a formal examination was set which covered criminal law and practice as well as general educational subjects. The service of a probationer could be dispensed with without formality but it was rare to be for failing the examination, as those deemed unsuitable were usually filtered out long before the end of the two years.

Great emphasis on probationer progress was placed upon getting to know as much as possible about the area and the people and to providing a good standard of service to the public. I found the guidance from senior colleagues and Supervising Officers firm but fatherly. Probationers were discouraged from getting married and even when confirmed in the post an application giving details of the fiancée had to be made and approved. Jarrow was considered a hard station and now and again a probationer would submit an application giving a variety of reasons for asking to be posted elsewhere; the applications were rarely approved.

One young friend of mine decided on an unusual course: he took a high-spirited young lady, well-known to young policemen, to the Annual Police Ball. Their flamboyant performance on the dance floor achieved the desired objective. The following day he was interviewed by the Superintendent and given strong advice about the sort of company he should keep and was told that in his best interests he would be posted forthwith to the other end of the county. He was delighted with the outcome which could have backfired but he was a good constable which probably saved him from dismissal.

As the whole of the county was foreign to me I was quite happy with working in Jarrow, which lies to the south of the River Tyne and was at that time very much in the public domain because of exceptionally high unemployment. The shipyards, which had been the main source of employment, had stood idle for a number of years. A section of the unemployed had organised a march on Parliament which became known as The Jarrow March. Ellen Wilkinson, MP wrote a book entitled 'The Town that was Murdered'. Nationally, Oswald Mosley was stirring up the Right Wing, causing public disorder; the Communists and the IRA were also active. Electricity installations were attacked and had to be guarded. Resentment against any form of authority was openly encouraged, resulting in disorderly conduct. Demonstrations and marches were sparked off by the slightest suggestion especially when the public houses were turning out. There was damage to property through drunken behaviour; shop and house breakings occurred but the method of policing kept those crimes very much in check. Breaking into electric and gas meters was more common and on occasion the culprits were the householders. Anyone spending or in possession of an unusual number of pennies was the likely culprit.

It would be unfair not to mention that the whole town was not a bed of violence and crime. The majority of the people living away from the troubled districts were well-behaved, cheerful, law-abiding citizens. The difficult areas were where a large number of people in poor housing had been unemployed for years and relied on unemployment benefit or means-test allowances. It was a breeding ground for resentment against authority and the police being the only 24-hour available service were the main target except when personal help was required. We gave first aid; we called out the ambulance to which every police officer subscribed – otherwise the patient was charged a fee, as mentioned above. We helped to fill in forms, draft letters and at such moments even the hardened, difficult, anti-authority characters were civil; but mutual respect or any suggestion of continued co-operation was, with rare exceptions, impossible, as they would have been accused by their neighbours of being police informers.

The novels of Catherine Cookson who was born and grew up on the eastern boundary of Jarrow gives a fairly true picture of the prevailing conditions. It was all new to me. I had left a quiet rural scene in Aberdeenshire and although I had read quite a lot of literature on slum conditions, I had not expected to experience poverty and its effect on such a large scale. Large groups of ill-clad men stood around the streets and obstructed the pavements, much to the inconvenience and annoyance of law-abiding citizens. There were arguments and fights, especially on days when unemployment and means-test benefits were paid out and at weekends. There was a hard core of drunken men who eventually went home and knocked their wives about, having spent most or all of their money. A child was usually sent to find the policeman on the beat and, when he arrived, the wife complained of being assaulted. The furniture and crockery were probably upset and broken and the man would rant and rave that his wife had not prepared a meal.

Domestic disturbances are impossible to settle: the wife wants the policeman to remain until the husband has sobered up as she knows full well she will probably be assaulted again for having called the police. Any suggestion of providing evidence of charges is rejected and there are occasions when they both ask the policeman to leave the house. Second or third visits to the same house in an evening were not unusual. In the event of the drunken and disorderly man appearing in the street, the only option was an arrest which wives resented. We used power of arrest under the Common Law for Breaches of the Peace when offenders were not in a drunken state. They were Bound Over to Keep the Peace and be of good order for a stated period. It was a most effective method of keeping order; the threat of prison for breaches of the order had a sobering influence.

There may be good reasons why Breach of the Peace seems to have gone out of fashion in England. It was a wonderful tool in my time on the beat and was much more effective than the complicated procedure for bringing alleged offenders to court under the modern ASBO legislation. The term 'zero tolerance' was unknown in the 1930s but in the tough rough areas of Jarrow that is exactly how police maintained a good standard of public order.

The Magistrates' Courts where most offences were and still are dealt with generally do a good job. However, in the best-run organizations there are black sheep. The rule at that time under which the Mayor or Chairman of a local authority on being elected automatically took his/her seat on the Bench, without any training whatsoever, was unsatisfactory. In the instance now described the mayor was politically ambitious and made no secret of the fact that he wanted to be re-elected. In the weeks leading up to the local elections, offenders appearing at Court where he was Chairman were being found not guilty, despite there being good evidence, and in many cases the punishment even to those with previous convictions was totally inadequate. The situation deteriorated when adjournments were requested to dates when he was scheduled to be on the Bench. The usual offences were for street fighting, being drunk and disorderly and for urinating in the shop doorways. After the public houses closed groups stood around until quite late and used the doorways as toilets.

There were numerous complaints from the local shopkeepers and business people whose doorways were being fouled. When we were paraded we were given firm orders to give the complaints special attention. We did so and reported the offenders but convictions were rare. One Sunday night the constable on the adjacent beat and I jointly raised the subject with our sergeant. He was a capable and highly-respected officer who held out little hope of matters being put right through official channels in the short term but he did express some thoughts and possibilities. The Mayor had a small shop situated at a well-lit junction which was therefore free from the attention of the offenders. Some time around the quietest part of the night my colleague and I urinated into the letter box of the Magistrate's shop! Apparently there was no complaint about the incident but on the Monday morning everyone appearing before the court which was chaired by the Mayor with the offence of urinating in the street was found guilty and fined the maximum of £2.00, which was about the week's wages of a labourer. The offences stopped; we kept our secret. Magistrates now have to undergo training before taking an active part in courts.

The River Tyne was fairly busy with ships importing and exporting a variety of cargoes and there was a 24-hour service of bunkering ships which were fuelled by coal. All seaports bring foreigners ashore and the majority of them have no intention of breaking the law but for a whole variety of reasons the police workload was increased. When the crew of a ship was paid off they had money to spend and they became the prey of local criminals. The approach varied: help to carry luggage was offered; seamen were guided to public houses or to places of doubtful repute, while more hardened criminals sometimes made a direct approach using knives and other weapons to execute robberies. Whichever approach was used the purpose was to part the rightful owners from their money. In the drinking establishments there were ladies expert at picking pockets whilst providing other services.

Experienced seamen usually tried to keep together to avoid trouble but those who had been at sea for a long time underestimated the effect of drinking and they would commit damage to property, brawl and eventually finish up in the cells. They were strong, hard men and took a lot of overpowering; normal handcuffs were not large enough to span their wrists which were enlarged with hard work and salt water. When they sobered up they had little recollection of the previous night's activities and were usually most apologetic. They paid their fines and the cost of damage without question but our muscles were often tender for a day or two afterwards. Whenever possible when we were approached or came across seamen the worse for wear through drink, we tried to usher them to their ships but the state of drunkenness coupled with language problems made the task difficult.

There were lighter moments when dealing with seafaring crews. It was not unusual for ships from the Eastern Bloc countries to have stewardesses. Usually two or three young ladies were accompanied by a formidable matronly figure who rarely took any part in conversation, but it was clear she was in charge. The girls would ask a policeman the directions to the lingerie shops. The language problems were confusing and to emphasis their needs they would lift their skirts and display their underwear which looked like sack cloth. An hour or so later on their way back to their ship, they would open their shopping bags and show their purchases which usually included underwear of a daring style! They would thank the policeman and sometimes reward him with a kiss on the cheek, which was enjoyable.

The local merchant seamen could also be a problem by committing offences under the Merchant Shipping Acts. Each seaman has documents with photograph, personal particulars and a complete record of the ships he has served upon, including any convictions against the Acts. The better shipping companies would not engage those with a bad record but there were companies trading in unattractive cargoes and paying poor wages which did. There was a legal obligation for companies to provide an advance note to the value of £5.00 to provide for his family and for the purchase of food and essential personal items whilst at sea. Cheques were normally cashed by the local tradesmen except when there was knowledge of previous convictions. If the cheques were cashed and the seaman did not turn up at the appointed time, an offence was committed which normally resulted in a term of imprisonment. There were no authorised organisations to provide assistance to the convicted, who could not get their cheques cashed and could not join their ship without provisions.

One morning I was on reserve duty in the office when I was instructed to keep a look out for five seaman and at a given time to line them up ready for the Superintendent and his Staff Officer. I checked their identities and the Superintendent, Mr Josh G Hammond, a 20-stone, well-over-six-foot blunt Yorkshireman, gave them all a severe dressing-down reminding them of their responsibilities to their families and promising them that they would spend the remainder of their lives in prison if they let him down. He cashed the five cheques from his personal bank account and they went on their way. Many years later when he was in retirement I mentioned the incident to him and asked him if he had ever been let down and what made him give in to their pleadings. He said he had never been let down and the reason he so acted was because of the likelihood of suffering to the wives and children.

Mr Hammond was a strict disciplinarian who rarely expressed praise and was frequently misunderstood, but when those under his command had problems he was helpful. There were many young constables from his command in the armed forces during the 1939-45 War and he regularly wrote letters in his own handwriting wishing them well. In the case of married men either he or his second-in-command would make contact with the wives and make appropriate reference to their well being. He retired to live at Darlington where I was posted in the rank of Inspector in 1952. I saw him about the town regularly and we enjoyed chatting and later when he suffered from cancer I visited him in hospital. Eventually he knew he would not recover and he went to see the then Chief Constable with a prepared document for his funeral arrangements. In those days, police in uniform turned out in strength and marched in tribute to their colleagues or former colleagues. A couple of days before his death he asked me to look after some aspects of his affairs and invited four officers, including me, who had served under him in Jarrow and who were now Inspector or Chief Inspector, to be his pall bearers. He was the same clear-headed, positive individual as he always had been and he faced death with great courage. I was proud and honoured to have been asked, or looking back, commanded, to do his final bidding; he was still the same strong decisive character.

Drunk and disorderly men are difficult to handle but women are more so in a different way especially when they are short and fat. I was not long out of my initial six months' training when on a sunny warm afternoon, a crowd was gathered in the main shopping street and on investigation I found a woman lying on her back obviously drunk, ranting and raving streams of foul language. Although traffic was light in those days the road was blocked. I tried to remove her from the road but when success was in sight she wriggled free, ran back and lay on her back in the middle of the road kicking her legs in the air which disclosed that her clothing was merely a thin dress. The scene caused great amusement to the crowd and amid loud laughter all sorts of advice was given me.

After I had made more attempts to remove her from the roadway, a chap who hired out handcarts arrived and helped me to lay her on the cart. Surprisingly she stayed there on her back, continuing to kick her heels and exposing most of her body. Embarrassment does not cover the way I felt but I wheeled her all the way to the police station, which was a long way, where neither she nor I were made very welcome. The police matron was called out and dealt with the woman who was well known. She had form for acting and performing when drunk. She was Irish in her fifties and when she appeared in court next day she started to sing an Irish ditty and tried to establish a rapport with the magistrates who knew her. She pleaded guilty and was asked if she admitted having 127 convictions. She chastised the Clerk of the Court for having got the number wrong and told him in no uncertain terms that she had 129 convictions. She expected to be sent to jail but she was bound over to Keep the Peace and left the court smiling. I returned the handcart in my own time wearing civilian clothes but I was left with a lot to live down.

Giving evidence in a Court of Law under oath is a nerve-racking business and although in the course of my career I gave evidence hundreds of times it was not a duty I approached lightly. Waiting to be called to the witness stand were the worst moments for me. Once started, my confidence increased and I was thankful to have been blessed with a good memory and needed to refer to my notes only in complicated cases. Officers were required to record in their official notebooks, in chronological order, all incidents, details of interviews and occurrences. In the event of an officer using his notebook to refresh his memory in court, the magistrates and the defence had the right to inspect the notes. If the notes appeared to have been altered or varied from the version given on oath, the officer was subject to detailed cross-examination and at worst an investigation into the possibility of perjury. Notebooks were made up in the street in all weathers and entries could become blurred. Supervising Officers frequently inspected and signed notebooks: timing and dating the entry with a signature was a good safeguard. The notebook if properly used was the lifeline of a policeman. Some solicitors were known for bullying in an endeavour to annoy and upset inexperienced policemen, thus causing them to be confused and throw doubt on the truth. In these circumstances it was important to think carefully before replying to questions and to display a modicum of decorum.

I had just started my shift at 2.00 pm when on passing a house and corner shop I smelled an escape of gas. The front door was locked so I went into the back street and scaled the wall into the yard. I found the husband in the kitchen with the gas oven turned on. He was unconscious. I dragged him into the open air and performed artificial resuscitation for virtually an hour until he regained consciousness. It was hard work and I was saturated in sweat; I had shouted for help but was not heard. His wife arrived and we got him to hospital where he remained for two or three days. He was then charged with attempted suicide. The court imposed a Good Behaviour Order and he returned home. Later when I was passing the shop, his wife called me in and thanked me for saving her husband's life, offering me a packet of 20 Woodbine cigarettes valued at four pence, which I declined explaining that I was a non-smoker. It was apparent from the state of their health and the condition of the house that they were in extreme poverty; 20 cigarettes would have been a generous gift in their circumstances and it made me feel very humble.

On a winter's evening when the snow was falling, I found a small dog whimpering in the street. There was on the collar an address to which I took the dog. The old couple were delighted: they thanked me and despite my continued refusals they pressed a half crown upon me. I entered the facts in my notebook and explained the incident to the Inspector who was marking me off duty. Wise man, he held out the Police Orphanage Charity box and endorsed my notebook accordingly. On leaving the station I was derided by my colleagues for being naïve. Of course I was fully aware there was no suggestion of bribery, something that had been drummed into us to resist. It has always embarrassed me to be beholden to anyone.

During the early hours of the morning on night shift (10.00 pm – 6.00 am) there is invariably a period when it can be difficult to keep awake: the legs get weary, the officer finds a place to rest, intending it to be for a brief moment and usually he is up and on his way quite soon. Now and again the officer fails to wake up and is absent from checking off-duty. In these circumstances the night shift and the relieving shift commence a search in the interests of safety. On the night I now recall, I was on the riverside beat from which the ferryboat, *A.B. Gowan*, operated to and from the Northumberland side of the river. The timetable was every 20 minutes from 4.45 am until 12.15 am. The police knew the crew through having to check for wanted persons and troublesome passengers.

I went aboard the boat at 4.45 am for the first journey of the day and off we went to the other side. Immediately on arrival, a River Tyne Police launch came down the river announcing by megaphone that all river craft had to remain stationary. Then the riverside lights went out. In gloomy darkness we could see four or five tugs moving *The*

King George V battleship on her way for her first sea trials. The precautions were intended to keep the progress of building naval ships away from the prying eyes of possible enemies. I did not get back to my beat until 6.15 am and was still a mile from the police station to which I ran. The Inspector asked no questions and barked an order that I would be on night shift for a month. I did not query the order and on the way out it dawned upon me that he had assumed I had fallen asleep on the beat which was fortunate for me. If the truth had been known it was possible that disciplinary charges might have arisen because I was off my beat without good reason or authority.

On Saturday nights there were two dance halls virtually opposite each other in Ellison Street. The entry charge was usually sixpence and the girls got in free. Two policemen were allocated to the task of keeping the peace outside the two premises from 10.00 pm until the people dispersed. Fights were frequent and disgruntled drunks refused entry caused problems. On this occasion, PC Jock Humble, a top Scottish wrestler, was with me when we were called to one of the halls. There was a terrific melee taking place and the central figure, a big bruiser of a man, was lashing out at all and sundry. We went either side of him and threw him out down the steps on to the pavement. There were loud cheers and we realised something was amiss. We had thrown out the bouncer who was employed to prevent disorder! He got up and it turned out he was the sparring partner for Bruce Woodcock, a well-known heavyweight boxer. We eventually calmed him down and we made an agreed brief record of the incident in our notebooks.

By the end of 1938 all kinds of naval ships were being built on the Tyne, bringing about a change in the livelihood of many people. Men previously out of work or on part-time work were now working twelve-hour shifts and there was an influx of labour to the area. It was very good for the people at large and for the shopkeepers but workers having so much more money to spend did bring problems. There were whole families of fathers and sons who had grown up during the depression and had never worked, for whom it was difficult to find a niche. Some who did not or could not adapt to the changed circumstances remained unemployed. There were probably good reasons why they could not change their way of life and fend for themselves but the situation was that some were flush with money and others were surviving on means-tested hand-outs which brought about discontent. There was an increase in drunken behaviour and there were more calls to deal with domestic violence. The political agitators became more active and infiltrated groups outside the public houses at weekends.

On Saturday 13th May 1939, disorder broke out on a large scale in the town centre where there were four public houses within sight of each other. The disturbance started with a young man who through his drunken behaviour was the centre of attraction. He refused to take police advice and two policemen managed with great difficulty to get one wrist hand-cuffed. However, with his behaviour and interference from bystanders, he broke free. My colleague and I, on the adjacent beat, on becoming aware of the disturbance, arrived to find the offender being carried shoulder-high and waving the arm with the handcuffs attached. On arriving at a good pace we grabbed him and dragged him on to a nearby through-road. Fortunately a motorcar stopped and we unceremoniously pushed him inside and sat on him until we got to the police station. In the act of getting to the car we were kicked and punched and damage was done to the vehicle by his violence. It was eventually fully restored for the owner and he was thanked for his services but declined publicity for fear of reprisals. As we left the scene, shop windows were being smashed and goods looted.

We knew the man, aged about 26 years, whom we had arrested, had previous convictions and had been discharged from the navy some years previously for misconduct. He was a bundle of strength and it was quite impossible to carry out the normal documentation. We handcuffed him to the rungs in the middle of the cell for his own safety. As the door was shut upon him he was shouting and trying to do handstands. We informed the Inspector the extent of the disorder and told him additional police help was necessary.

My colleague and I hurried back to the scene and found a sergeant with an injured knee in a shop doorway. As a temporary measure we managed to carry him into a house to be cared for. There was still a solid crowd and four police officers were standing back to back, advising the crowd to calm down and go home. Their advice was being ignored and missiles were being thrown at them and increased on observing that we were the two officers responsible for finally arresting the original offender. Some of the agitators tried to maintain the aggression by shouting and implying that we had killed the prisoner. These rumours revived hostile attitudes and it took little encouragement from the leaders for a mass march towards the police station. The two of us remained together and tried to beat the crowd to the police station and give the alarm, by using back streets, but we were too late.

The then modern building housed the Superintendent and his family at one end and his second-in-command at the other end. By the time we got there several windows of the Superintendent's house had been broken; stone and bottle throwing was taking place; police reinforcements were arriving and lining up. Josh Hammond, the Superintendent, came out with an officer carrying a box to give him greater height, which the Superintendent mounted and through a megaphone read The Riot Act followed by the order, "CHARGE!" We shouted as loud as we could and charged with our batons, ignoring the stone and bottle throwing. During the remainder of the night we patrolled the town and dispersed, by force when necessary, groups of three or more loitering in public places.

Next day, Sunday, the main streets in the town centre were closed early in the evening to vehicular traffic. Thousands of people and agitators from surrounding towns swelled the numbers assembling in one of the main streets. A strong force of police arrived. The crowds took to the pavements, and the police patrolled in pairs about eight yards apart. When there was the slightest indication of hostility by movement or voice of the people crowded together on the pavements on both sides of the street, we snatched them without warning and removed them from the scene. After the first two or three were dealt with in this manner there was complete silence and the crowds gradually drifted away without a murmur. The following weekend a fairly large number from outside the town came, many of them probably out of curiosity, but there was no local support and the weekend was virtually trouble free.

On the Saturday night of the riot, 28 of the alleged offenders were locked up and others were arrested by warrant in the days that followed. The reading of the Riot Act was effective as the focal point in breaking up the riot but had no significance in law as it was not read by a magistrate. We were all trained in Durham by officers with knowledge and experience of industrial disputes. The police had given the agitators and troublemakers a bloody nose by a show of strength and positive action which I believe had a sobering effect upon the regular trouble-makers and the political agitators appeared to be less active thereafter. The old-fashioned wooden truncheon is I believe an effective tool for dispersing rioters: policemen being lightly armed can move about swiftly, duck and weave at speed making plenty of noise and thus putting a measure of fear into the opposition, breaking them up into smaller parties making dispersal easier. The modern method of protecting policemen with shields limits their mobility, presenting static targets reminiscent of bygone battle scenes. Of course we took a few knocks but the only officer on the sick list on this occasion was the sergeant injured in the initial stages of the riot and he was soon fully fit for duty.

The end of two years as a probationary constable was approaching with the requirement to pass a written examination. It had been a busy time and I had derived a great deal of satisfaction from most aspects of police work although there were things one wished could have been done to improve the lives of the less fortunate. Wife-battering was commonplace by young men who spent earnings or unemployment benefit on drink. On the occasions police were involved, the excuse usually given was that the wife had not prepared a meal. The wives had no money to buy food and the children, young and many in number, also suffered. There were wives who retaliated in a variety of ways: shoplifting was a favourite, as were incurring debts and using false names and addresses to obtain goods. Surprisingly most were extremely loyal to their husbands, probably because in those days there was no alternative or means of support to which they could appeal.

Debts were common and Orders were made by the Courts to recover the money by distraining upon the goods in the household. I happened to have very good lodgings with the bailiff and his wife. He was constantly requesting the presence of a policeman, solely to keep the peace, when he was executing the Court Orders. It was administratively convenient for me to be so detailed which was an eye-opening experience. Getting acknowledgement and entry to property was difficult: doors would not be answered, entries were refused; there were threats, bad language and occasional assaults and on gaining entry there were no goods of value upon which to distrain.

The incident I now relate was even by expected receptions a bit different. The bailiff and I were making our way up a steep stairway to a flat when the occupant, a slim, good-looking young lady, known for entertaining seamen, appeared on the landing right above our heads and addressed the bailiff as "a bald-headed old b.....d." She issued a torrent of foul and abusive language and lifted the only garment she wore up to her chin, inviting the bailiff to take the money owed, "out of that." I was learning fast. His reply was appropriate and left little to the imagination.

What made me feel really helpless were children of tender years with dirty faces and ragged clothes in the street during the night asking for pennies for the gas meter to warm milk for babies. Policemen were not well paid but there were occasions when I could not resist parting with a penny or two. Colleagues regarded me as a soft touch and warned me that the news would get around and the scroungers would put their children up to spinning me lies. However, in an unintentional and unexpected way, I reaped benefits. Now and again a mother of young children would surreptitiously pass me information about the whereabouts of wanted persons and tips about those involved in crime. My most memorable arrest arising from that source of information was when I was directed to the rear of a lock-up fish and chip shop where I found two young men in the enclosed yard about to break into the premises to steal the contents of the gas meter. To catch criminals red-handed is the ambition of every young policeman; I was just as thrilled as the culprits were frightened.

In two short years I learned a great deal about people and how to deal with the public from all walks of life. The policeman on the beat was required to record the movements not only of criminals and suspected persons but anything unusual. Policemen also got to know the movements and habits of good honest citizens and a sound understanding could develop by merely passing the time of day with them. When crimes and offences were committed the culprits were frequently detected through a combination of notebook entries and good relationships built up with reliable members of the public. Of course we had to be aware of informants giving false information but more of that later.

A Declaration of Intent and War-time Policing

Policemen on rotating shifts find it difficult to socialise and take part in regular activities with members of the public at large. Therefore the tendency is to spend free time with colleagues: soccer, athletics, the cinema and occasional dances were popular. We did not spend much time in public houses for the good reason that we could not afford to do so. As single men we lived in lodgings approved by our superiors. Some of the landladies tried their hand at match-making and on birthdays and on special occasions arranged house parties with usually an equal numbers of young ladies and policemen.

During my two years as a probationary constable I was able to visit my home in Aberdeen on only two occasions because of the limited time off and the cost of train fares. However, Mother, a prolific letter writer, kept me abreast with the family news. I had been well received in Durham and had made good friends. My life in the police service was satisfying but much of my free time was taken up with studies and I had deliberately not got seriously involved with any young lady. Whilst I was still undecided as to how I intended spending my free time, I was introduced to Lucy Brunt on 8th August 1939. One problem was solved: we married in wartime on 6th December 1941 and as I write we have completed 65 years of marriage which was marked with a congratulatory message from Her Majesty the Queen, with her photograph.

The German nation led by Adolph Hitler had been threatening war in Europe for some considerable time. In September 1938 Neville Chamberlain PM went to Munich on a peace mission and when he stepped off the aircraft upon returning, he waved a document for all to see and gave an assurance there would be "Peace in our time." In the meantime Hitler continued aggression by annexing Austria, Bohemia and Moravia. Britain was quite unprepared for war. The promise of peace was generally regarded as of little value but it did provide a breathing space for a start to be made to re-arm. On the Tyne, shipyards which had stood idle for years were again in use. A new rolling steel mill was built on what had been Palmers Shipyard to make plates for the construction of warships. The police service was busy training officers on how to deal with incidents arising from enemy attacks. A proportion of the training was carried out on Sunday mornings when there was least activity on the streets.

By September 3rd, 1939 my training was complete and I was the only policeman on duty in the centre of the town on that morning. Poland had been invaded on 1st September and it was expected that the Prime Minister would address the nation on the 3rd at 11.00 am. As the hour approached the streets were silent, with most people tuned in to their radios. I had arranged with the caretaker of the Town Hall and his wife to listen to the broadcast. We waited. He and his wife were behind the iron grille gates with their portable wireless and I was on the steps outside. The waiting passed slowly but eventually the expected bad news came, the Prime Minister announcing that war had been declared upon Germany. Within two to three minutes of the declaration the air raid sirens sounded which was the signal that an air raid was imminent. The street remained quiet for about 15 minutes until the sirens sounded the All Clear.

The immediate reaction from the nearby terraced street where there was a dense population was a rush of families towards the Town Hall demanding the issue of gas masks to which they were entitled and had been promised. The anger was made worse by the fact that it was common knowledge that some local authorities had issued or were in the process of fitting and issuing masks. The caretaker tried by telephone to get attention from senior Council staff but help was not forthcoming. According to the caretaker the only masks available, as far as he was aware, were those especially made for the protection of young babies.

It was within my knowledge that some members of the Salvation Army had been trained in fitting those masks. A message was sent to the nearby Salvation Army hall. Two ladies with nursing experience and trained in fitting baby masks responded immediately and we sent messages to other people so trained, eventually making a small team of six. Between us we thought it would be worth trying to allow three adults, each with a baby, into the Town Hall at any one time. I tried to tell the crowd what we were doing but they were not ready to listen and the angry scene continued. When the three mothers reappeared with their babies and masks there was a gradual reduction of threats to storm the Town Hall and as the day wore on the noise subsided somewhat although a large crowd remained.

I was relieved late in the afternoon; apparently I had not been missed at the police station which was understandable as all officers whether on or off duty reported there when the sirens sounded. They were busy being briefed from the special orders which hitherto had been confidential to the senior officers. I am quite sure that those who heard that broadcast still remember it, and how they felt, and where they were, on that fateful Sunday morning. I still remember every detail and the surge of fear which went through my body when war was declared; what followed was equally frightening.

The work of the police increased and changed with the outbreak of war and the introduction of Emergency Laws. The immediate task was dealing with aliens. Most German families had already returned home but there were a number of aliens on police records of other nationalities in the category to be detained and placed in secure accommodation. Additionally, beginning from the invasion of Poland, merchant ships of all nationalities sought refuge in British ports. The Tyne became packed with ships not going anywhere and they remained there for some time.

The crews spent time ashore ambling about the streets; some had money to spend, some did not. They were expected to return to their ships overnight. The police did their best to help them back aboard but it was difficult, for there were language problems and not all of them had adequate identity documents. A curfew was imposed which to the best of my memory covered the twelve hours between 8.00 pm and 8.00 am. Among those seamen were those who had no desire to return to their ships and hoped they could find refuge ashore. Towards the end of most days the police gathered those still not aboard their ships and herded them in small groups to the police station. They were charged with breaking the curfew laws and appeared at court the following morning. On pleading guilty through interpreters they were usually fined one or two pounds sterling. They remained in custody until a representative from the ships paid the fines. By and large they were frightened and worried people, friendly with police, but control was essential as their presence provided opportunities for enemy agents to infiltrate and remain in the country.

All premises had to be completely blacked out during the hours of darkness which was not easy to achieve at short notice. Police spent much time giving advice and help. As Air Raid Wardens became more available the police task of dealing with the blackout was lightened. Getting about the streets in a complete blackout was hazardous: hand torches were permitted. Vehicles were not allowed to use headlamps and sidelights were dimmed, showing only sufficient light for other road users to see them approaching.

Within a short time of the declaration of war, German bombers came regularly during the hours of darkness and dropped bombs in the area. No doubt their targets were the shipyards where battleships and other naval craft were being built. The Tyne is curved and, coupled with effective camouflage including dummy ships, the intended targets were difficult to locate. Initially there not many anti-aircraft and searchlight units in the area and the bombers got through, resulting in dwelling houses being hit. One such raid occurred in Napier Street, Jarrow just before midnight, resulting in many deaths, casualties and the destruction of a number of dwelling houses.

I was on night duty on that beat and quite near to where the bombs dropped. The explosions tore a gap in the terraced street. Amid the dust and debris there were cries of people in pain and calls for help. At this early stage of the war rescue services were limited which necessitated the immediate rescue work to be carried out by willing neighbours. It was a dangerous task as part of the damaged buildings had to be torn apart with bare hands by tugging and pulling, thus increasing the risk of falling masonry and other debris. We managed to get a number of people out alive. Some of them were injured to varying degrees, but the death toll was high and two or three families were wiped out completely.

At this time not all the air raid shelters had been built but even where they were available there was some reluctance on the part of members of the public to use them. This attitude soon changed when it was realised that everyone was vulnerable. Police on duty were required to remain on patrol in the open and only visited the shelters if their presence was requested. In addition to the dangers from falling bombs, the spent, fragmented anti-aircraft shells could and occasionally did cause serious injuries. Steel helmets were essential protection. The raids continued, causing casualties and damage but as time went on the density of the anti-aircraft batteries and searchlight units increased and became more effective in detecting and dealing with enemy aircraft.

Regular policemen were placed in the reserved occupation category which meant they could not resign even if they were eligible for a retirement pension. However, military reservists were liable to call up and most had been recalled to their units by mid-November 1939. The result was that the police ranks were greatly depleted of young officers. The problem had been foreseen and in the months leading up to the commencement of war there was a recruiting drive for suitable candidates of an age unlikely to be conscripted for military service. They were to be appointed 'Temporary Constables' and would not be included in the reserved occupation category. The response was poor: police wages were low compared with unskilled labour being paid overtime working in the shipyards and factories where the demand for labour was high. The high wastage from the small numbers recruited was disappointing.

Long hours, with no overtime payments, were the order of the day for regular officers. Occasionally, if things were quiet, a couple of hours off would be given at the discretion of the officer in charge of the shift. When there were air raids we were required to report at our normal place of duty and we did so willingly. However, on our one day a week off duty we thought it harsh to have to remain within the bounds of the responsibilities of our normal stations. After representation the requirement for those going beyond the normal limits was to submit a report in advance and await approval. That system was an obstacle, especially to single men whose plans were more flexible than married men and with further pleas it was agreed that if we intended leaving the bounds of our operational station it would suffice to record the details in a station counter book.

The new arrangements were an improvement but it did result in a few of us having narrow escapes in getting back to our stations in reasonable time after the sirens had sounded. We frequently went farther or elsewhere than we intended when recording our intentions and when the sirens sounded there was no transport. On one occasion I ran all the way from Newcastle, a distance of about seven miles and after changing into uniform I crept quietly into the background with others on reserve and my late arrival went unnoticed. There were other scrapes and a variety of reasons was given. As a last resort the excuse of being asleep and not hearing the siren was used. The senior officers no doubt had the measure of us and gave brief advice. Occasionally if it was apparent that an officer was taking undue advantage, an extra night shift or two was the punishment.

We accepted whatever punishment was awarded and congratulated ourselves on the occasions we had not been found out! We did work hard but we enjoyed a few hours' relaxation in our limited free time. Air raid duties had priority but there were still more than enough traditional police duties to be carried out. There was more money about with long hours being worked in the shipyards and factories and much of it was spent in the public houses. There were probably more cases of assault, damage and drunken behaviour than in peacetime. We also had to cope with the continuing presence of alien seamen.

There was a feeling of togetherness: people were more friendly to each other and there was greater co-operation with the police than before the war. Families spent more time in their homes which reduced the incidence of house breaking and theft from houses. Police were often the bearers of sad news arising from death and casualties within the country from air raids, and also from the Armed Services. At that time and for a long time afterwards a high number of merchant ships were being sunk and it often fell to the police to inform families of the loss of husbands, sons and fathers of young children. This duty necessitated a sympathetic approach and on occasions first aid had to be applied. When possible we would seek out good neighbours or friends to accompany us and be present when we were breaking the bad news. Many lives and dreams were shattered; loved ones and breadwinners never to be seen again.

Policing the War

This chapter is included after much anguish and soul-searching as it is a part of my life which I have kept to myself. Sworn to secrecy has always meant just that to me but over the years the task involved which I write about has been written about and discussed by others identically involved and in any case it is all about past events which now expose no threat to the security of the nation. People of my generation were brought up during and in the wake of the First World War to regard the defence of the British Empire as our first duty in life. Therefore colleagues of my age discussed how we could be of greater service to the country: the general feeling amongst us was that we should be in the armed services. We were not being given much news about the war in Europe and what we heard was not very encouraging. In January 1940 one or two of us made application to be released from police duty to join the armed services. Our requests were turned down and we were informed that we were needed on the home front looking after and dealing with the people affected by air raids. We were reminded it was an important and dangerous duty of which we should be proud. It was more or less what we expected but I decided to put in a similar application at the beginning of each month.

February and March came with the standard rejection replies. I submitted another application at the beginning of April. My Superintendent said he would forward it as usual to the Chief Constable with his comments but he thought it was a waste of time. In the meantime it was common knowledge that the war was not going well in Europe and additional fortifications were being built around the coasts and navigable rivers. A week or so after my April application, my Superintendent asked me to report to the Deputy

Chief Constable at Durham on my weekly rest day. He emphasised that I must not mention to anyone what I was doing and I was required to go in plain clothes. His last advice to me was not to make a note of the event. Going to see the Deputy Chief Constable at that stage in life filled me with trepidation and it no doubt showed; my Superintendent added that I was not in trouble and gave me a reassuring smile.

I kept the appointment with the Deputy Chief Constable who made reference to my persistent applications to join the armed forces. He was friendly and asked me to meet two men in grey suits whom he called into his office. I spent the day with the two men, being given lunch and a £1 note to cover my travelling expenses, which was generous. It was explained that there must be no record in police accounts of the meeting or of expense claims. They said they were looking for people to carry out tasks connected with the war and they had to be satisfied about the suitability of people selected. I was not given any idea of what the tasks might involve. I answered what I thought were hundreds of friendly but incisive questions. The only feedback I was given at the end of the day was a comment that they thought I had a good memory which would be essential as nothing I might be involved in could be committed to paper.

Within a few days I had a letter from a gentleman in Aberdeenshire who had been one of my referees when I initially joined the police. He had previously written and wished me well but on this occasion there was a hint that he thought I might be in some kind of bother. It was obvious he had had a visit from someone asking about my background. I was then young and naïve and it was not until years later that I became familiar with the term, 'Positive Vetting for Security purposes', which is what I had experienced.

Within a short time of my visit to Durham, my Superintendent informed me that the headmaster of the Grammar School would be pleased to see me on a confidential matter. I asked no questions. Subsequently I had a meeting with the headmaster at the Clock Hotel, Hebburn, which was situated a few hundred yards over the Jarrow Borough boundary and about five minutes' walk from my lodgings in Albert Road. Our meeting was in a small room which was completely private. The manager of the hotel kept a good house and charged about half a penny per drink more than the normal public houses which was a good way of maintaining standards. Policemen found it a suitable place to go to get away from unwanted attention, as did the headmaster. He had a friend from industry with him: we talked and we got to know each other that evening. Another meeting was arranged. Confidentiality was emphasised and the need to continue to be seen to be living a normal way of life.

At our next meeting the possibility of a German invasion was discussed. It was disclosed that there would be no surrender and it was anticipated that the civil authorities and the police would be required to continue to serve the public. There was however a possibility that the enemy might disband normal services. Whatever happened the plan was that in addition to the tiers of fighting and defence forces there was to be a sprinkling of people trained for the purpose of sabotaging the work of the enemy at every opportunity. Those so trained would be expected to operate without supervision or orders and take what action was appropriate as opportunities arose. The people selected for this task must continue to live and work in the locality in which they would operate or if necessary as a last resort go underground and continue harassment of the enemy. A whole lot of the difficulties and problems which might arise were put to me before I was asked if I would undertake such a task. I accepted the challenge.

Training in my off-duty time commenced immediately with an hour or two now and again at irregular intervals. Meticulous training was given in the handling and use of explosives and where they were available. Skeleton keys made of brass, giving access to explosive magazines, were provided as steel keys can trigger explosions. Additional skeleton keys were made available, which concerned me because policemen are not allowed to have them; the consequences of being found carrying them was a serious offence under the Police Discipline Code. My trainers advised me on how to disperse them and keep them hidden along with other tools and materials. A complete knowledge of the geography of the streets was demanded and the mental noting of likely bolt holes should dangers loom. To this day I can still recall blocks of streets as they were then. For example, the streets, James, Clayton, Mackintyre, Wear, Berkeley and Bladen were bounded on the north by Great Western Road, on the south by

Grange Road South, on the east by Ellison Street and on the west by an industrial site. I was tested on the use of skeleton keys by entering certain premises and bringing out an article or used envelopes with the addresses thereon. There were sufficient explosives available to blow up the oil refineries on the River Tyne and other industrial establishments.

The situation was deteriorating in Europe and between the end of May and 4th June 1940 there was a mass evacuation of the armed forces via Dunkirk. A few days later on 10th June the Italians declared war on Britain. Italian ice-cream parlours were closed and families had to leave their homes to be detained in secure accommodation; it was a sad time, for they were friendly and co-operated with police requirements. Once again the River Tyne was overwhelmed with ships seeking shelter, which brought about extra work concerning alien seamen. Air raids continued and there was grave concern that the country might be invaded. The nation was shocked and spirits were low. Families did not know if the soldiers who did not escape at Dunkirk were alive or if they were prisoners of war. The Royal Air Force was doing an excellent job in fighting off German air attacks but the Royal Navy was having heavy losses. Merchant ships were being sunk with essential supplies of food and other necessities.

Ration cards were in use for the purchase of food, clothing and other items. Housewives had a problem in trying to eke out family rations and queued up at butchers' shops early in the morning in the hope of buying sausages and pies made of offal which was not rationed. Fashion clothes disappeared from the shops and items of clothing such as nylon stockings and lingerie were only obtainable from under the counter at a price and the surrender of clothing coupons. The black market flourished. Thefts of ration cards and clothing coupons were frequently committed within families and were difficult to resolve. Serious offences were dealt with by police and the courts.

By the spring of 1941 there was less tension in the air as it was beginning to appear an invasion was less likely, the belief being that Hitler had missed the opportunity to make the attempt. Although there was no question of abandoning the sabotage plans, my training took a change of course. The headmaster turned my attention to the history of the peoples of Europe and specifically the high numbers and nationalities of those who had settled in the United States of America since the end of the 1914-18 War. Reading material was provided and we had tutorials on the subject. It was readily apparent that the families of the immigrants of that time would be of military age. It posed the question whether that had any relevance to America's apparent reluctance to join in the war against Hitler. Some politicians and journalists were critical of America for not taking part, although the USA was supplying Britain with food and other supplies and their ships were being sunk in doing so. At the time I did not associate the subject discussed with anything which might involve my future. I was given a comprehensive mathematical test paper which I completed and was informed the results were good. Shortly after the test two men in grey suits spent a couple of hours with me. The questioning was wide-ranging and conducted in a friendly manner. It may seem odd now that I did not question the purpose of the interview but the circumstances were different in wartime Britain. Slogans were everywhere, one of which was 'Careless talk costs lives'.

Therefore I was surprised to be given confidential advance information that quite soon there would be an announcement inviting applications from serving police officers to join The Royal Air Force Volunteer Reserve to be trained either as pilots or navigators. Their release from serving in a reserved occupation was conditional on their achieving either of two qualifications and if for any reason they were unsuccessful or their services were no longer required, they would be discharged to return to their former duties. At the same meeting they told me that the mathematical examination was the educational test for pilots and navigators. The next surprise was being told that a flight had been arranged for me at a nearby RAF Fighter Station with the explanation that it would be a waste of time if for any reason I was unfit for flying duties. The flight was early one morning in a two-seater aircraft in which I was treated to a variety of aerobatic manoeuvres. Now and again the pilot would ask on the intercommunication system if I was all right. When we landed the pilot apologised for giving me a rough ride but he had been briefed to ascertain if I had the nerve and stomach to fly.

When the conditions for joining the RAF VR were announced, Bob Dobson, a friend and colleague, and I made immediate application and we were accepted with effect from June 1941. He was of course unaware of my brief experience in the air. There was a tremendous response from serving police officers to become airmen. After documentation and preliminary tests Bob Dobson and I swapped our uniforms for a different colour of blue in September 1941.

Policeman to Pilot

While waiting to join up, normal police duties were undertaken. There was some relaxation in the long hours worked which gave me more time with Lucy. We had been keeping company for nearly two years. Lucy was working full-time and was also a volunteer air raid warden so that our meetings were frequently broken up with the noise of the air raid sirens. People looked after each other and were very thoughtful. They would leave their front doors ajar to enable people caught out in the street to shelter. On more than one occasion we would throw ourselves into a passageway and find ourselves on top of people already there. It was good fun and we laughed a lot at our escapades in the blackout! About the only places of entertainment still functioning were the cinemas but when the siren went the audiences took to the shelters. In daylight hours we walked a great deal, keeping within a reasonable range of our reporting posts; we could both run very well in those days. Immediately after my being accepted for the RAF VR, we were engaged: we had no plans for marriage. It was a sad parting. We knew not what was ahead.

For the first few weeks in RAF uniform we spent much of our time in the classroom with periods of drill and physical training. We were Aircraftmen Second Class (A/C2) and, according to the drill and PT sergeants, who also were mainly pre-war professional footballers, the lowest form of humanity. We did bait them a bit now and again merely to enliven the proceedings! Most of the intake were young men of about 18 years of age who had not previously lived away from home and they needed help and guidance which the older amongst us gave them. Eventually we were dispersed to a number of small airfields to commence our flying training and to continue class work. It was a testing time: we flew Tiger Moths, with the objective of reaching solo standard in about eight to ten hours' flying, which if not achieved, except on rare occasions, meant discharge or being moved to undertake a navigation course. Others were relegated to courses for air gunners or to ground duties. Fortunately I made the grade.

In the meantime we had progressed to become cadets with the pay of Leading Aircraftsmen (LAC) which meant an increase. Durham County Police Authority were kind to policemen serving in any branch of the armed services and made our salaries up to 75% of our police pay. Most police authorities were generous to some extent but frequently the time came when the earnings of individuals increased to the point where they no longer qualified for the authority payments. We were recognized as Air Cadets by wearing a white flash in our caps and documented as U/T (under training) pilots. We joined holding units pending the decision where we were to be posted for the next stage of our training. There were insufficient facilities in the United Kingdom and air crews were being trained in South Africa, Canada and America.

At this stage I was taken in secret to a place where there were four RAF cadets, ex-policemen, unknown to me or to each other. We were briefed by Sir Winston Churchill PM on the task required of us and the importance of confidentiality as any breach could be harmful to UK/US International relations. The plan was the result of a joint personal agreement between Roosevelt and Churchill. It appeared a simple enough assignment for an experienced police officer and provided one kept one's counsel it should not impinge upon flying training. We were told no record of the briefing would be made so in effect no such meeting took place.

Looking back on this incident, sixty-plus years later, I suppose it seems strange that I was not struck by the significance of this audience with the Prime Minister. As I saw it, I was simply doing my job and it took me a little time to realise the importance of being entrusted with such a task. I never told anyone about having met Winston Churchill on that special occasion until I mentioned it to my wife, Lucy, three or four years into the new Millennium. I do indeed consider it an honour to have had a private audience with probably one of the most significant men of the 20th century.

Towards the end of November I was included in a draft scheduled to sail for Canada around mid-December and given promise of leave. I immediately wrote to Lucy proposing we should be married before I left the country to which she said yes. Time was short. There were few telephones available but thankfully the postal service was very good and most letters arrived the day after posting. Lucy and her friends had spent all their clothing coupons. It was impossible to find the sort of outfits normally worn at weddings but it was not an obstacle as neither fashion nor celebrations were available to the many others in similar situations. The normal requirements of Calling the Banns on three consecutive Sundays and other formalities were set aside in wartime. Our best friends Winnie Thompson and Francis Charles (Charlie) Davis were Bridesmaid and Best Man. We were most grateful for their help and Lucy's family in making arrangements at short notice. So on 6th December 1941, ten days after my proposal, we were married at Christ Church, Jarrow.

Mr and Mrs Rennie

When we came out of church we were cheered by a large gathering of local people wishing us well. After a brief celebration with Lucy's family, we spent the night in Edinburgh on our way to have a few days with my family in Aberdeenshire. We travelled by rail with service travel warrants for which I was most grateful as I had only the sum of £4.19.6d left! We were mad but at the same time it was a mad world.

On the night of our wedding the Japanese bombed Pearl Harbor which brought the Americans into the war. It immediately crossed my mind there might be a change to my posting to America. On reporting back to my unit along with others returning from leave, we were informed the sailing which was due before Christmas was postponed. Whilst waiting we asked for more leave of absence which was refused. We were kept occupied during the hours of darkness on the face of the South Cliff at Scarborough, supposedly guarding the coast: we had no weapons, and it was pitch black and perishing. With the help of a friend, a London and North Eastern policeman and the kindness of a Post Office driver, I sneaked a weekend home to the surprise and delight of Lucy.

Eventually I joined *The Banfora*, originally a French ship and sailed from the Mersey early in the New Year; the ship was quite unsuited for the North Atlantic. It was really a cargo ship with a cabin or two. We set sail with *The Rangitaiki* a New Zealand ship. The two ships sailed together without escort. The following day about 11.00 am an RAF plane flew over and around the two ships, dipping a salute before flying out of sight, which we were informed meant we were on our own.

The Banfora had a skeleton crew and the cadets undertook a variety of duties. There was an anti-aircraft gun mounted at the stern upon which four or five of us were given brief training. It was fortunate that we were not called upon to fire the weapon in anger! There were a few cabins up front which were strictly out of bounds to cadets. About the only member of the crew with whom we had regular contact was the cook, who was noteworthy in producing thick-skinned sausages in the morning and stew for lunch and supper always accompanied by tea. We dipped our mugs in the tea bucket and our mess tins in the stew buckets as otherwise we would have spilled everything because of the pitch and roll of the ship. We were advised to sleep in our clothes which we did, except for our shoes, in hammocks in the hold. There was hardly any space between us and we soon kept our shoes on rather than have sweaty feet in our faces.

Photo taken in Scarborough to give to Lucy

After a couple of days there were only three or four of us not suffering sea-sickness. The mess and stench was such that even though it was cold and often wet we spent the nights crouched on the deck. We encountered a heavy storm which lasted for several long days, making the sea-sickness last longer than expected. During the storm the ship pitched and rolled with the two twin screws remaining out of the water for some considerable time. It was frightening. When the storm abated *The Banfora* had engine trouble and was out of control for about 24 hours, during which time *The Rangitaiki* circled us until the engineer, an old Scot, who used to come on deck now and again for a breath of fresh air, got the engines going again. The following day *The Rangitaiki* had engine trouble and *The Banfora* did the circling. Thereafter the speed was reduced to nurse the engines. In the meantime the weather on deck was perishing; we sort of worked out from the sun that we had gone far north, probably to avoid enemy submarines. The delays resulted in the journey taking nearly twice as long as scheduled. The rations and drinking water were in short supply but the stew kept coming!

We were a dirty, scruffy, smelly lot when we finally crept into Halifax, Nova Scotia, through a bank of thick fog. In later years Sir John (Sandy) Willison, an old colleague, reminded me of that journey when he was entertaining audiences with tales, a favourite being that old sailors never die they just smell that way.

There was a story going round the ship that there were two senior German officers being carried in one of the forward cabins to be detained in a prisoner-of-war camp in Canada. It was deduced from the story, whether rumour or truth, that their presence ensured a safe passage preventing attack from submarines. It certainly was a relief to put our feet on dry land. We went by train to Trenton, Ontario, to a large transit camp where we cleaned up with the inevitable 'Free from infection' inspection examination and where we enjoyed wholesome food.

After a short stay at Trenton, about 300 cadets boarded a troop train for the journey to Georgia in the USA which was expected to take three to four days. We reached as far as Quebec one afternoon and after an hour or two of inactivity at the railway station we realised something was amiss. Four of us, ex-policemen, all Scotsmen, enquired when the journey was likely to restart and were informed it would not be before 8.00 o'clock the following morning.

We slipped away quietly and made our way to the city centre. It was a wonderful sight: there was snow on the ground, and the whole place was brightly lit showing up many fine buildings. It was a tonic after being used to the blackout at home and the rough sea journey which we had recently experienced. We enjoyed looking round and admired the Heights of Abraham in its flood-lit splendour. We had something to eat and drink; we were not drunk but we were in high spirits! It was still early in the evening. We could not understand why the streets were so quiet. Someone suggested we perform a sword dance on the snowy ground to keep warm. Just as we started fooling about, children and adults started to drift past. The girls were beautifully dressed, all in white. We stood still but did not attempt to speak to them.

Very soon four young policemen appeared and despite our protestations we were ushered to a nearby police station. They asked for identification but we made little progress as their French was not our French and in any case they were not inclined to converse with us. We tried giving them information and explanations for our presence in Quebec. Finally one of them spotted from our documents that we were Scottish. We were then asked to sit down while a telephone call was made. Shortly afterwards, a tall man in civilian clothes, obviously their superior, arrived and addressed them in French. Then he turned to us and putting on an exaggerated Glaswegian accent and confirming our situation told us he was a lieutenant in the Quebec Police. He had served in France in the First World War where he met his wife and subsequently emigrated to Canada. He took us to his home nearby where we met his family and were overwhelmed with their hospitality. They rallied round other people of Scots origin and there was soon a full house. We were plied with questions as to how things were in the United Kingdom and in particular their places of origin in Scotland, still referring to them as 'home' although they had been in Quebec for over 20 years. It was a wonderful evening.

We were escorted back to the railway station quite late at night. We asked the reason for our behaviour and presence being queried and were informed that the police had been contacted by people passing on their way with their children to Notre Dame Cathedral. Apparently it was a Saints Day, of which there were many, and it was the custom for the normal social and street activities to await the conclusion of the Cathedral proceedings which explains why the place was so quiet. We went on our way the following morning and were informed the reason for the delay involved a dispute because the driver was not a member of the appropriate union.

As we travelled south, rumours and counter rumours abounded as they do in these circumstances. Disappointments were expressed by some that they were not to be trained in Canada from where there were glowing accounts from earlier cadets. My friend Bob Dobson was delighted when he was selected for a Canadian course which he enjoyed and gained his wings in a relatively short period of time.

There were broadly three types of establishment where flying training was taught in America. The most popular was mainly manned by civilian instructors where the atmosphere was more relaxed and there was a better social life. The Naval Air Force personnel were trained at Pensacola in the Gulf of Mexico and there were British cadets there in training but not in large numbers; they were not enthusiastic about the place because of strict discipline and limited freedom. The American Army Air Force trained American West Point and British cadets on identical lines to the West Point Military Academy which is the equivalent of our Sandhurst. There was a book with the title 'I Wanted Wings', written by a former cadet, circulating among us on the train, the reading of which did nothing to calm our nerves.

We finally arrived in Georgia and were made comfortable in a tented camp during which time we were given thorough medical and dental examinations similar to those which we had undergone when joining the RAF VR. Not all had recovered from the long sea and train journey and the generous portions of rich food to which we were not accustomed caused stomach upsets and diarrhoea. Physical training commenced immediately, conducted by university-qualified civilians and in a short time we were in good shape again.

Our studies commenced with the theory of flight and other related subjects all of which we had covered thoroughly and been tested on in the UK. Similarly, although we had all passed the solo test, we had to start again from scratch; our pleas and production of our log books with the appropriate entries were disregarded.

One good aspect of staying in that camp was that we were allowed out in our free time and were able to meet and mix with the local people. They were friendly and generous to us in the coffee bars. From their conversation they assumed we were training to go to war against the Japanese. We explained that although we were at war against the Japanese we would be returned to serve in Europe and we were surprised that they seemed to have scant knowledge of the war there which had been going on since 1939.

Eventually our flying training commenced with highly-capable civilian instructors. There were no limits on how many hours were allowed to reach solo standard but it was much more generous than in the UK with the RAF. Surprisingly there were a few cadets who did not make the grade and were returned to Canada. We were quite aware that we would not all get through the course but the rejection at this stage of cadets who had previously reached the required standard was bad for morale.

At the end of four weeks we were dispersed into different camps and joined up with West Point cadets. The ratio was probably about four or five Americans to one British. We were allocated beds in dormitories with a West Point cadet either side. We were fully integrated and would be known as West Point cadets with a requirement that we address each other as Mister. Our American colleagues had joined West Point when they were 18 or 19 years of age and for the past two to three years it had been their life. They had few privileges, limited leaves of absence and were well-conditioned to the strict discipline code, known as the Honour System which was completely different from the British Military method of maintaining good order and military discipline.

The Honour System involved the award of de-merits by the cadets reporting themselves for minor breaches of discipline. Regular Officers and Honorary Cadet Captains also had the authority to award de-merits. A chart was on display in each dormitory upon which the de-merits were recorded. Each cadet was allowed seven de-merits per week free of punishment. Over and above that number the punishment was 15 minutes' marching for each de-merit incurred. The marching took place in an enclosed square surrounded by offices occupied by Regular Officers attending to their daily duties. Cadets were required to march at 90 paces per minute and when the pace slowed down orders would be called by the officers through open windows to quicken the pace; the scene was reminiscent of a prison exercise yard. Cadets booked themselves on and off for these punishments which were carried out in their limited leisure time. If a cadet accumulated a large number of de-merits it could take weeks to eradicate them. It was hard work marching in the heat and humidity of Alabama, Georgia and the Carolinas where the camps were situated.

In the early days of the course I did my share of marching, usually for minor infringements of which we were not aware. To my knowledge the USA cadets never complained or questioned whatever was asked of them whereas the younger UK cadets found the rules frustrating and made their views known or deliberately defied them. Their high-spirited harmless pranks were not appreciated and resulted in the award of more de-merits. The older among us did our best to keep them out of mischief by talking to them and giving advice. I believe that if the rules and obscure breaches of conduct had been explained beforehand there would have been a better understanding and less frustration for the benefit of all concerned; as it was we learned by default.

The atmosphere was not conducive to getting to know our American cousins as easily as we should have done because the conditions were a barrier. About half-way through the year-long course, I was made an honorary captain with appropriate badges of rank and the responsibilities and authority of Regular Officers which included use and supervision of the de-merit charts. The honorary rank gave me the privilege of being confined to the dormitory instead of the marching punishment but a handicap was that if I did not ensure that the requisite number of de-merits were awarded, the balance was credited to me with the accompanying punishment! I soon learned and decided a different method of awarding de-merits for which I expected to be challenged. Each day I inspected the de-merit chart and awarded de-merits to those with few or none against their name and at the end of the week I reduced the number of cadets in-excess of the seven permitted awards. The results were that awards were being given more than usual but fewer punishments ensued. A few weeks passed without comment from the Regular Officers before it was noticed that the number of cadets marching off de-merits had declined. I was asked to see the Commanding Officer and much to my surprise he complimented me on having created a better understanding between USA and UK cadets and for improving the standard of discipline in my company. No mention was made of my bending the de-merit rules; I had taken a chance and got away with it!

Now and again we participated in American sports which were about the only outlet for social discourse. The PX (Post Exchange) shop, like our NAAFI, was available for the purchase of our domestic needs and there was an abundance of coin-operated Coke machines about the place, but there were no social facilities or centre for getting together and relaxing. There was a bar in a section of the PX which was available to other ranks but was out of bounds to cadets. The temptation to take risks and have a beer on a warm steamy evening appealed to two or three of us older cadets, while the younger ones enjoyed Coke. We found a way of getting there by tipping the other ranks employed in keeping the place tidy to leave a set of overalls in a place where we could find them. We put them on, strode into the bar and enjoyed a couple of pints. The consequences of being found out were not to be thought about. The food was generous and well-prepared but the dining hall visits were disappointing, as meals were consumed quickly with scarcely any conversation.

Having re-qualified to fly solo we moved on to the next stage of training at a large military camp. The instructors were USA officers and one or two from the RAF. We continued classroom studies covering aeronautics, navigation and other subjects more related to the American army than to the needs of Royal Air Force personnel.

The aircraft were two-seater, single-engined and more powerful and faster than the ones we had previously flown. We practised exacting manoeuvres with the guidance of an instructor over the inter-communications system until we reached the standard to fly solo that type of machine. The aerobatic manoeuvres which were challenging and enjoyable gave us confidence and taught us the necessity for maintaining a high standard of safety. There were strict procedures on the action to be taken to ensure there were no obstacles or other aircraft about before changing course. Taking off was relatively easy compared with ensuring smooth landings which we practised until we got them right. We referred light-heartedly to this exercise as 'circuits and bumps'; there was no place for the bumps which were heavy landings resulting in the aircraft bouncing along the ground and, in the event of strong cross-winds, turning the machine over.

A serious hazard when flying in this part of the world were the cyclones. They were seasonal and occurred regularly and without warning in the afternoons when the temperature was high. Terrifically high winds and rain developed whirlwinds causing columns of black dirt to swirl into the sky for hundreds of feet. They were frightening and it was essential to be on the alert and to take immediate avoiding action as no aircraft could survive them. Even if it appeared you were not in the path of a column, there were dangers as they weaved about changing course. Fortunately there were a number of emergency landing fields marked on our maps and flying windsocks to which to divert. The torrential rain usually continued for some time in the wake of the storms but the water, sometimes ankle deep, soon dried up in the hot climate. There were occasions during severe storms when light aircraft, unless strongly anchored, were carried into the air and found elsewhere wrecked. Casualties did occasionally occur in these circumstances.

As we progressed we were taught formation flying, the lead pilot being in charge of the three which made up the flight. He controlled the pilot on either side of him by hand signals and a known wiggle of the wings. We found it much easier in maintaining formation and direction to fly close to each other and when we were well away from our base we had fun lightly tapping the wing of the lead adjacent machine. It was certainly not the most sensible thing to do but there were few opportunities to let off steam on this long, highly-restricted course where relaxation and light relief were rare.

We moved on to fly more powerful aircraft and put into practice our navigation skills learned in the classroom. We plotted courses, taking into account wind speeds, magnetic variation, weather conditions and distances. We fed the information into manually-operated calculators which when flying were strapped on above the knee. We were instructed in instrument flying which we practised with some trepidation as it is in effect flying blind and very much by the seat of the pants. Night flying caused some uneasiness and it was a relief when I passed my first solo flight in the darkness. Each flight was entered in our log books and senior instructors gave us what were called Check Rides regularly throughout the course.

Those who did not make the grade were required to pack up their kit immediately and we could return to our dormitory and find an empty bed space. It was an ongoing occurrence and we were all aware there would be a number of us who would not make the required standard. The reasons varied, one reason given, which we thought harsh, being lack of moral fibre (LMF) the individual's record being endorsed accordingly.

Before posting to our final stage of training we were individually interviewed by a panel of two USA officers and a civilian, who we thought was a psychiatrist by the nature of his questions. My turn came and the questions revolved around responsibility, management and whether my preference was for acting alone or being in charge, controlling and giving orders to others. They were apparently trying to assess if cadets were best suited as fighter or bomber pilots. I was listed for training on multi-engined aircraft and a potential bomber pilot.

The technique for piloting twin-engined aircraft was different but not difficult; the trickiest exercise was landing on one engine which was practised as an emergency measure. When cadets were considered capable of flying without an instructor, two cadets made up the crew. One was detailed pilot with responsibility for ensuring that the proper procedures were adhered to and the other the co-pilot. It was interesting work: we were given map references for quite long flights usually triangular and with landing and take off from other airfields. The trainee pilot was responsible for preparing the details of the flights for the information and approval of the control tower staff. The machines were not fitted with radio; therefore it was important for the flight plans to be prepared with care. Cadets getting lost were removed from the course.

We began looking forward to the end of the course with great expectations and apprehension. My final Check Ride was about two weeks before the conclusion of the course. The following day my Company Commander informed me I had qualified which was a great relief. I was delighted. I did one more flight as co-pilot to another cadet the following day and he subsequently passed his Check Ride. It felt good to be in company with other successful people as there were still those not making the grade at the eleventh hour which was demoralising.

The American wings, a metal badge, would be awarded at the Passing Out Parade. RAF personnel would, after returning to the United Kingdom and having passed a flying test, be eligible to wear the coveted Brevet of the RAF. Additionally an advance tactical course was necessary before participating in operational work.

During the course I had occasional meetings and communication with the Security people relating to the task for which I had been briefed. There had been no problems and about three weeks before the end of the course I had a final and amicable meeting at which I was thanked for my services. I believed I had done all that was asked of me, which was to ascertain the attitude of officers of German descent taking arms against the country where many of their grandparents lived. My experience indicated strong loyalties to the United States of America. In the meantime the attack on Pearl Harbor had occurred.

A Bump to Earth in a Khaki Suit

Two days after I had qualified as a pilot I was interviewed by two RAF Officers. They apologised for not keeping an appointment which had been arranged for the previous week. After some small talk they drew my attention to the terms of my engagement in the RAF VR which limited me to be trained as a pilot or navigator and if not suitable or not required I would have to return to the reserved occupation of a police officer. They then talked about arranging a voluntary transfer to the Army to perform security duties of a highly confidential nature. I could not believe what I was hearing and told them I had qualified as a pilot and had been recommended for a commission in the rank of Pilot Officer. I sensed by their reaction that they were unaware of the situation and the meeting was adjourned.

When we met next morning I was informed there had been a misunderstanding which they declined to explain. I was then informed there was an excess of trained pilots and navigators and that air crew had the option of accepting ground duties in the RAF, but I was ineligible because of my conditions of service. They informed me that since I had left the police service there was no longer a strict adherence to policemen being in a reserved occupation and that certain age groups were now being called up for military service and they proposed arranging a voluntary transfer to the Army. I explained the situation to my Company Commander, an American Officer, but could not inform him of the security element in which I had been involved. Next morning he confirmed my name had been deleted from the pass list and the recommendation to become a Pilot Officer.

That evening I sought out another ex-policemen who was in the complex in another company. He was equally upset: he had been grounded without a Check Ride and without notice. He knew of another ex-policemen and when we found him, he too had also been grounded without a Check Ride. They had been seen by the RAF Officers and informed their best option was voluntary transfer to the Army for security work. Up to that time I had never hinted or mentioned to anyone my confidential briefing in the UK but as we were sympathising with each other it dawned upon us that we had been serving the same purpose.

I recalled a remark made by the headmaster of the Grammar School when I was saying goodbye to him, to the effect that once you were involved in security affairs it was for life. I had a final meeting with the RAF Officers; they were persuasive and reminded me of my previous security training, pointing out that it would be useful to my future in the Army. There was nothing I could do to deflect them from their purpose. I refused to agree to the proposal and I left the meeting disappointed and bitter. I realised the intention had been to have me grounded before my final Check Ride and that it would have happened if they had kept the original appointment. They were obviously working to orders but I think they made a clumsy job of it. I asked my Company Commander for leave of absence explaining that I was not in the mood to remain in an atmosphere where there would be celebrations to which they were entitled. He readily granted the leave and said he was appealing on my behalf.

Three of us went hitch-hiking to the south eventually reaching Miami with the help of kind truck drivers. The people we met were kind and generous. The highlight of our jaunt was when somehow or other we found ourselves at a Grand Party held by or for film stars and entertainers of that era. The only name I now remember was Martha (the mouth) Reay, no longer in her prime – but she knew how to party! My objective was trying to drown my sorrows and there was an abundance of the right sort of liquor which helped.

On our way back to camp we ran out of a lift in a small town in late afternoon and when trying to get lifts were approached by two Highway Patrol Police Officers. After a chat they offered to take us out on to the open road where they suggested we would have a better chance of vehicles stopping. We accepted the offer and they left us. Within 10-15 minutes darkness fell, there being no long gradual sunsets in that part of the world. We knew no one would stop for us in the darkness as the road was unlit, so we knocked at the door of a shack which was lit. The occupants were black and on answering our knock slammed the door and extinguished the light within. They probably thought we were Ku Klux Klan members, then known to operate in the south. We were left in complete darkness on the edge of a tobacco plantation; the smell of rotting vegetation in that humid climate was dreadful. We lay down on the grass verge but it was impossible to sleep or rest as the insects kept biting wherever they could find flesh. When daylight finally arrived we looked a right mess, the pain and swelling being intense. The sick bay back at camp put us right in a day or two. We cursed the Highway Patrols.

The author marching with West Point and RAF VR Air Cadets in the Heroes Day Parade, Georgia, USA, on 17th July 1942.

The Passing Out Parade was over; the Inspecting Officer being General George Marshall. My friends rushed to tell me that my name had been called out at the Parade. My Company Commander handed me the metal Wings and said he had put my name on the Parade list but he had been unable to get me re-instated on the Pass List. I thanked him for his unselfish action, knowing that he probably risked censure. I was still bitter and I handed back the Wings badge and asked him to drop it in the Everglade Swamps next time he was flying over them. We parted good friends. I knew that as my name had been removed from the Pass List there was small chance of winning an appeal and it would probably take months marking time in America awaiting a decision. I had studied and worked hard to become a pilot and I was now in a position to be labelled a failure. I accepted the inevitable voluntary transfer to the Army. My two friends felt equally cheated and were bitter but as they had been denied a final Check Ride there was nothing they could do about it. If their circumstances had been the same as mine we would have stood together and appealed.

Within a few days arrangements were made for us to travel by rail to New York and board *The Queen Mary*, then engaged in conveying troops to Britain. I shall never forget the tearful and emotional scene as we sailed out of New York, the setting sun lighting up the Statue of Liberty. We stood on the top deck shoulder to shoulder with the American soldiers repeatedly singing their National Anthem, their right hand on their heart in the traditional manner.

The Queen Mary was unescorted and depended upon her speed and a constant zigzag course to evade the submarines. I think we took only about four or five days to reach the Clyde but in that overcrowded ship it was difficult to tell night from day. We were extra passengers but we found an odd corner and were given numbered meal tickets and informed to expect to be served with food every six to eight hours. After the first food issue it was usually about twelve hours between meals. The queue was constant. We had our mugs filled with tea or coffee and were advised to help ourselves to as much food as we wished, mainly hard-boiled eggs, cheese, sausage and bread. A common complaint was constipation referred to as 'egg-bound'. We had nothing to do except guard our kit which was very necessary and it was impossible to exercise. Before leaving America I had given away all my RAF kit except the essentials to make space for the purchase of things for Lucy which were unavailable at home. The items included nylon stockings, silk lingerie, perfume, hair clips and many other things which were much appreciated.

We entered the Clyde in late afternoon and by the time darkness fell an air raid was in progress with anti-aircraft guns blazing away and searchlights weaving about in the sky. It struck terror into the hearts of some of the troops and needless shots were fired from the top deck.

We were aware of one casualty, killed by what is now referred to as 'friendly fire'. On arrival we were put on a train and spent a night at West Kirby. After documentation we got four weeks' leave of absence. It was wonderful to be re-united with Lucy. It had been a long 15 months. We had been together for only a few days after our wedding.

After leave of absence I reported back to West Kirby in preparation for discharge from the RAF VR. My friend Mac in similar circumstances was there and on 18th March 1943 we were issued with travel warrants to take us to Shrewsbury. I did not think that one day I would live there and serve in the rank of Deputy Chief Constable of Shropshire. We were supplied with the usual food for travel, two hefty sandwiches, one with cheese, the other with egg, and a rock cake. We arrived at Shrewsbury about lunchtime and looked for somewhere to eat our sandwiches; the only place available was a public house. It was busy with motherly ladies taking a break from factory work and drinking pints of beer. We were in RAF uniform. They gave us a warm welcome and refused to let us pay for our drinks. We both had bad memories of what had occurred in America and at that moment we were not really enthusiastic about joining the Army. As a result, we stayed drinking much longer than we should have done before setting off on foot to find Copthorne Barracks, the home of the Shropshire Light Infantry.

Eventually we arrived mid-afternoon in a jovial mood and reported to the Guard Room. We said we were volunteering to join the Army, which was basically true, but we did not produce the appropriate documents and we were not believed. There was a bit of banter during which the Regimental Police Sergeant did his best to send us on our way. He was a tolerant chap and eventually suggested we take a nap in the guard room which we did. A couple of hours or so later we woke up and produced the necessary paperwork. We expected and deserved trouble, but we apologised most profusely and much to our surprise that was the end of the matter.

The Shropshire Light Infantry marching pace was 120 paces per minute which did not fit very well with people the height of six feet. The short stay at Copthorne covered the basic induction course and included various tests to ascertain the suitability of recruits for further training. It was explained that four regiments, the Cheshires,

Manchesters, Middlesex and the Royal Northumberland Fusiliers were to be trained as support troops, their main weapons being Vickers medium machine guns and 4.2 inch mortars. Precise and accurate calculations, planning, range-assessing and map-reading with a good knowledge of mathematics were necessary as the long-range weapons would be firing over the heads of attacking infantry. I opted for the Royal Northumberland Fusiliers (RNF) thinking there might be a possibility of, at some stage, being posted to Fenham Barracks, Newcastle upon Tyne, that being the home of the regiment. In fact the only occasion I ever visited Fenham Barracks was after I had left the Army and returned to police service in Durham. The occasion involved arresting a fusilier for a house-breaking in the Bishop Auckland area and I thought it best in the circumstances not to mention my connection with the regiment.

The personnel selected for the four regiments were trained at 24 Machine Gun Training Centre (24 MGTC), The Dale, Chester, to which I was posted. Initially there was infantry training which included exercises in North Wales, sleeping in a bivouac. On the third week at The Dale we set off for one of the camping exercises in a convoy of 30cwt. trucks with about 20 soldiers in each. On one of the many sharp bends a truck went over a bridge and down a steep embankment. There were broken bones and some bleeding. I was in the following vehicle and with my background and experience automatically slipped into doing what I would have done as a policeman. After attending to those with bleeding wounds, we used wooden fencing to make splints to support broken limbs and cut up blankets into strips to secure them. The next stage was assembling makeshift stretchers with rifles and greatcoats to get the injured to the top without causing further injury.

On returning to The Dale I was ordered to see the Commanding Officer. All sorts of things went through my mind as to the reason for the appointment, one of which was that I had possibly overstepped the mark in directing operations at the scene of the accident in the presence of a captain, a lieutenant and two or three NCOs; who had all worked hard and willingly and were dirty and sweaty like all of us. The Commanding Officer thanked me for my services at the scene of the accident and promoted me from fusilier to lance corporal, unpaid, forthwith. There were not many perks with the rank; the one most valued was getting the occasional pass to sleep out at a local address when Lucy would join me from Tyneside. At that time leave of absence was frozen except for overseas posting so the weekend pass was a real bonus.

The Dale was a well-run establishment: the discipline was sensible, the training was of a high standard and we were kept busy. A good standard of fitness was necessary as the weapons were heavy to handle. In addition to the usual physical training, outdoor exercises and foot drill, everyone in the camp under 45 years of age, including the officers, paraded each Saturday morning in battledress and army boots and at 11.00 am the Commanding Officer, not a young man, signalled the start of a ten-mile road run. No time limit was set but we soon learned to be competitive if we wanted a hot shower. Quite a number of soldiers were filtered out as the course progressed because they did not achieve the demanding standards and were posted elsewhere.

Whilst at The Dale I was recommended for a Commission and spent a few days with an Officer Cadet Selection Board made up of the most senior Army ranks. The questions were many and varied. We were given situations which were a test of leadership qualities and included extensive physical challenges, with us usually finishing up getting wet and dirty. We dined with the officers; it was a great treat to be served at the table. Having survived the first stage, I was off to Wrotham in Kent for a few weeks on a final selection course. The weather was cold and wet with a mixture of snow and frost and a constant south-east wind. We were outside all day and often half the night, our clothes becoming muddy and rarely dry. The accommodation was in Nissen huts, cold and miserable places. It was a test of endurance and some dropped out without completing the course.

Alton Towers in Staffordshire, where I was posted as an Officer Cadet, is, as I write, a quite different place from what it was in 1943. There had been a serious fire pre-war which completely gutted a fine old house. During the first few weeks on infantry training, we slept on the ground floor which had neither doors nor windows. It was not a hospitable place but thankfully we moved on to better quarters. The intake comprised a mixture of 18 and 19-year-olds, and more mature men, including ex-policemen, then eligible for call up. Some of the younger men were still growing and developing and despite their best endeavours they found the going hard. The more mature among us would help by carrying part of their equipment, especially towards the end of the day when they were near exhaustion. The Regimental Sergeant Major, a hardened old soldier, did his best to destroy the morale of the youngsters. One or two of us tried to reason with him but to no avail and we told him we were going to inform the Company Commander; he disregarded our warning and we did see the OC but there was no change in his behaviour. Eventually we got hold of his cap, cut the diced hat band into little squares and put them in an envelope in the OC's office. Of course there were questions and threats of withdrawing privileges but as we had few of them, mass punishment was not imposed. We realised the Army did not want publicity and the Sergeant Major was replaced by a sensible chap who dealt with the youngsters sympathetically.

After completion of infantry training, the work was challenging and interesting, enabling us to learn a variety of skills. We went out and around the public roads in Staffordshire, driving track vehicles in convoy. They were skittish in snow, frost and on cobblestones and I can recall the panic we caused at a T-junction in Leek. Control was lost on the cobbles: the track vehicle spun completely out of control and a queue of housewives waiting for the butcher's shop to open flung themselves to the ground. Fortunately there were no casualties and when the ladies got up they made their feelings known in a spate of unladylike language. Another exercise was cross-country map-reading in groups of three, covering a distance of about 15 winding miles in the course of a day. We reached a farmhouse where we were generously treated to food and home-made cider with which we were not familiar. As we set off again on a hot summer's day every step felt like a hammer blow to the head!

We also spent time in Wales, in and around Radnor Forest, using live ammunition. The farmers were usually friendly and helpful which was in their interests as they depended upon our signing their claim form for loss of sheep. There were occasions when more sheep were killed on paper then existed in the first place; diplomacy was needed to reach amicable agreements. We did meet a proclaimed Welsh Nationalist who did everything in his power to obstruct our operations and spoke only in Welsh until we refused to sign his exaggerated claims, when we discovered he could speak and swear in English.

We also escaped exercises, which could be a lot of fun, living on our wits on what we could find on the land. I was on one of those exercises when our son was born. Edna, my sister-in-law, sent a telegram to Alton Towers, the contents of which were relayed to another Cadet Rennie in the Manchester Regiment. He was young and single and thought it was a hoax. He was in Yorkshire, I was in Wales and it was not until we returned from our exercises that I knew I had a son, then ten days old.

The six months at Alton Towers had its lighter moments some of which I have mentioned. We left as Commissioned Officers, physically fit, technically well-trained and with a good grasp of our responsibilities and an awareness of our dependence upon each other. We had played harmless tricks upon each other and on the training staff which were taken in good part. Life was so different from the sombre atmosphere which I had experienced for a year as a temporary West Point cadet.

On leaving Alton Towers after being commissioned in the Royal Northumberland Regiment and a brief leave of absence, I reported to a military training unit at Sedbergh School in Yorkshire, which the Army used during the War. There were about 20 officers from a variety of regiments on the course. We were referred to as volunteers, which was news to most of us, and informed that we were on a commando-type course with an emphasis on security matters. Survival training involved living on the land for long periods, with given objectives, during which time we tried to kill anything that moved, eating and, when possible, cooking what we caught. We pilfered eggs and chickens from farm buildings and covered our tracks by leaving scenes as if there had been an attack by foxes; it was a wonderful test of our field-craft skills and stamina.

Anti-interrogation training was given; infiltration of enemy lines and getting back safely with prisoners was practised and there were occasions when incidents became a bit too realistic. One Saturday morning we were driven to Manchester Ringway where we were taught the rudiments of parachute jumping, first from a static position and, on the Sunday, from an aeroplane. The intention was for everyone to achieve a minimum of two jumps from an aircraft but the weather closed in and a few managed only one jump. There were one or two with broken limbs but I was fortunate and completed the two jumps. Of course we realised we were not qualified as paratroopers but it was comforting to have the experience should the need arise. A bonus was that we had learned to fall in such a manner that injuries could be minimised and there were occasions throughout my life as a police officer when that skill saved me from possible injuries. The people on the course had a wealth of knowledge, experience and skills which we shared.

When the course finished I was posted to Aldershot where I joined three other officers. None of us knew why we were there and we gained no satisfaction from asking questions. We kept ourselves reasonably fit by running around a football ground. After about two weeks I was posted to Anglesey in North Wales and joined a large number of support troops living under canvas. I became a Platoon Commander and was happy with the job of improving our skills. However, that did not last long. I was directed to take a contingent of 30 soldiers, not members of my platoon, to France as reinforcements. We went by train and landing craft infantry (LCI). The weather was rough and most were seasick, but the journey was otherwise uneventful. The troops went to a holding unit and I was at a loose end for a day or two while trying to get some recognition of my presence there. Eventually it transpired I should have been posted direct from Aldershot some weeks earlier. There had been an administrative error in sending me to Anglesey and in the meantime there had been some concern about my whereabouts!

On Active Service

I became a member of 30 Corps, commanded by General Horrocks, a wonderful soldier and a gentleman, and normally wore the corps identification shoulder flashes, the Ardennes Boar. In addition I was issued with a pass signed by General Montgomery, Commander in Chief of 21 Army Corps, authorising me to wear any dress whilst operating within 21 Army Group. On the occasions when irregular dress was appropriate, I begged, borrowed or helped myself to garments suitable for the purpose.

My duties in Europe were varied and wide-ranging, with a good proportion of my time spent on detachment with non-commissioned officers. Therefore there was little time for the ceremonies and life in an Officers' Mess. However, I was well provided with a vehicle and a driver/handyman, Corporal Bill Alderson, a native of Sunderland and a married man with two children. He was a tough, hardened soldier who had spent time in the desert. He looked after my laundry, uniform and boots and frequently cooked our meals. He had the happy knack of trading our compo rations when in friendly territory, which was a nice change although I believe we ate cat killed in our honour by an old lady in Belgium in whose home we spent a comfortable night. Being looked after was a luxury for me after being so long in training doing all my own chores.

The personnel with whom I worked were mostly NCOs with experience of active service which I lacked. Nevertheless we soon got the measure of each other and their support and loyalty was most gratifying. Not only did I get to know them but also quite a lot about their families. One of the duties of officers on active service is to censor, by reading and endorsing, the personal letters to wives, sweethearts, children, fathers and mothers. When I was so engaged I always felt I was intruding on a very personal and intimate part of their lives. Nevertheless it had to be done and it did mean being in a privileged position. There were occasions when it could be helpful in the event of a family problem.

My specialist army training and police experience provided me with an excellent background to deal with the tasks in which I was involved. In the advances and reverses crossing and re-crossing country boundaries on the way through Europe, the reception by the various nationalities was exceptionally warm. However there were places where the Germans had been in occupation for a long time: some had married or had families with local girls and there were those who had done business and profited from the occupation, thus providing bonds and loyalties. There was understandably the question in some minds as to which side would eventually triumph. The Dutch-German border threw up these sorts of problems.

There was a troublesome leak of information about army formations and movements on the approaches to the bridges leading to Nijmegan and Arnhem. Normally the source of the problem was known and we were suitably briefed but in this instance no background information was available. With a small contingent we kept observation on the bridge at Grave and stayed quietly working in a baker's shop on the fringe of no man's land overlooking the bridge. The culprit was, to our surprise, right under our nose. He was aged about 40 and used a tradesman's delivery cycle with goods in the front carrier which never appeared to be disturbed. He would travel around the Allied formations which were assembling and then cycle across the bridge into the German zone of operations. He did this twice per day until detected, whereupon he was dealt with accordingly.

On the other hand there were Germans who disliked the Hitler regime and there were probably a number of sleepers listening illegally to British broadcasts and were well intentioned and helpful as the war progressed. There was a three-storey black and white house-cum-shop and workshop in Hamelin, the town in the Pied Piper legend, where the owner, a very old man and his daughter, probably in her sixties, asked for protection. They believed the German army had been tipped off that they listened to and sent messages to London. They certainly had all the necessary radio equipment skilfully secreted in the loft among the many lengths of briar wood which they used for making smoking pipes. In the event the German army was abandoning the town as there was a risk of their being sandwiched between the Russian army and the Allied forces. Two of us stayed a couple of nights on the premises for which the man and his daughter were most grateful. We really had no other option as the German army filled the road outside on retreating.

We occasionally helped people to get back to safety from difficult situations and in those sorts of incidents we were usually provided with precise information upon which we could plan and act. On one occasion two of my men were unaccounted for in the Dutch district of S-Hertogen-Bosch which was a contentious military area. We received information from a Dutch source that the soldiers might be in a Nunnery and that the nun in charge liked an alcoholic drink. Officers on active service were allowed a bottle of whisky per month. My bottle was intact and I took it with me to the Nunnery where I received a warm welcome from the very elderly lady of Irish origin in charge. We had a drink with a lively chat and eventually on her command youngish ladies in long cloaks appeared, all smiles, with the two missing soldiers scrubbed clean with laundered uniform. The event took some living down within our small unit! The great thing is not to panic in unusual circumstances. I had not reported them missing and therefore no record of the incident was recorded. The lady in charge thanked me for the whisky which I left her.

On 16th December 1944 the Germans counter-attacked the American forces in the Ardennes and the whole of the front was destabilised for some considerable time. The Americans lost substantial stores and armour and there were English-speaking Germans wearing American uniforms advancing with the retreating Americans. A substantial force was assembled in 30 Corps and were soon on their way to help to stem the attack. In the meantime I was sent ahead with a contingent of about 20 men and accompanied by a similar-sized detachment of Royal Engineers. We were a lightweight force and could get there in a reasonably short time, the purpose of which was for the engineers to set up wire cages in the form of prisoner-of-war detention centres into which retreating soldiers and bogus officers could be channelled. Our work was with the American forces in establishing identities. The weather was atrocious: snow, ice and severe cold were as much an enemy as the Germans and many soldiers perished solely due to the adverse weather conditions. It was a serious and determined counter-attack by the Germans and if they had been successful the consequences could have resulted in their reaching the Low Countries which by that time were considered safe.

After our initial task was completed, the Americans requested that I should stay on, which I did for the next few weeks. My driver remained with me while the remainder of the contingent returned to 30 Corps. My position was described as Liaison Officer with the CIA Agents. The work was of a highly-confidential nature and was somewhat similar to what I had been doing. My previous experience with the American forces was beneficial to the tasks and to our relationship with each other which was very good. We did have different methods of tackling incidents which we discussed freely, with the result that combined plans prevailed. Their personal kindness was at times embarrassing. They issued me with American-type clothing and uniform to enable me to blend in with the American soldiers when necessary. I still had my own jeep but unfortunately it was damaged by a land mine, which did not do me much good either! My left ankle, right shoulder and right hip were jarred and painful for a while but I remained on duty. In recent years recurring pains have reminded me of the incident and a replacement hip has been necessary. The jeep was damaged but would have been repaired if with a British unit. The Americans issued me with a Willys Jeep, which was much superior to the Ford which was placed on the scrap heap. I did not even have to sign for the new vehicle. My driver regarded his time with the Americans as a bit of a holiday: they looked after our laundry and we were fed like fighting cocks. It was also a wonderful experience which I enjoyed, and from which I learned a great deal.

When the Prime Minister made his first visit on to German soil during hostilities, I was responsible for arranging his journey and safety from the outer boundary of 30 Corps into Germany, a distance of about 20 miles and back again. There was very little time to reconnoitre the road and the place where Churchill would stop. Secrecy was essential for his safety which meant that we had only 24 hours to cover every likely eventuality. The roads and stopping-site chosen were of a rural nature but there were dwelling houses and hamlets adjacent to the roadways. A curfew was in force as the area had only recently been vacated by the German troops but we gave the people a reminder by sending a vehicle along the route and addressing them over a loud speaker.

My plan was to have four outriders in front and four behind. I would lead in the Willys Jeep with an interpreter, driver and one other, making four in the vehicle and another jeep immediately behind the VIP's car which was the open tourer normally used by General Montgomery. The motorcycles would be our standard BSA machines with which the riders were fully familiar. However, some bright spark at the eleventh hour sent us four Harley Davidson machines with the instruction that we had to drive at high speed in the interests of safety. The roads were deeply rutted and pitted from lack of maintenance and artillery shelling and were quite unsuited for Harley Davidson motorcycles as they are much lower to the ground; furthermore I did not have anyone familiar with riding the machines. The gear change is on the other side from what the riders were used to and they needed time to get used to these strange American machines. I knew there was no point in explaining my objectives or to make alternative plans. I decided to retain the original number of riders on the BSA machines and four brave chaps volunteered to ride the Harley Davidsons with the instructions to fall out if the road conditions proved too difficult. On the day we set off at the appointed time and within half a mile, one Harley Davidson rider had come off. It later transpired he had a broken leg. I ordered the other three to fall out and we managed nicely with the BSA machines. The driver of the VIP car found the driving on the potholed surface limited his speed and the journeys were completed without further problems.

Churchill, who was accompanied by General Montgomery, got out of his car and whilst standing on German soil urinated and said something to the effect that he would have preferred to have stood there and shat on Hitler's face. He did not linger long and on the return journey to the outer end of 30 Corps boundary, I pulled to my right, stopped and stood up in the jeep giving a salute as I expected the car to join the waiting escort and continue the journey without stopping. However, it stopped right opposite and adjacent to where I was standing. General Montgomery stood up in his vehicle and gave me a salute. He thanked me and the escort, handed me a packet of 200 Robin cigarettes and asked me to give 'the boys' a smoke. I did not smoke then but I was later informed that the quality of the cigarettes was so poor that even the prisoners-of-war thought twice about using them.

While I am certain that he did not recognise me from our previous encounter, Churchill beckoned me to his side of the open-top motorcar. I jumped to the ground and on going round to him he spoke to me and said the Americans were grateful for the work done with them in the Ardennes. He added his thanks and made an oblique reference to my time in America, expressing his satisfaction. I was surprised and impressed, and somewhat tongue-tied. Obviously someone had done their homework in providing the information of my identity and posting to America. What a gift Churchill had for making people feel special.

Any feelings of elation by the events of the day were quickly dispelled when I was informed that on the outward journey I had, through the vehicle public-address system, reminded German families walking on the road that a curfew was in force. Apparently I had used coarse and uncomplimentary language because of my lack of ability with the German language. My defence was that it was effective.

Bremerhaven is a port at the mouth of the River Wesser and during the war was an important submarine base. Towards the end of hostilities senior officers, scientists and others were known to be leaving the country for Argentina and other South American countries, some because they might be put on trial, others to sell or practise their skills elsewhere and it was believed valuables were being transported. The Royal Navy was trying to blockade the passage of submarines but the area was heavily mined. The intended escapees were believed to be waiting in the Bremerhaven Police Station which was fairly adjacent to the submarine pens. At about 24 hours notice I was detailed to put a party together, take the police station and detain the wanted people from escaping until such time as the advancing troops of the 52nd Scottish Lowland Division arrived. In the normal course of events I would have arranged a reconnaissance with the Army Air Corps Lysander serving the artillery but there was heavy fog and time was short. The information given was that there were about twelve VIPs waiting to leave the country, but there was no information available on the numbers of police likely to be encountered or the size of the building. The population of Bremerhaven was said to be about 120,000, so on my knowledge of police stations in the UK, I assumed it would be of modest size. How wrong I was!

To get there without detection was essential and therefore a small party was more likely to be successful. I decided on about 18 personnel including an interpreter and a signalman, with the remainder lightly-armed for ease of movement. We had been promised smoke-screen cover but in the event it was not necessary because of the thick smog for which I was glad as the smoke-screen would have drawn attention to the activity in the area. We got on our way and stopped short of the hostile boundary for refreshments and a couple of hours' nap. We left our transport in charge of one man and set off about 2.00 am.

It was a very dark night and thankfully it was still foggy. We had to feel our way stealthily by touch of fences and buildings along the streets. On arrival just before dawn, the party was complete except for Bill Alderson my driver/batman. The scene was uninviting: there was a high stone wall surrounding a large solid-looking building like a fortress. There was a heavy oak door with an inset trapdoor and a quick look around the boundary revealed an extensive parade ground. There was no way our party could storm the place.

Fortunately there was a public telephone kiosk on the pavement close to the outer wall and it was still in working order. The adjutant eventually answered in English and in my conversation with him I gave the impression that we were a substantial force and suggested we be given access as we wished the occupants no harm. Next the Chief of Police came on the telephone speaking reasonably good English. He asked a number of sensible questions and eventually the gate was opened and we were admitted just as dawn was breaking. He insisted on taking me to his office and drinking schnapps. It turned out that he had been a POW in the First World War and spent a considerable time in Yorkshire. It was apparent he disliked the Hitler regime and when I explained our mission was to stop certain people thought to be in his station from fleeing abroad, he expressed his pleasure and offered his full co-operation. He had an armed strength of 300 policemen in the building but on the arrival of senior army officers he had lost his authority which annoyed him very much. They had taken over part of the premises and were giving him orders. He thought there were about 50 of them, which was quite different from the information given to me and quite frightening. He agreed to lock off the section they occupied and to assist in guarding them. We cut off the telephone to that part of the building. The Police Chief insisted on removing the bolts from their rifles and placing them in our custody, together with small arms, explaining that the practice was in accordance with the Geneva Convention, of which I had little knowledge. Throughout the time we waited for the arrival of troops of the 52 Lowland Division, which I believe was about two and a half days, he fed me and plied me with schnapps and because of the lack of sleep and the amount of alcohol consumed, the time factor was hazy.

As soon as the area was made safe there was an unseemly scramble of American and UK Security people trying to grab and persuade the intended escapees to co-operate. The Police Chief wanted a formal surrender of his force and again quoted the Geneva Convention. I tried to persuade him that policemen were not normally regarded as part of the Armed Services but he insisted they were within that category as they were armed and trained riflemen. The whole of his 300 men, dressed in their best, assembled in three ranks with their rifles, without the bolts, and on the steps of the approach to the station he went down on one knee and presented me with his sword which he said was now mine. A police photographer took photographs of the ceremony and the column set off marching to report to the nearest POW Camp. However, he was a determined and proud old man and I arranged for two outriders to lead the march and a jeep at the rear in case of illness, as some of the policemen were not that young. They were rejected at the POW Camp and the late Bob Ward, then RSM of the 52nd Lowland Provost Company who served with me in the Durham County Constabulary, sent me a message jokingly asking me if I knew the difference between a soldier and a policemen. Before leaving Bremerhaven I returned the sword to the Chief's Office and wrote a note thanking him for his unstinting help. I felt I owed him that as without his friendly co-operation our mission might not have succeeded.

What of the missing Bill Alderson? There was no body so we assumed he was a POW, which was confirmed five weeks later with the cessation of hostilities in Germany. He was granted 28 days' survival leave and in the normal course of events would be posted to a Reserve Pool and subsequently to a new unit; the system was referred to as Y listed. I received a personal letter from him, the gist of which was that he was sorry he had a pee against a wall but he had kept quiet. What he was referring to was that on these sorts of operations, I had trained the troops to stand with their back against the wall when urinating so that a full view of anyone approaching was readily apparent, and that if attacked they should try and keep quiet so that the presence of other officers would not be compromised by going to their aid and endangering the object of a mission. He told me he was merely the width of the street away from his colleagues when he was seized by two soldiers. He stuck to his rights by refusing to give them other than his name, rank and number. After some questioning he got the impression that they thought he had got lost in the fog. I wrote, thanked and congratulated him, adding advice. The day his survival leave expired he appeared in my office in Hanover. He had used all his skills and training to return without being detected. It took considerable time and persuasion to have him officially posted to his original unit. I was delighted to have him back: his loyalty was typical of the soldiers I was proud to serve with during my time in Europe.

San Bostal Prison Camp was situated towards the southern end of Luneburg Heath, not far from where the 2nd World War armistice was officially declared. For some weeks there had been news of atrocities in death camps across Europe. The largest and most notorious are well known and still referred to 60 years later. There were many other camps where unlawful killings took place and San Bostal was one of them. We had just sorted ourselves out after taking over Bremerhaven Police Station when I got a map reference to go to San Bostal as quickly as possible. We joined up with a party of Royal Army Medical Corps personnel commanded by a captain who was a qualified doctor. Our total number was about 30.

We found a dreadful scene: the stench was beyond belief. There were skeleton bodies all around and it was difficult to distinguish between the alive and dead. The only sign of the Germans was the body of a woman in officer's uniform lying in the open. We learned the German Guard had quite recently departed and the prisoners had stabbed the woman officer as she was struggling to get on the last departing vehicle. She was an exceptionally large person which apparently hindered her progress and cost her life. We were informed she was a particularly cruel person. There were a few recently-arrived merchant seamen whose ship had been captured off the north-west coast of Germany a week or so earlier. They were still in good shape and went on their way.

The building made of coarse wood was a ramshackle structure and it was apparent that it had been expanded from time to time. The prisoners' quarters were not waterproof and the two-tier bunks contained many dead and dying skeletons. Those more mobile were staggering or crawling on the grass in the open. Their bodies were emaciated, with maggots and other vermin. The only immediate help we could give them was a generous application of de-lousing powder. They were filthy: most were naked as the rags about them and on the beds were dirty and covered in vermin. There was no food. We shared ours with those able to eat but all we could do at that time was totally inadequate.

We thought it would help if we could provide soap and hot water but we needed more hands to do the work. At first light I sent our vehicles to collect as many able-bodied people aged twelve years and upwards and bring with them cleaning material, disinfectant, bleach and buckets so that their bodies could be washed and bedding laundered. No males were found but quite a large number of women were assembled and did our bidding for the next three days. Many were frequently physically sick but all the prisoners were washed and made a little more comfortable. We also asked them to carry out the bodies for burial purposes.

The Medical Officer considered it would be unwise and unsafe to consider sending the prisoners to a hospital because he feared a serious outbreak of typhus and other diseases would create an epidemic. Our main task was to prevent them leaving the camp; it was a difficult and unrewarding task as they could not understand why they had to be so confined. We were given a number of different injections each day and we were delighted when sufficient reinforcements arrived on the fourth day. It was quite long enough for even fit young men to undertake the sort of work we were doing and we withdrew. We had had little or no sleep and I was very much concerned for the health of the troops, but fortunately we got away with a clean bill of health.

As far as we could ascertain, the people sent to the camp were from other labour camps and when they were no longer able to work they were sent to San Bostal to die through neglect, lack of food and health care; some were also beaten. They were still quite young. It was fairly obvious from the attitude of the German women that they had little if any sympathy for these unfortunate people. I spoke to them frequently and without exception they denied all knowledge of what had taken place. I pointed out that some of their dwellings were in sight of the camp and that they must have seen much of what was taking place. When I mentioned the dreadful smell which they could not deny, there was no explanation. They resented me for arranging their collection but they worked hard at the unpleasant and distasteful task; I had no regrets for my action. Although we were only on the site for a relatively short period, the sights and smells remained prominent for a long time and can still be recalled.

A great deal has been written about the airborne attack of Arnhem and no doubt historians and journalists will continue to give the event attention. My memories of that beautiful sunny autumn morning on 17th September, 1944 are of standing on the banks of the Rhine looking up for what seemed hours, watching the continuous stream of gliders overhead. There were a great many troops doing the same thing. The success of the operation meant so much to all of us. We were ready and waiting to move and there was an unusual quietness among the troops. When it became apparent that things were not going well, our plans for attack were amended to rescue work. It was a sad and disappointing operation never to be forgotten.

Eventually other plans were made for the crossing of the Rhine, involving the forming-up of a large number of divisions under the command of General Horrocks of 30 Corps. It required comprehensive planning and control of movement over roads which were churned up. The heavy pieces of artillery had to be winched into place, packing them together sardine fashion; it was a masterly piece of work. The Germans continued firing artillery across the river but nothing on the scale of the 30 Corps' bombardment which commenced when ready and continued night and day for many days. The Reichwald Forest, south of the river, contained fine mature trees but the shelling from both sides reduced their height bit by bit until even the tallest remains were only about man-high. The amount of shelling made the forest an unhealthy place and I was unfortunate to be hit on the right knee by a piece of German 88mm artillery. It was not serious and only momentarily interfered with my work. I thought the shrapnel had all been picked out by my driver and me, until nearly 60 years later when I had a knee scan for another reason and small particles of shrapnel were found; it still remains without trouble to me.

The final crossing of the Rhine was twice postponed for 24 hours, during which time we billeted ourselves in the cellars of badly-damaged dwelling houses which were otherwise occupied. The cellars provided excellent champagne and other good wines which was good for morale and kept the tension down. When the time came we were in good spirits and set off in amphibians, most getting to the other side with a minimum of casualties. Within 24 hours the Royal Engineers did a marvellous job of laying, under fire, a Bailey Bridge across this wide fast-flowing river and by next day traffic was using the bridge.

After an operation with a small number of men I recommended to my Officer Commanding, Hamish Mackintosh MC, of The Cameroonians, that Corporal Dunlop be recommended for a Military Medal to which he agreed and added that he was recommending me for a Military Cross. After some time, the response from higher authority was that it was not policy to approve the two medals as recommended. Hamish tried hard with the support of the other senior officers to get them to re-consider the decision, without success. It had to be one Military Cross and one mention in dispatches. The choice was mine. I sincerely believed Corporal Dunlop was worthy of a Military Medal. My mention in dispatches was eventually published in the London Gazette on 8th November 1945.

8th May 1945 ended the war in Europe and the surrender of the German Armed Forces. It was a pitiful sight to observe a defeated army marching back to their barracks. Some saluted, others lowered their heads and they were tired-looking, old and young, very young men in shabby outfits. Within a week or so of the end of the war, I was posted to Hanover with about 40 Military Policemen, 25 or so of whom were stationed in Hanover and the remainder in outposts. The building used at Hanover was a house in the suburbs with large cellars which were made into police cells by the engineers. The city centre had been virtually destroyed by fire storms as a result of incendiary bombs dropped by the Royal Air Force.

At Hanover on cessation of hostilities with best friend Charlie Davis

Our primary duty was to seek out and identify those suspected and wanted for questioning about war crimes. If in the suspected category, they were passed on for further investigation. Dutch and German English-speaking police officers were employed as interpreters. Visits to prisons and police stations revealed prisoners detained without any record of why they were in custody or for how long. In such circumstances they were released and the details recorded. We raided houses of ill-repute in conjunction with the full co-operation of the German medical authorities, the purpose being to reduce the spread of venereal diseases to our troops. It was a problem.

We set up and manned an Information Centre in the middle of the city, which was helpful to members of the forces as well as the civilian population. When news filtered through to the Germans that the Russian army was advancing eastwards, they were alarmed. The adjustment to the front was a political decision which led to the creation of East Germany. German ex-servicemen lined up and volunteered to join the British Army to fight and stop the Russian advance. For two or three days, until they accepted the situation, large numbers refused to disperse so counter books were provided where they recorded their personal particulars on the understanding that if required they would enlist to fight the Russians. I sometimes wonder what happened to the books.

A variety of situations cropped up from time to time and we dealt with them in the best way we could. We had no terms of reference or rules and no-one could or would give us any. As far as I am aware our unorthodox method of policing was never challenged. The German people in Hanover were friendly and in season the children brought us tomatoes, other fresh vegetables and fruit. The children enjoyed our chocolate rations and I suppose we might have been in breach of army orders which prohibited fraternisation but we never found anyone who could provide a definition of the word.

On our first arriving in Hanover, a large labour camp was brought to our notice. There were a number of different nationals and quite a numbers of Jews. The occupants were short of food and there were no immediate means of supplying them. A search revealed six pigs ready for slaughter at a German barracks. The Jewish leader spoke English. I asked him if he would enjoy pork for his supper. After smiles and exchanges with a colleague, he agreed to eat such a meal, explaining that he did so only because if he declined it would be unfair to the others. I went and spoke to the Adjutant backed up by two of my staff and butchers from the camp and asked if he cared to contribute the pigs to the starving people. He refused but agreed he would not resist if we removed them. Months later when I was being demobbed, I was presented with a pigskin holdall from the camp which I treasured and used for many years.

There was a move to repatriate the displaced persons to the countries of their origin. The Russians dictated the conditions and eventually a convoy of American 6 x 6 trucks was arranged, driven by black American servicemen and two military policemen, not above the rank of corporal, to navigate. The convoy set off with 200 people, 20 to a truck. Within two to three weeks a number of gypsies re-appeared in camp. Others trickled back, but it was over five weeks before the trucks returned. Our two military policemen reported that the Russian forces stopped the convoy from time to time and repeatedly checked the particulars of the occupants. The checks lasted for several days. Though there was a ban on carrying and using cameras on the journey, photographs were obtained secretly and showed drunken Russian soldiers displaying wrist watches, strapped side by side, extending from their wrists to their elbows on both arms. The thoughts were of what happened to the rightful owners? Another convoy was mooted but as far as I know the plans did not reach fruition.

By the autumn of 1945, a great many Service personnel had been released to return to civilian life. Some had attained positions of responsibility quite different from their pre-service lives and although there was a duty on employers to re-engage former employees, many declined the opportunity, believing they could do better for themselves. However, there were disappointments: expectations were too high and pride was sometimes an obstacle to realistic clear-thinking. The Services with all its faults did look after people, but comradeship was missing in civvy street and promises of welcome back to better lives could be elusive.

When I was offered Class B release, conditional on my returning to Durham County as a constable, I was delighted. Commissioned Officers do not get discharged from the Services: they are placed in reserve and as far as I am aware I remain in that category. I trust the Armed Services are not depending on thousands of Old Crocks like me in the event of an emergency!

I have included some examples of my involvement in Wartime 1939–45. Like so many others, I had dreamed of what was ahead when it all started. I never regarded that period of my life as other than temporary and when the job was done and demobilisation was in sight, I was impatient to return to my beautiful wife and to my fine toddler son whom I had rarely seen and of course to my chosen career as a policeman. My thoughts are frequently with those who did not return.

My unit gave me a farewell party, which I shall never forget, when I was leaving to be demobbed. It concluded with my being carried shoulder-high on to the train where they had reserved a compartment to which I would not normally be entitled. They put my kit beside me with a generous supply of food and drink and some 30 hours later I was just about returning to the land of the living when the train reached the French coast. They were wonderful men: they had worked hard and loyally which made me proud to have served with them.

Back to the Beat

There were occasions during the long years of military training when I thought I would never be able to justify the massive costs incurred. However, on reflection, I did work hard and never had an idle day after my arrival in France. The University of Life had taught me a great deal and I was longing to return to being a policeman which was my life's ambition.

On 1st November 1945, I was granted leave from the army for the remainder of the month. Lucy had rented a flat in Wansbeck Road, Jarrow and despite household goods and furniture being rationed, she had made a comfortable home. In our four years of marriage we had been together only during brief periods of leave. Alex, our son, a fine, sturdy, active lad was two years of age and we had to get to know each other which took time. Rationing, lack of adequate transport and other shortages did not bother us. It was a wonderful month which passed all too quickly.

At the beginning of December, I reported for duty to the Divisional Police Headquarters, Jarrow, where I had previously served. Josh Hammond, the Superintendent who had been prevented from retiring on pension because of wartime regulations, had left but his second-in-command, Chief Inspector William Dodds, was still there. He and other old hands welcomed me and two others, returning the same day, but it was sad to learn that a number of our former colleagues had become casualties.

It was readily apparent that there was much work to be done and that there was a serious shortage of policemen. The law-abiding citizens came out of their homes and welcomed us with cheers and good wishes. Police pay was low compared with that of many people who were at that time being paid overtime rates. There were resignations from officers not allowed to resign during war and from newly-appointed recruits. Ex-servicemen also found it difficult to settle down, especially those who had been doing special duties of one kind or another, often on a loose rein.

Thankfully our supervising officers were forgiving when we played pranks, which pre-war would have had serious consequences. An example of the sorts of things we got up to during the night, when all was quiet and most people were in bed, was challenging each other to reach the roof of buildings. We had special-issue service boots which made it relatively easy to climb up with the help of the drain pipes. One fine morning, about 4.00 am, three of us were on top of the Jarrow Town Hall catching pigeons when we spotted Sergeant Dent, a capable and highly-respected officer, leave his bicycle and saunter down one side of the Town Hall; we quickly nipped down to the street level on the opposite side. A suggestion was made that we hide the sergeant's cycle, but the idea was rejected and it was decided to ride it to the police station, class it as found property and that is what was done. We did work hard; we were needed on the streets and our high spirits were more or less overlooked. In fact Chief Inspector Dodds related to another Inspector that we had brightened the place up since our return!

Our supervising officers were highly experienced and one by one we were posted to other stations with good reports and good wishes; we had to be split up and we accepted the situation with good grace. My turn for posting did not come about until April and in the meantime I brought quite a number of offenders to justice, some of whom were known trouble-makers in pre-war days.

An amusing incident occurred involving two brothers with criminal records. Although they were registered as merchant seamen they had spent the war years on sick or other benefits. Their life-style was scrounging and threatening people, especially foreign seamen and of course getting drunk, committing assaults and damage to property. This particular afternoon about 3.30 pm, which was half an hour after the public houses closed, they went to the Labour Exchange and demanded benefit money to which they were not entitled. I was called and found them a bit the worse for drink, arguing with the Exchange Staff and refusing to accept their decision. After my threats of locking them up, they left the premises and as the Exchange staff did not wish to take further action, that, as far as I was concerned, was the end of the matter, apart from an entry in my official notebook.

About half an hour later a sergeant and two policemen approached me and asked if I had seen two men, whom they described, and for whom they were looking as they had a report that they were intent on murdering the Mayor of Jarrow. The signal-man at a level crossing had telephoned the police station and reported that two men the worse for drink were looking for Rennie and were going to kill him. The Mayor was named Rennie, no connection with me, and the signal-man had assumed they had been referring to the Mayor. We found them nearby still the worse of drink and causing disorder. We took them into custody and charged them with being Drunk and Disorderly. They were subsequently bailed to appear at court and when they did so they were smartly turned out. One of them was wearing a three-piece suit which I immediately recognized as having belonged to me! I had given the suit to a charity organisation, to provide for people whose clothing had been lost through enemy action, when I left the police service to join the armed services. When the court case was over I tackled the individual and he admitted to having obtained the suit by false pretences. It was typical of him and others like him who had spent the war at home drawing sickness and other benefits. He and his two brothers endeavoured to keep out of my way thereafter.

In 1937, when I joined the police service, Police Regulations stipulated that officers were not eligible to sit promotion examinations until they had completed four years' service. Examinations were suspended during hostilities but a number were promoted without having qualified by examination. It was a practice which was unpopular with others, who had so qualified, but were bypassed. The passing of examinations does not lead to automatic promotion which is usually by recommendation and appearance before promotion boards. My situation in December 1947 was similar to that of many others who had served in the Armed Forces, in that there had been no opportunity for us to sit the examinations.

On the expectation of my return to the Force, Chief Inspector Dodds had put my name forward to sit the first available examination which was arranged for the beginning of 1946. Policemen returning from the

Armed Services were given a one-month residential refresher course. Unfortunately the course to which I was allocated was scheduled for after the date of the examinations! The examination entailed two full days of written work. The first day was on educational subjects with the option to take the Sergeants' level or opt for the higher level for Inspectors. I had been entered for the latter and I passed with good marks. The second day covered questions on Police Law and Practice for which I was ill-prepared, having been out of the police service a number of years. I did my best with the morning paper and assessed my chances of passing the examination as doubtful.

Over lunch I deliberated and thought that although I might scrape through on the morning paper I would have to do better on the afternoon paper. On being issued with the second paper, I decided the best course for me was to pull out as I did not wish to get a pass with low marks. The result would be permanently on my record and if I just made it or failed it might be an obstacle to future promotion. I returned my question paper to the Chief Invigilator, with whom I had previously served. He did not ask why I was withdrawing from the examination; he did try to make me change my mind but I offered no explanations. He said he would record the reason for withdrawal that I felt unwell, explaining that by doing so I would not be marked as a failure. He was a kind and wise man for which I was grateful.

In the meantime, I was posted to another division and for the next year I studied hard and also undertook a correspondence course. In 1947 I sat the police promotion examination and was placed first with a pass mark of 95%. I was delighted and reflected that my decision to pull out the previous year was right for me.

In April 1946, I was posted to be the local constable at Tindale Crescent near Bishop Auckland, County Durham. The Force removal van driven by PC Hope conveyed me and our furniture to Hare Street and Lucy with our son used public transport. We had no opportunity to view the house which was rented by the police authority and had been the local police house for many years. It was two-up-and-two-down with a scullery and a concrete backyard, situated in a back-to-back double row of identical houses. Cooking was by means of a coal fire and a gas oven. The fire smoked when the wind was in a certain direction and there was usually insufficient gas pressure to be useful. There was no hot water system, bathroom or flush toilet. The dry toilet was in the backyard and had a seat for one adult and another for a child alongside. The midden was emptied once a week and the stink remained in the atmosphere for hours and hours dependent upon weather conditions. There was a candle-type telephone in the entrance and it was expected that the front room would be used for interviews. Disappointment did not fully express our feelings.

Lucy, unpaid, was expected to answer the telephone and deal with callers if I was not about. She was very good at dealing with members of the public. She soon learned that items reported stolen might be lost, the difference being that stolen property was recorded as a crime and included in statistical returns, whereas lost property was merely entered in a ledger. It was the ambition of every officer to keep the number of undetected crimes as low as possible.

The beat included farms, a number of small holdings, a drift mine, a long-established factory producing sanitary and bathroom ware, owned by Shaw and Knight, a brickyard, gas works and several other industrial units. A new trading estate developed at the end of the war produced ladies' clothing, buttons and other domestic items which were then in great demand. There were quite a large number of dwelling houses making a total resident population in the region of 8,000; the daytime population was in the region of 17,000. The A68 road which carried quite a volume of heavy vehicles connected with quarries on the Upper Tees went through the centre of the beat.

Another important industrial unit was the Railway Engine Works which operated 24 hours per day, engaged in collecting and delivering coal to the centres, west and north of the county. The many engines were constantly in need of maintenance and repairs involving high-value metals were a temptation to thieves. Unusually for County Durham, there were no public houses on the beat but there was a large modern Workmen's Social Club which was visible from my front window. It was well-managed and caused no problems. There was an Isolation Hospital about 200 yards from my front door and I had to deal with the post mortem on coal miners who died from pneumoconiosis, referred to as stone lung. The pathologists had to assess the degree of illness which contributed to the deaths and their reports were important in settling the amount of pension for the wives and children so affected. Most of the people were or had been coal miners and working with them was a new experience for me.

As in any community there were curious people and busy bodies wanting to see and test their new policeman. Initially they would come with trifling questions, a favourite being that they wanted me to make telephone calls for them because they did not know how to operate the call box which was in the middle of the small town and about 80 yards from my door. When this occurred I took them along to the public telephone and showed them how to make calls, explaining that it was better they knew what to do in case I was not available in an emergency. One lady came regularly reporting clothing missing from her drying line and returned the following day with a friend informing me the item had been found. They wanted to see what we had in the house; we were always pleasant but kept them at arm's length unless the matter was genuine.

Most families had coal-mining connections and were granted free supplies of coal. The loads arrived by horse and cart and were tipped in the back streets. The amount given them was generally far too much for their needs and there was barter and trading which often took place during the hours of darkness. Even giving it away was not officially permitted and only came to light when neighbours or families quarrelled. I refused to get implicated and advised the complainants to seek advice from the Colliery Manager.

Our second child, Margaret, was born when we lived there and it was difficult with our inadequate heating systems to provide sufficient hot water to deal with nappy-washing. Disposable nappies were then unknown. The lady living directly opposite across the back lane was married to a colliery blacksmith. They were a lovely couple whose family had grown up and left home. Instead of breaking the rules about giving coal to those not entitled, she gave Lucy bucketsful of hot water but was careful to do so when I was out. Apparently it was an acceptable practice.

Lucy with Alex and Margaret

Officers detailed to work the sort of beat to which I was posted had a 24-hour responsibility and to a large extent selected the hours to suit the operational needs of the area. In recent years, I hear and read of what is often published as a great new idea of appointing Community Officers; I wonder how many claims have been made that the wheel has been re-invented! That is what we were and we attended to every aspect of work requiring attention. We had one rest day per week and one free evening from 6.00 pm to 12.00 midnight each week, subject to the exigencies of the service which meant you could be called out at any time and it did happen. Overtime payment was unknown.

My sergeant lived at West Auckland, a distance of two to three miles. I rarely saw him but we telephoned each other when necessary. He had seven other constables for whom he was responsible, working the same type of beat. The next cog in the wheel was the Sub-Divisional Inspector with a police station at Shildon, and above him a Superintendent at Divisional Headquarters, Bishop Auckland.

I wanted to take my time before rushing in and being misunderstood. However, an opportunity presented itself the first Sunday I was in occupation. A mother came to the door about 3.30 pm and asked me to go and deal with her 21-year-old twin sons as they were the worse for drink. They had thrown the dinner on the walls and were generally causing trouble. The house was on the main road and people had gathered outside, where the bad language and noise were plainly audible. I gave them advice and told them that if there was a recurrence they would be in serious trouble. On my returning home, a brief look at the notes provided by my predecessor showed that it had been a regular custom over a long period of time for him to settle similar rows on a Sunday afternoon.

The next Sunday, the mother arrived with a similar tale and on this occasion I told them they would be reported for using indecent language which could be heard in the street. The summonses were issued and for the next week or so until the date of the hearing the mother and the sons pleaded with me to take no further action. Eventually they asked me to write letters on their behalf pleading guilty, requesting the court to excuse their attendance to avoid losing a day's pay because they had a mother to support. It cost them £2.00 each; they gave me the money on pay day and I paid it into the court. They thanked me, and we parted on good terms; the mother was less friendly for a long time but she admitted that the Sunday misbehaviour had stopped.

The beat records showed that a number of pedal cycles had been stolen over a period of time and also phosphor-bronze bearings from the engine sheds, each valued at £500. Those were the sorts of crimes I was keen to detect but I knew that until the local inhabitants weighed me up it would be difficult to find people willing to trust and help. The engine shed staff and train operators were continuously about at irregular hours and one morning at about 2.00 am I stopped a man on the roadway outside the site. He told me he had just returned from Tebay in Cumberland and was going home to bed. He appeared nervous and ill-at-ease and when I asked him what he had in his haversack, he collapsed. I helped him to his feet and walked with him to his home which was nearby. He told me that he was very concerned for having broken the law and it transpired he had been given a small package of home-cured bacon by a farmer during the time the train was having an additional engine attached to take the train over Shap Fell.

It was a regular occurrence: lumps of coal were dropped off for the benefit of the farmer and eggs, bacon and other home-produced rationed food was given to the train crews. He also told me that he was a Lay Preacher and he was afraid that he would not be able to face his religious friends again. I explained that I was looking for the people stealing the phosphor-bronze bearings from the engine sheds and for anyone else committing crimes and was not interested in his few rashers of bacon. He thanked me profusely and although I saw him about the place from time to time we never exchanged glances or words. Within a week or so of the incident, there was a note through my door giving an address of a family repairing cycles in their garden shed. There is little doubt who the informant was. The end product was that I locked up a father and two grown-up sons for a number of thefts of a variety of goods as well as for stealing cycles, a number of which were returned to their owners. The ice was broken and I sensed I had been accepted by the community.

Detection of offences and information of crimes from informants kept me busy. Many of them were of a petty nature by employees of both sexes stealing from their places of employment. There were not many house-breakings but there were plenty of sneak-in thefts as doors were rarely locked. I received anonymous letters from women complaining that their husbands were gambling their wages and they were barely receiving sufficient money to provide for their families. The local street bookmaker was named and it turned out that he was the man who had sold me Rhode Island hens which were excellent layers. It was said he bragged that he was safe from arrest because of the deal with the hens. I chose a day when well-known races were scheduled. I changed into overalls and found him openly taking bets in the street. He had three betting clocks for timing the receipt of the bets: they were expensive, and he pleaded with me to leave two of them at home before I took him to the police station, but I refused. He was fined and his clocks confiscated. Apparently he had not worked for years and was drawing some sort of sick benefit.

There were complaints of Indecent Exposure, Indecent Assaults and one or two more serious sex offences which I dealt with. The problem, as I saw it, was that the colliery houses were small; there were large families of both sexes being brought up in overcrowded conditions which probably contributed to the unsavoury behaviour.

The police service was seriously under strength and I was taken off the beat for weeks at a time and attached to the CID. There was plenty of crime to be investigated at Bishop Auckland. It was good experience for me but the people at Tindale Crescent continued to expect me to attend to their complaints when I returned home. I did my best, often working long hours.

On the weekly market days at Bishop Auckland, the public houses were open all day as with most towns and there were arrests for drunken behaviour. The miners were making good money and although rationing of food and clothing was still in force, the women had lots to spend, much of which was spent on unnecessary goods displayed on the market stalls, There were women travelling the markets and stealing purses and handbags in the crowded conditions. There were not many police women in the Service at that time but we were fortunate to have in the CID at Bishop Auckland, Freda Gauden. She could dress up and mingle with the other women unnoticed and I remember one market day she arrested seven women in the course of a few hours for stealing purses and handbags. Two of us remained in the office and processed them as they arrived.

It was the practice at that time, when offences of that nature were committed, to search the houses of the accused before we bailed them. In many cases we found dresses and clothing stolen from the multiple stores, with the price tickets attached. The articles were sold among the neighbours at prices less than on the price tags; they were delighted with the bargains which were otherwise unobtainable because of clothes rationing.

Of course there were many who took care of their money and used it wisely. Miners' wives were traditionally in charge of the household purse, as it was the practice for the husband to take his pay packet home, unopened, on a Friday and place it in his wife's lap; she then handed him his spending money!

Sir Hugh Dalton, Chancellor of the Exchequer and Member of Parliament for Bishop Auckland, had been the driving force in establishing the clothing and other factories situated on my beat. A large proportion of the workforce were survivors from the Jewish labour camps in Germany and other European countries. I have previously mentioned helping to acquire piglets for consumption by starving people in a detention camp at Hanover. One day about lunch time, I was on duty in uniform walking along the pavement on the opposite side of the road from the factories when I saw two figures rushing towards me. They put their arms around me and kept repeating 'le Capitan'. They had been in that camp. It was wonderful to see them so happy, and no longer skin and bone and of course no longer in tattered garments.

Many of the refugees wished to become British citizens which is a complicated and time-consuming process with innumerable questions to be answered, documents to be examined and authenticated. Hugh Dalton sponsored their applications and I was given the task of doing some of the work; my previous brief knowledge of the documentation in the labour camp was helpful. The work involved the joint checking and signing of forms with the Member of Parliament. He lived at Etherley which was not far from Tindale Crescent and we usually met at weekends when there was a need. When he wanted to see me, he always telephoned personally and one Friday morning I received a call from him: it was readily apparent that he was upset. He told me he would be unable to see me that weekend as an incident had occurred which would attract publicity and he wanted to get back from the House of Commons and explain what had happened to his wife before an announcement on the radio at 6.00 pm that evening. He was concerned that his action, which he did not then explain, might mean he would no longer be acceptable to sponsor refugees. He was passionate about helping them to a better life. He explained that the news item would clarify the situation and wished confidentiality to be maintained in the meantime. The news revealed that he had let slip an item of significance concerning the forthcoming budget for which he was responsible. He chose an honourable course and the news item included his voluntary resignation. During our association, politics were never mentioned and he treated me with the utmost courtesy. I felt honoured to be his confidant.

I was sent on an Advanced Driving Course in preparation for starting an experimental section employed on mobile crime patrols, with a roving commission in that we had to study serious crime patterns and patrol the appropriate areas. We wore civilian clothes and carried police headgear which provided us with the power to stop vehicles, there being no obligation to obey signals from anyone in civilian clothes. It must have appeared odd when we put on a police cap and on alighting we were in civilian clothes, but it was the only way we could operate as opportunities arose. We had some good arrests and passed useful information to others to follow up. After three months the section was made permanent and full-time officers appointed.

I thought I would get back to full-time duties on my beat but I was appointed Acting Sergeant at Bishop Auckland. It is an unenviable situation, highlighted by wearing two stripes on the arm in place of three stripes on each arm as regular sergeants.

Despite the fact that I was absent from my beat quite a lot, I was on good terms with the majority of the local inhabitants. At the approach of Christmas, when I answered the door, the Chairman of the local Workmen's Club and a colleague were standing there smiling with a large decorated tray. There was a dressed goose, a bottle of Newcastle Brown Ale, a bottle of port, Christmas pudding and cake. The Chairman asked me to accept the gifts with the best wishes of the Club Members. I had no connection with the Club. I had never had cause to visit it and I knew that Workmen's Clubs would not accept policemen as members. I explained that it was quite impossible for me to accept the presents, however well-intentioned. I thanked them for their good wishes and walked back the short distance with them to the club and waited while, at my request, they endorsed the action taken in their Minute Book. I had experience of keeping observation of clubs using false identities when seeking confirmation of offences to support the granting of warrants for raiding the premises, and the obvious dangers of being obliged to such organisations. There is no doubt the act of giving was intended to be seen by the public and could well have eroded my authority or worse. In any case my nature would not allow me to be beholden in such a manner. Lucy agreed with me wholeheartedly although we could have had a different Christmas lunch from that we were able to afford on police pay! The news of such an incident soon got about and for some years I was known as the man who did not eat Christmas dinners!

Life continued at Tindale Crescent as before. The tittle-tattle reaching me about the Christmas lunch was mixed and amusing. The people who were anti-club thought it was a good idea to put the Club Committee in its place, whereas others had mixed comments, but none of them appeared critical of my action.

On holiday at Butlins circa 1954/5

Promotion to Sergeant

In June 1948, I had an interview with my Superintendent when he informed me that the Chief Constable had approved my promotion to the rank of sergeant. He congratulated me and wished me well. I was to be posted to Barnard Castle which was in the same territorial Police Division under his command. I had a good rapport with him and looked forward to the task ahead. By this time I was credited with almost eleven years' police service as a constable and it might be thought by some that it was slow progress and I was just a plodder. My thoughts were that, compared to many others in my situation, I was fortunate to have been given opportunities during the past two years to deal with such a wide variety of police operational work. I was confident to accept the responsibilities of the rank which I have always considered to be a very important link in the chain of command and is probably the most difficult to achieve.

The first step up the greasy pole for promotion is the rank of sergeant: to get there is not easy, there being approximately one sergeant per ten constables. In my day the sergeant was rightly regarded as the most important leader at the sharp end of events. The majority of constables on the beat were young and inexperienced but they were and still are the officers first confronted with the most serious crimes and offences demanding immediate action. The initial action is important: the decisions then taken can and often do have far-reaching consequences. The High Courts frequently spend much time and money on deciding the rights and wrongs of such snap decisions.

In the times of which I write, beat officers were provided with handcuffs, a whistle, notebook, torch and a two-foot folding ruler to take measurements at the scenes of road accidents. As mentioned earlier, I must admit to still having in my possession the two-foot ruler which was issued to me in Durham and is still very much in use though not for the original purpose. There were no personal radios to call for advice or assistance. In cities and in some of the larger towns there were police boxes connected to main police stations and public telephone boxes were occasionally used.

The method of working beats, that is, being at previously nominated places at specified times, was called making 'points' or 'meets'. The time between making points was usually 30 minutes and the time spent there was five minutes, during which supervising officers could confer, giving advice or information as necessary. Additionally, an officer of the shift, designated on reserve, would make contact and disseminate information about wanted persons, stolen cars and anything upon which immediate observation or action was required. On a busy night it could be a hard task being a reserve officer. He would go from point to point and on return to his station further messages were available and off he went again; I still have memories of swollen, sweaty feet. Supervising Officers would inspect and sign notebooks under the last entry with the time, date and place. Considerable emphasis was made that notebooks had to be made up at the time or as soon after the occurrence as was practicable. Solicitors and barristers in courts made great play on when the notes were made and more so when it was their only line of defence.

Sergeants were expected to have a wealth of knowledge on all aspects of police procedure, in maintaining control, and ensuring that the best use was made of a frequent shortage of manpower. Some officers needed a push, while others might be too keen, wasting time on trivial matters. In taking into account the strengths and weaknesses of those in his charge, due attention had to be paid by the sergeant to the welfare of the men and their families. His duty was to be out in the thick of things, providing the best service possible to the members of the public: even the simple task of giving members of the public directions on request was considered an important aspect of duty and was a good way of getting to know people.

We had only a few days between my being notified of my promotion and moving, so there was no opportunity to view the house, but we did learn that it was much better than the two-up-and-two-down in which we lived. On 1st June 1948, we moved and I was granted the following day free of duty to help put the place in order. It turned out to be a Victorian house in a good neighbourhood with helpful neighbours. Much needed to be done which was typical of the state of houses in the aftermath of the war. However, it was a luxury to have a flush toilet and a bath!

We remained in the house for two years until it was sold by the owner and we were moved into a local council house. Furniture and many other items including food and clothing were rationed but we managed nicely. Our son started school and Lucy took him there and back with his sister in the perambulator. The daily journey attracted attention, with her tall slim figure and blonde hair streaming behind her as she scurried down the hill and around the corners, gathering innumerable young children on the way; she loved children and they responded to her.

Although our social life was limited there were happy days on a Sunday when I was free: we went to the seaside at West Hartlepool on coach outings with Geordie Maude, the owner and driver of an old Bedford bus. Occasionally we would get a baby sitter and attend Police and Military Dinner Dances. There was a period of six months in 1952 when I was on a course and was able to get home only four times. I had more than enough of institutional living during the war and I missed Lucy and the family very much. It was equally hard for her, left to bring up the two children on her own. Nevertheless we had happy memories of our stay at Barnard Castle.

The Sub-Division was in charge of a Chief Inspector with three sergeants, one at Staindrop and one at Middleton in Teesdale. My responsibility was the town and a number of farms and military camps. The authorised strength of my section was ten uniformed officers but because of shortages and young policemen being attracted to better occupations, we never had more than seven or eight and one detective constable.

I was appointed an Inspector under the Diseases of Animal Acts which entailed the checking of animal movement records on farms and supervising the movement and transport of animals at the local auction markets. It used to concern me that because of the pressure of work I was unable to give as much attention to that aspect of my duties as was desirable. Fortunately there were no serious outbreaks of infectious diseases during my term of office. There were two or three cases of anthrax which affected individual cattle and could be dealt with in a few days, including the burning of the infected carcass. I was however asked by the local Sanitary Inspector to take over the disposal of a human being who had died of the disease. The deceased was of Irish origin and had lived in a flat in Barnard Castle. His occupation was to look after and feed the Lartington Hunt based across the river in the North Riding.

The disposal and control of animal bodies was not then well defined and the hunts accepted them free of charge from the farmers, whence they were cut up and fed to the hounds. The man who died was experienced and would have been well aware of the cause of death of an infected animal but he obviously took a chance and suffered the consequences. Apparently the local undertaker who knew the consequences of anthrax infections refused to accept the body for burial from the Sanitary Inspector. I refused to take any part in the disposal of the body and finally between the three parties cremation was agreed and the Sanitary Inspector took over the cleansing of the flat and the destruction of clothing and bedding. We never did trace any relatives, which was probably just as well.

The main and virtually full-time work of the police was in dealing with military personnel. There were four military camps on the Durham side of the Tees and one across the river, Deerbolt Camp in the North Riding of Yorkshire. The camps were all within walking distance of the town which was the local recreational centre for the troops. They were usually fully occupied, each with different regiments, changing regularly. The total number of troops could be up to 50,000.

Conscription was in force and quite a number of the conscripts disliked being in the armed forces. Some of them committed crimes in an endeavour to avoid postings to such places as Suez, Malaya and particularly Korea. We liaised with regiments as they arrived and asked for pay days to be staggered so that they were not all paid on the same day of the week but with the best will in the world Thursday and Friday nights followed pay days and there was still money available for Saturday nights. On these three nights of the week we had to deal with street offences of drunken behaviour, fighting and damage to property. Concurrent with the street disorders, shop-breaking and house-breaking offences were being committed. We also had to deal with sexual offences. Fighting between regiments was common-place.

Dances were held in the Witham Hall which was only about 100 yards from the police station and our presence was needed there most nights. Ladies were usually admitted to the weekend dances free of charge. One Saturday night on being asked to go to the hall, we found a pitched battle between soldiers of the Border Regiment of Scotland and the 35th Light Anti-Aircraft Regiment of Wales. I arrived with two constables but we were completely ignored and the fighting continued. We sent a message asking the two Regiments to send their Regimental Policemen with transport.

In the meantime I asked the band to play the National Anthem. The fighting stopped immediately and we used the time to usher the women out of the hall. As soon as the National Anthem came to an end, the fighting re-started and I think the anthem was fully played three times more until the Regimental Police arrived. Those most difficult and the worse of drink were loaded into the trucks and went on their way to the respective guard rooms. There was no point in our locking them up, or trying to do so, as we knew the punishment they would receive would be more appropriate at the hands of the military commanders. The incident was dealt with by a brief entry in the Occurrence Book and the following day when the Chief Inspector looked at it, he remarked that he presumed it was not a serious matter as there were no prisoners!

Amongst the conscripts there were a number of young men who had been released early from Borstal and similar institutions on condition they served in the army. They were the real criminals who committed serious crimes within the camps and also against private property in the town. Those crimes were reported to police irrespective of whether committed on army or private property.

Jack Collinson, with whom I had worked in the CID at Bishop Auckland, had in the meantime been moved to Barnard Castle as a Detective Constable. He had served in the Royal Navy during the war. We had a lot in common and we were good friends. We developed a technique when interrogating hard cases which mostly brought satisfactory results. Jack was a first-class detective and eventually became a Detective Chief Superintendent in Durham. I missed him when he was promoted to sergeant and moved. He was a wonderful character and the last occasion I saw him in public was a few years ago at the Memorial Service for the late Alec Muir who had been our Chief Constable in Durham. I was walking down the aisle in the quiet Cathedral when his arms went around me and in full voice he exclaimed, "It's good to see you, you old bugger." All eyes turned!

The sorts of cases on which we worked jointly were those of a serious nature, the end product being the appearance of the accused at Quarter Sessions or Assize Courts, now replaced. Twelve hours' work on a day when we were on to something was not unusual. In addition to dealing with cases at the civil courts we gave evidence and supplied documents to the military authorities. The policy of whether soldiers would be dealt with at civil courts or the military was roughly that if there was no civilian involvement and property so involved, it was of a military nature, and the police would hand over the case.

Among the conscripts were frail young men usually from sheltered backgrounds who were really quite unsuited for military service. Now and again the policeman on the beat would come across such a conscript hanging about in a secluded position late at night. They had reached a point when they could not face the rough and tumble of barrack room life. They had not checked into their units by the required time and they were in real fear. We tried to deal with them sympathetically and took them back to their units, putting on record that they had lost their way. However, in most cases they were put in the guardroom to appear before their Commanding Officer.

Now and again there were more serious situations, with what I term the inadequate conscripts, resulting in attempted suicides. An 18-year-old conscript reported to his unit that he had been shot at while walking on a footpath in a wood near the town centre. The military brought him to the police station where I interviewed him and arranged his examination by the Police Surgeon. He had a recent scar on the outer side of his right forearm which he alleged had been caused by a man with a handgun. He was right-handed and to an extent this supported his story. His appearance was typical of an underdeveloped body but he spoke up well and stuck to his story. Details of the incident and a description of alleged assailant were circulated locally. Reinforcements joined me and we went to the wood with the complainant. He identified a place where he said he had been shot which was at a slight bend.

For the next six hours or so we searched the area for a weapon or other traces of an attack. From time to time I led him away from the spot he had indicated in an endeavour to establish if he could point out the same place each time as I was sceptical of the truth of the matter. In the meantime his army locker was searched and enquiries were set in motion to obtain background information of his home circumstances. He was adamant he had been attacked and from time to time he trembled and shed tears.

Within a short time of the commencement of the wood search, cold heavy rain fell and continued until dusk when we had to abandon it. We were soaked to the skin. I asked the other officers to go home and as the journey took me past where we lived I took the soldier into my home. My intention was to get dry clothes, take the complainant back to his unit and continue the enquiry the following morning. Lucy took charge, getting a basin of hot water which she placed before the young conscript and told him to take off his boots and socks. She advised me to have a quick bath and although I was reluctant to leave her she insisted. Within a few minutes I returned to find the complainant, still with his feet in hot water, supping mince, potatoes and vegetables, part of the lunch which I had missed! I joined in the eating and Lucy said he had something to tell me. He then blurted out that he had for some time contemplated suicide but had lost his nerve and he then thought up the idea that if he injured himself he might get discharged from the army. His background was that he had been a weakling child brought up by his grandmother. He had brought the weapon used, a small pellet handgun, from home. There seemed no point in taking action against him and I returned him to the army where he was promptly placed in the guardroom. I was most grateful to Lucy for doing, with her sympathetic manner and kindness, a better job at getting to the truth than her trained husband. It might be thought that it was foolhardy of me to leave my wife in such a situation but I knew she had the confidence to take charge. Thank goodness our two children were fast asleep upstairs.

On a Saturday night around midnight I was checking that things were in reasonable order before I went home. At that moment a telephone message was received to the effect that a husband was expected at his house with the deliberate intention of murdering his wife from whom he was estranged. It was a house where a mixed family lived and from which it was not unusual to get calls when there were disagreements. The usual remedy was to give strong advice with the threat that they would be locked up if the policemen had to return. PC Carles Harcourt, a good young probationer, was available and answered the call. I delayed my departure pending his return which was quite soon. He brought a young man with him and explained he had arrested him in the act of attacking his wife with the intention of killing her. The prisoner, good-mannered and calm, agreed with everything the constable said.

The background history was that he had married while a serving soldier at Barnard Castle some years previously. He was posted overseas to complete his term of service and had visited and stayed with his wife during leaves of absence. On his discharge from the army she refused to have anything further to do with him but she continued to accept financial assistance. He found work locally and endeavoured to persuade her to live with him. He eventually returned to his native Glasgow and found good regular work, continuing to persuade his wife to join him, writing letters which she did not acknowledge and paying visits which proved abortive, to the extent that she would not allow him into the house. He said he had knowledge of her association with other men but he was still willing to forgive her. A short time before his final visit he had sent her messages that unless she joined him he would kill her on his next visit. In preparation for his final visit, he resigned from his job in Glasgow, sold most of his possessions and gave up the tenancy of his accommodation. On arrival at Barnard Castle in the late evening, he telephoned the house and was answered by her sister. His wife refused to speak to him and he asked that she be told that he would be arriving shortly with the intention of killing her: hence the urgent call to the police. When PC Harcourt arrived he was already in the entrance hall and being barred from further entry.

In the Police Service you get a few puzzles to sort out from time to time. Here we had a prisoner who adhered to his intention to kill his wife and had made plans accordingly. The only thing he declined to tell us about was where he was going afterwards. He was a quite bright chap; he had some money and I formed the opinion he had made some sort of plan to disappear in the hope that he would not be traced. Whatever his intention we had a self-confessed prisoner and a victim without a scratch on her and as far as we could ascertain neither of them had had a glimpse of each other that evening. I searched my mind and had a quick look at reference books but got no further in formulating an appropriate charge.

After a few quiet moments I came to the conclusion that simplicity was the best course of action. Technically he had committed an assault, the definition being that positive steps to strike someone is an assault and to continue the action and strike the other party becomes an offence of Assault and Battery contrary to Common Law. When arrests for murder, attempted murder and unusual serious crimes were made it was Force policy to notify senior officers as soon as practicable and make arrangements for supporting units to preserve and search the scenes of crime for evidence. In this case no purpose would be served in calling out specialist squads. I completed the charge sheet in that, "He had assaulted his wife with the intention of murdering her contrary to Common Law."

I deemed it prudent to notify my Chief Inspector whose living quarters were an integral part of the police station. By this time it was around 1.00 am: we rang his bedside telephone, knocked at his bedroom door and the only response was snoring!. With considerable trepidation I entered the bedroom. There was no response when the light was switched on and I had to shake him by the shoulders to wake him up. He could hardly believe his eyes but he was a good chap whom I had first got to know when he was a Regimental Sergeant Major in the 52nd Lowland Scottish Division on active service in Europe. He came down to the office where I brought him up to date. His original reaction was that no such charge would be recognized. The prisoner was put in a cell. I went home and on returning at about 10.00 o'clock the following morning I found the Chief Inspector engrossed in studying Criminal Law books. After some discussion it was agreed that the appropriate offence was as charged. He notified the Divisional Superintendent and Dick Hall, the Detective Chief

Superintendent and was told there must be a more appropriate simple charge of Breach of the Peace. We countered by explaining that it was still his intention to murder his wife.

On the Monday morning we had him remanded before the magistrates to be detained for the next three days in the police cells. Frantic efforts and consultation took place with senior officers and solicitors but the original charge was allowed to stand. I prepared a report and statements for a decision to be made by the Director of Public Prosecutions. The subject was discussed and questions asked by those in the chain of command right up to the Chief Constable. The DPP asked to see me. I went to London and he asked whether I was convinced he would stand by his statements that he intended to kill his wife. My assessment of the man was that he would not change his mind. He was committed for trial at the Durham Assize Courts with a top barrister to conduct the prosecution. The prisoner was also adequately defended.

When the prisoner stood up in the court to be formally charged, there were eight varied Counts all including the word 'assault' read out. He pleaded guilty to the original charge and despite the intervention of his barrister and two or three adjournments including advice from the judge, he refused to vary his plea. I believe there was a lot of sympathy for him but with his intention unchanged he had to bear the consequences. He had been in custody awaiting trial for some time. He was awarded a prison sentence: I cannot now recall whether it was for one or two years. There was also a condition that he had to keep away from his wife and from Barnard Castle. The legal profession and police had very much hoped that the case would be disputed on a point of law and would eventually reach the highest courts in the land which would have settled the point for future reference. These odd incidents made life interesting and challenging, which I enjoyed.

The police have to deal daily with people with health and personal problems but the incident I now write about was quite unusual. One afternoon a smart young army captain came into my office and asked me to arrest his wife, who was not with him, and charge her with destruction of life. He was prepared to give evidence against her and he said he had corroborative evidence to substantiate the charge. He produced a recording machine and a tape which he began to play. He explained that the tape had been made while he was in bed with his wife and without her knowledge. It was readily apparent that the problem between him and his wife was concerned with different religious beliefs. He refused to stop the tape which indicated intercourse had taken place between them after initial questioning of his wife as to whether or not she had taken birth control precautions. She admitted having being so prepared which was her usual custom and left him in no doubt that she intended to continue the to do so. His allegation was that by using contraception she was guilty of murdering his child. It was obvious he had become obsessed to the point that there were no other thoughts in his mind. When I suggested he see his doctor and legal advisor he threatened to report me for neglect of duty. I had a cup of tea with him and explained that I needed to have legal advice before I could take action. We parted on the promise that I would take action. I immediately spoke with his Regimental Doctor and his Commanding Officer. They were well aware of his problems but seemed more concerned there would be adverse publicity now the police were involved. I expressed the view that it was time they took positive action to help him. He was admitted to a private nursing home forthwith.

Police work by its nature provides temptations to take risks and do things which are unorthodox. In many instances the consequences of being found out are not of sufficient importance to warrant further action, perhaps other than advice. But now and again there are challenges with which officers are confronted and which they believe can best be solved by operating outside the rules. On the occasion I now refer to I was quite aware that if I were to be found out there would be a strong possibility of being charged with serious disciplinary offences or even appearing before a court for the illegal possession and use of firearms. Army Camps are a magnet for stray dogs: the soldiers feed and look after them and they become pets. Unfortunately stray dogs do not settle down easily and there is a tendency for them to turn to sheep-worrying on moonlit nights.

A farmer complained that dogs had been chasing his sheep and had worried three of them. He had seen the dogs and scared them off but was unable to get within shooting range. We did not have the resources to keep a full-time watch but I was sympathetic to his plight.

I discussed the problem with a friend of mine who was a Regimental Sergeant Major at one of the camps. The next fine moonlit evening we set off with two army rifles and ammunition. Three dogs soon appeared and were making towards the sheep. We shot the three of them and quietly retreated to camp to replace the rifles.

Next morning when I saw the farmer he was delighted to find the dead dogs. He asked no questions but on inspecting the bodies we were surprised to find that two of the dogs were of an unusual breed and appeared to have been well groomed; the third was a normal stray. In the normal course of events the farmer would have buried the carcass and that in all probability would have been the end of the matter. We realised that two of the dogs were different and that there might be a hue and cry about their disappearance.

On going to the nearest camp I learned that a lieutenant had bought them abroad and had been authorised to have them at the camp after their period of six months' quarantine. His batman was supposed to look after them, exercise them on a lead and in no circumstances were they to be allowed to run free. Having established that he had disobeyed orders, the servant was promptly placed in the guardroom. The lieutenant assumed they had been shot by the farmer and wanted to know the full details and even mentioned seeking compensation.

I asked to see the colonel, a wonderful Irishman, whom I had already met in the course of duty. I took him into my confidence and he then sent for the dog owner. He reminded the lieutenant of his responsibilities and pointed out that he was liable to be sued for a substantial sum of money unless he made reasonable compensation and he advised the lieutenant to settle the matter there and then to avoid publicity to the regiment. The lieutenant asked permission to telephone his mother as his bank account was low. In the meantime I had lunch with the colonel and when I left the camp I was in possession of a very substantial cheque made out to the farmer which pleased and I think surprised him. It was a small farm; they just about made ends meet. They wanted to do something for me but I declined their offers settling for a glass of some sort of home-made wine which made me see stars! My RSM friend and I had a quiet drink in his Sergeants' Mess and considered ourselves fortunate to escape detection for our doubtful deeds.

On one occasion I asked a Sergeant Major to cancel the demobilisation of about 250 soldiers and place them in detention. The following morning there was a full face photograph of me on the front page of 'The News of the World' with uncomplimentary comments and questions. The unit involved was a Demobilisation Centre responsible for equipping clothes and clothing coupons to soldiers being discharged from the army. Every few weeks, about 250 soldiers were dispatched on a month's leave. Arrangements were made for them to be entrained at a railway halt near the camp. We received a report from the unit that certain premises had been broken into and thousands of clothing coupon booklets were missing. A brief visit to the camp indicated the scale of the thefts and I realised that it would be impossible for any individual to carry that sort of weight. The soldiers were already at the halt awaiting their train.

It would have been difficult to search each soldier and keep control of the situation by searching them where they were, so I asked the RSM, who was present with Regimental Policemen, to cancel their leave and march them back to Camp. He said he would do so if I first advised them that they were to be detained on suspicion of being involved in breaking and entering and the theft of booklets of clothing coupons. I addressed the soldiers forthwith. They voiced their objections but were marched back to camp where each man was required to turn out his kit and be subject to a personal search. We recovered a large number of clothing coupon books from over 100 soldiers. Most admitted buying them from other soldiers and were detained. The remainder were transported to Darlington railway station to continue their journey home. In the course of our enquiries we established that the breaking and entering was committed by two permanent staff and a further quantity of clothing books and several hundred pounds were recovered from them. The Army dealt with the soldiers who committed these offences.

During the latter part of that Saturday, the police were inundated with telephone calls from Members of Parliament and the Press. It transpired that the nephew of a Member of Parliament was one of the soldiers involved. In the Sunday morning newspapers there were varying accounts of what had taken place. 'The News of the World' had a photograph of me on the front page with uncomplimentary remarks challenging the legality of my actions. Legal or otherwise I believe our joint action was justified.

On one occasion I was caught for disobeying instructions by Eric St Johnston, Chief Constable. At that time petrol was rationed and in order to get as many miles as possible per gallon, there was an instruction that, except in an emergency, police vehicles must not exceed more than 45 miles per hour. I was driving the 10 hp Hillman, not by any means a fast vehicle, with Jack Collinson as my passenger. We were trying to get to Bishop Auckland to arrest three men who we believed were on the last bus from Barnard Castle to Bishop Auckland and we had good reason to believe that during market day they had stolen handbags and purses from several people. It was dark and when we were about half-way on our journey and travelling as fast as the car would go, we recognised in front of us and going in the same direction the Chief Constable's car. I drove on past him; we had a fairly good idea that he would recognise the police vehicle.

We reached the main Bus Station at Bishop Auckland just as the passengers were disembarking and detained our three suspects, finding purses and other property belonging to other people. We took the three prisoners to the police station which was nearby and no sooner had we got them inside than the Chief Constable and his wife followed. He first asked who was driving the car now parked outside. I admitted to being the driver and tried to explain the purpose of our journey. He wanted a report on his desk as soon as possible. Eventually, I managed to explain that we had arrested three well-known criminals for a number of offences of larceny from the person. He queried whether or not the journey was an emergency, at which his wife spoke up and remarked that he was lucky to have such clever policemen! That was the end of the matter.

During the summer when regular units were otherwise engaged, the camps were occasionally occupied by Territorial Regiments for a couple of weeks or so. One such was the Shropshire Yeomanry, then equipped with tanks. On the morning after they arrived, we received a call to the effect that the Officers' Mess had been broken into and bottles of alcoholic drinks had been stolen. Jack Collinson accompanied me to the scene where we met the Commanding Officer, a short man with heavy dark eyebrows, wearing battledress and the badges of a Lieutenant-Colonel. He was hopping mad and cursing everyone within sight. We listened for a moment or two and realised he was more concerned about adverse publicity than the value of the stolen property. I advised him to refer Press enquiries to the police.

We tackled the permanent staff at the camp, a handful of soldiers, whose duties usually were to keep the grounds tidy, clean the lavatories and such-like. We had had previous dealings with them and two of them admitted breaking and entering the Officers' Mess and stealing the drinks. We recovered some bottles buried under leaves and in toilet cisterns. The culprits admitted having sold bottles to soldiers and also that there were a couple of cases in the ration truck which had left early in the morning with the tanks en route for a firing range in Cumberland. The two culprits were put in the Guard Room and we made our way to Cumberland, catching up with the tank convoy just as it was entering the camp. With the help of the officers we turned out the belongings of every soldier and searched the vehicles. We recovered a number of bottles and left the regiment to deal with the offenders.

When we arrived back, the Press were seeking information and I informed them there had been a breaking and entering at the camp and that items of Mess silver had been stolen but were all recovered and the culprits were being dealt with by the army, adding that the procedure was normal with crimes of this nature committed by service personnel within military establishments. The explanation was accepted and the only publicity was a brief entry in the local newspaper. Many years later when I was a Superintendent in Durham, Alec Muir, my Chief Constable, suggested I might care to apply for the post of Deputy Chief Constable, Shropshire, which I did and was invited to appear before a Selection Board of the Authority. Members of the Board asked me a number of questions but the only comment the Chairman made was that he noted from my application that I had served as a Sergeant at Barnard Castle, which I confirmed. I was appointed to the post and it was not until later that I realized the Chairman had been the Commanding Officer of the Shropshire Yeomanry at their Summer Camp at Barnard Castle. The subject was never mentioned but from time to time I have given thought to the coincidence.

Promoted Inspector

I was qualified for promotion and selected to attend a six months' course at the Police College which was for potential Inspectors expected to reach higher rank in time. I completed the course at the end of June 1952 and was promoted to Inspector. I took up that appointment at Darlington a few weeks later on 5th August.

By this time, a programme of building standard police houses was taking place and we were the first occupants of one of four new houses built at Houghton le Skerne on the outskirts of Darlington. It was a pleasant place to live and there was a good school nearby. There were good shops and adequate amenities including a swimming pool where Lucy taught the children to swim.

The Police Division incorporated Newton Aycliffe, the first post-war new town to be built in the country. The busy A1 road cut through the town centre creating traffic problems and bringing undesirables whom we could have done without. The population of the old Quaker borough was about 85,000 in 1952. The main Industry was engineering: bridges were built and locomotives and wagons were constructed at the extensive railway works. The police workload was high and the cells were frequently filled to capacity.

It was a useful and popular place for HGV drivers to stop overnight and Bed and Breakfast on their journeys north and south. Travelling criminals begged lifts, stopped off and committed a whole variety of offences: shop-breakings and house-breakings were commonplace. There were also crimes and offences generated from within the local population. The troops from Catterick Camp in the North Riding and from Barnard Castle kept us busy at weekends.

On reporting to my new station I was welcomed by Superintendent Charles Middlewood under whose command I had previously served. He had no specific instructions and he gave me a free hand to do whatever was necessary to improve the standard of policing which he considered had not recovered from the war years owing to the continuing shortage of manpower. He was a good policeman, a capable leader and by repute a strict disciplinarian. I was happy with my brief.

The general duties of an Inspector are to arrange adequate cover with the available strength, briefing the shifts with relevant information when parading them for duty and when practicable de-briefing them at the end of their shifts. Prisoners had to be brought before the courts within 24 hours or released; therefore evidence had to be prepared and scrutinised forthwith for completeness and accuracy. Inspectors also prosecuted in courts which I very much enjoyed; solicitors were only engaged when prisoners were being committed for trial and in highly contentious cases. Inspectors could get bogged down with paperwork and become office-bound. My intention, which I believe I managed to keep, was to spend as much time as possible with patrols, giving support to those at the sharp end and so gathering information and knowledge of the area.

My first shift was from 10.00 pm on a Friday night. I was on the point of leaving the Station when a patrol car stopped at the front of the building. The crew of two were struggling with three prisoners and shouting for assistance. I grabbed one young man and hustled him inside, and on the way asked directions to the Charge Room as I had little knowledge of the building. I pushed him inside and hastened to help with the other two struggling prisoners. On returning to the Charge Room I found that the original prisoner was missing. He had jumped through an insecure window on to the street below, a height of about 25 feet. Fortunately, the patrol officers had taken possession of his RAF pay and record of service book which told us he was from Croft Airfield, a distance of about eight miles. He was overtaken on the outskirts of the town and charged with the other two prisoners with taking and driving away a motor vehicle without the consent of the owner. I did not charge him with the offence of escaping from police custody as I considered an open window an open invitation.

The night shift Inspector was required to submit a report with a resume of occurrences. I included details of the escape, accepting responsibility. When I next saw the Superintendent he asked me why I had included the incident in the report bearing in mind that the prisoner had been re-arrested. I explained that to have excluded the item might have created the impression to those under my supervision that I was being dishonest and I thought it was better that a correct version was on record, as in course of time a different story might have got about.

In large towns there are usually a number of homeless people and tramps sleeping out, some of whom are from good backgrounds, others from broken homes and ex-servicemen finding it difficult to settle down. The relationship between them and police is generally good but now and again there are complaints about their presence and they have to be moved on. They are expert at finding warm places adjacent to furnaces, bakeries and those sorts of places. On really cold winter nights when they are not feeling at their best, they try to find a cheap lodging for a night. Many of them are filthy, smelly and lousy and therefore unacceptable.

Prior to the Health Acts of 1948, Local Authority lodging houses, known to the users as Spikes, were strategically placed about the countryside and within about a day's reach from one lodging house to another. Bed and breakfast was free. There was a limited time for which they could stay and before being discharged there was a requirement for them to perform some chores. By the 1950s, a large number of the lodging houses had been closed and there was a continuing policy to close the remainder. By 1952, there were none in Darlington. The only place was the Salvation Army Hostel where the charge was two shillings and six pence for bed and breakfast. Social Services did not exist and the police were the only people to turn to for help. We had no funds for this purpose and it was not infrequent for police officers to have a whip round and take the person to the Salvation Army Hostel. Even then there were quibbles and objections because of their being smelly and filthy.

There were other groups of down-and-out people living more or less permanently under railway arches and similar places, existing on scraps and drinking meths and red biddy. They existed in a haze and we left them in their wretched existence unless we received complaints about their presence or behaviour. A few of the tramps had convictions for petty thefts of food and milk and, unable to pay fines, were sent to prison which they enjoyed in bad winter weather and particularly over the Christmas period. We knew one or two who gave glowing accounts of being well fed and entertained at Christmas in prison. They were cleaned up and voluntary organisations provided them with a change of clothing and presents upon being discharged.

One such person arrived at the police station about 11.00 pm on 23rd December with a brick in his hand, threatening to go outside and break a shop window. We gave him food and tea but he kept coming back into the station asking for a policeman to witness him breaking a window. A bright young detective, named Whittaker, who eventually became a Detective Chief Superintendent sat falsely as a magistrate and held a mock court binding him over in the sum of £2.00 to be of good behaviour. He still refused to go away until he had been served with the appropriate form. The detective found a friendly truck driver with an empty vehicle who was travelling south on the A1 road to take him in the back. He was foul and unfit for a seat beside the driver which was another reason why we did not want him in police cells. The following night, 24th December, we received a call from the neighbouring North Riding Police reporting that this man had surrendered to them. I was brought into the picture then and it was arranged that a patrol car would meet half way and transfer the so-called prisoner to Darlington. He wanted to go to prison so we had a whip round, raising the required £2.00 and took him to the local Salvation Army Hostel where he spent a few days over Christmas. Before moving on, he called and asked that the magistrate who paid his fine be thanked for his kindness. The North Riding Police were none the wiser and it was an item which I did not include in the Night Report.

Complaints of metal thefts from engineering works were common and particularly phosphor-bronze journals from the railway works. The site covered several hundred acres with security fences around the perimeter but the weakness was that secondary public roads and little-used tracks were immediately adjacent to the fencing. Within the site, railway lines criss-crossed everywhere and were used for moving materials in wagons. The stolen property could best be removed from the site by wagons containing the metal being manoeuvred right up to the outer fences and at a given time and pre-arranged point the stolen property could be passed over to a waiting vehicle, the final operation being executed in a minute or so.

The reader may think it would be a simple task to catch the perpetrators red-handed. However there were many obstacles in the way, for example, the extent of the site and the hundreds of wagons scattered about which needed a trained signaller to move them to a previously-arranged point. In addition, the wagons selected for movement of stolen property were marked with a secret code by the thieves. The workers were organised into gangs, usually made up of seven men employed on a particular project. It was common knowledge that it required the involvement of a number of people to get the stolen property to the point of leaving the site. Union representatives challenged the business of anyone they could not identify on entering the Main Gate which was strictly controlled. If a policeman called, he was not allowed within the Works; if he made a move to do so a strike was threatened. Therefore, informants and under-cover methods had to be employed.

Secret police emergency plans were made in readiness to take action in the event of stolen goods being passed over the fences. I happened to be the night shift Inspector when the plans had to be implemented. It was a timed operation, the intention being to arrest the thieves as well as the receivers. The names and places of work of the suspects and their place of work within the site were known to police. My main job was to protect the three detectives accompanying me, with the help of three uniformed officers. None of us got beyond the Main Gate, which was not unexpected. A cry went up that police were on the premises and by obviously pre-planned arrangements the whole of the night shift walked out and sat down on the A1 road, completely blocking traffic. I have no confirmation of the number involved, but a three-shift system was in operation and it was said there were about 10,000 on each shift. It was then after midnight on a cold but dry February night. There was no point in even attempting to move them or to ask them to do so. When the day shift arrived at 6.00 am they also sat down on the road.

I remained on duty long after finishing time, which was 6.00 am, and I was wondering how long the sitting protest would last when, at about 7.30 am, a real wet north-east blizzard started; within an hour there was slush on the roads and water running in the gutters. Gradually the road cleared as the soaking protestors drifted off without a word! The weather had done a much better job of clearing the road than the police could have done! The operation was a complete success and a number of people were brought before the court later that day. The traffic problem was not unusual and well-defined diversions were implemented while the road was closed. Darlington sorely needed a by-pass, but had to wait until the sixties for a new motorway.

There was plenty of work in the post-war years and extra income was made by people working overtime. Illegal betting houses were thriving and the laws governing public houses and clubs were in some instances being ignored. We were receiving anonymous letters purporting to come from wives, alleging that their husbands did not arrive home on Fridays which was pay day and when eventually they put in an appearance they had little or no money for the needs of the wives and children. In those days workers were paid weekly in cash. I was under no illusions that police activity would not stop the hard-core gamblers and drinkers who would find other places to continue their way of life. Nevertheless, I believed that police action would be beneficial to families and family life.

Initially it was easy to keep observation and get sufficient evidence to apply for warrants to raid the premises as no action had been taken against them for many years. A number of places were raided and the offenders brought before the courts. It was surprising how light the penalties were: they were not a deterrent. Within a few weeks we repeated a raid on premises previously raided. On that occasion the court fine was somewhat increased, and other similar establishments began to realise we meant business.

These places are havens for prostitutes and provided they don't ply their trade in the street or run brothels, no offences are committed. We received a complaint from a householder that a particular named prostitute was active immediately outside her house and there were disturbances involving the clients. The householder had warned her that she was going to notify the police of her conduct but the advice was ignored. It was a simple matter to get the evidence and charge her accordingly. When she came before the court the case was adjourned for no apparent reason. It was suggested that consideration be given to charging the person with being Drunk and Disorderly or Breach of the Peace; the suggestion was rejected. Eventually the woman pleaded guilty to the original charge. The result of the adjournment and delayed proceedings brought more publicity than if the case had gone ahead at the first hearing. The reason for the shilly-shallying was that, as far as memory went, there had been no such previous convictions upon the borough for prostitution and the belief was that the conviction would bring disgrace.

The Superintendent attended regular meetings with the councillors and senior officers of the authority which included magistrates. On returning from one of the meetings he came into my office smiling and asked me where I would like to be posted. He explained that the raid on betting houses and public houses and clubs had brought disrepute upon the town, the last straw being the offence of prostitution. The Superintendent was asked if I could be moved from Darlington on promotion or by any other means. He explained that his officers were carrying out his will and pointed out that arising from these raids there had been a great many letters of appreciation from members of the public. Whether or not there would have been more pressure from the 'City Fathers' will never be known, as about this time I was instrumental in the arrest and charging of a magistrate on a charge of Gross Indecency with a teenage boy who had been dealt with before a Juvenile Court. Approaches of the kind referred to merely confirmed my determination to carry out my duty without fear or favour, giving my best to the public at large and to encourage those under my supervision to do likewise.

Shortly after taking up duty at Darlington I was on duty in uniform in the town centre where I met a sergeant and a constable. It was dark and soon after 10.00 pm when a man came running round the corner and told us that a policeman was lying on the ground getting a good hiding. We sprinted round the corner and within about 70 yards found a violent scene. A uniformed constable was lying face down on the road trying to protect his head with his hands from blows being rained down upon him with a weapon, which turned out to be the officer's truncheon. A second man was kicking his body. The sergeant and the constable took the attackers to the police station and I accompanied the injured officer to hospital. I remained with him throughout the night and for some time was joined by his wife. He was never unconscious and remained talkative while he was being medically examined and treated.

He was a fit young man in his twenties but almost completely bald. To the best of my memory, 17 wounds were readily identified as having been inflicted by force with the truncheon. The skin was broken at the points of impact and had rolled back leaving wounds of up to about one and half inches in length, exposing his skull bone unprotected. Surprisingly, there was not as much loss of blood as one would have expected. He suffered aches and pains in other parts of his body owing to having been kicked a number of times. He had no fractures and the doctor expressed the opinion that he was fortunate in having a very thick skull, otherwise the consequences from the head wounds could have been very serious.

I went to see him later the same day and found him in good spirits and asking to be allowed home. His memory appeared to be unaffected so I tried to get him to relate the sequence of events leading up to the attack. I was unable to elicit from him the reason why he became so involved and of the circumstances of how one of them got possession of his truncheon. He did not or would not provide the details asked and throughout the court proceedings the matter was never clarified. The Defence Barrister endeavoured to establish that he had drawn his truncheon without good cause and it had been forcibly taken from him and used in self-defence. There were no bruises or marks on the two accused to support the theory. The police and prosecutors made the point that even if the accusation was true their conduct could not be justified for carrying out the determined and savage attack upon the officer. The hospital doctor and I were the principal witnesses at the trial. The injured constable did not have much to contribute. The accused were originally charged with attempted murder but they were found guilty of Grievous Bodily Harm and both sentenced to stiff prison sentences. I was left with the question which I still ponder, why and how the constable's truncheon came to be in possession of one of the assailants. Truncheons are gripped tightly in the hand and held in place with a strong flexible leather loop around the thumb. The constable had been trained in the use of a truncheon; he was strong and had previously used his truncheon in anger. It would have been extremely difficult for it to have been removed by a third party from his truncheon pocket housed in a specially-made pocket within his trousers.

In course of time I perceived that the officer was not highly regarded by his colleagues, which is frequently an indication that something may be wrong. He was a tremendous worker, making many arrests and reporting people for summary offences and he was a useful chap to have by your side during a rough-house. His paperwork had to be carefully scrutinised as he had a tendency to exaggerate. He was not always on the shift for which I was responsible and I became aware that the older Inspectors kept him in the office doing the telephone duties during night shifts. They explained they were uneasy about the aggressive way he sometimes went about his duties and it was evident they did not trust him.

Inspector Leslie Wearmouth, a colleague and good friend, agreed with me that it was undesirable to discriminate against him and when he was on our shifts he shared the street patrols with his colleagues. However, we decided to keep a close watch on his activities. On two occasions I refused to accept charges against persons arrested by him and brought to the police station. One I remember was for being drunk and disorderly and for assault upon police. I considered the prisoner was not drunk and he appeared to me to be an unlikely chap to assault a policeman. The constable invariably accepted my decisions without demur. A worrying aspect of his life were the many occasions when he reported unfit for duty, suffering from bruises to his hands and face and occasionally limping. His explanations were that he had accidents riding his bicycle. When he was missing from my shift, I made a point of paying him a personal visit or arranging for a sergeant to do so. He had the wounds to prove he was not malingering.

Darlington was a place where shop-breakings and house-breakings were high but we had a reasonably good record of detections except for the breaking into terraced houses over the previous few years. The offences took place on dark evenings on Fridays which was pay day, the intruder gaining access by climbing over the backyard walls and forcing entries. On occasion two, three or more houses adjacent to each other would be attacked the same evening: it was apparent that it was easier to climb over the dividing walls than the outer yard walls. The breaker confined his takings to cash. Special watch by plain-clothes observations were unsuccessful. I had an idea and set about secretly and in my own time building up a picture and graphs of the terrace house break-ins, which matched the dates with the occasions upon which the officer reported sick. The information collated provided a good reason to consider him a suspect. I prepared a detailed paper and suggested that Headquarters CID be asked to form a team of officers from other divisions and, unknown to the suspect, to keep him under observation during the hours of darkness on Friday evenings. The Superintendent endorsed my suggestions and because of the sensitive nature of the document asked me to take it to HQ and hand it to a Detective Superintendent.

Charles Middlewood, my Superintendent, was on the point of retiring. His replacement was not known to me but within a short time of his arrival my friend and colleague, Inspector Leslie Wearmouth, was posted to Houghton le Spring Division. He had quite a lot of service and raised no objections to the move as his new post was likely to be less stressful. The new Superintendent saw me and in a conversational manner mentioned that the officer I suspected of crime had a good record of work and I should not to be too hard upon him. No mention was made of my suspecting him of house-breaking; I was surprised but further discussion on the subject was declined. The next thing I received was a memorandum from the Chief Constable's Office directing that I be posted to Stockton Division to perform similar duties. I sensed there was a reason, unknown to me, for the proposed move so I asked for a personal interview with the Chief Constable, Alec Muir. He listened to what I had to say and it transpired that he had no knowledge or background information of the document I had prepared suggesting the suspect be kept under observation. The Chief Constable being a perceptive chap cancelled my posting and the suspect was posted to the same Division as Inspector Wearmouth.

We conferred and made arrangements for the suspect to be kept under observation as much as practicable in his new surroundings. The second day after he arrived, he was caught wheeling a sack of stolen potatoes home on his bicycle. A search of his home revealed fishing gear stolen during shop breakings at Darlington and a few trinkets connecting him with the Friday night house-breakings. The Chief Constable asked me to see him and said he had come to the conclusion that I was the only person in the Force who knew the man. I was directed to take charge and supervise the case for Court. Furthermore he asked me to give the evidence of character of the accused upon conviction and to serve the dismissal notice, which I did within a few minutes of his being sentenced to a substantial term of imprisonment.

I could have queried the underhand manner the whole affair had been dealt with but thought no useful purpose would be served in doing so. My conclusion was that instead of laying on an observation team, a decision might have been taken to interview the suspect with my paper as background knowledge. If they had consulted me about their intention I would have informed them that he was an astute hard-boiled character who would withstand interrogation. Apparently he convinced them of his innocence and complained that I had been harassing him. He declined to make a formal complaint, no doubt, in the knowledge that if he had done so it would have resulted in his many shortcomings being revealed and assessed. If he had not been brought to justice I have from time to time thought that I might have finished the remainder of my service in the rank of Inspector.

In an industrial environment there are invariably accidents, fires and explosions necessitating police attention. There was in my time at Darlington one really frightening incident. About 2.00 am a series of loud explosions and fires lighting up the sky for many miles occurred at the Bakelite Factory at Newton Aycliffe. Roof tiles were flying from the nearby dwelling houses and landing a considerable distance from where they originated. Three men were rescued from the factory and sent to hospital. Thankfully at that time of night nobody was about in the streets but bedroom lights were showing and we used a patrol car with public-address advising people to remain indoors. The explosions stopped after about two hours but fires raged and there was the possibility of renewed explosions.

Bakelite, which was being produced, was the forerunner of plastic. The method of production was very much an industrial secret and the only information I could get as to the cause of the incident was that there had been a leak from a faulty joint. It was the simplest and briefest report which I ever had to make covering a disaster of this magnitude. The Company, American-owned, arranged the immediate repairs to the dwelling houses. It was a miracle no members of the public were injured.

There were really no day-to-day problems of bad discipline but we had an ex-Guardsman who had been on active service throughout the war who found the demon drink hard to resist. Time and again he had been helped and given advice but to no avail. One night about 1.00 am he was brought singing to the Station in uniform by two men who half carried and dragged him up the steps. They had found him sprawled in a shop doorway with a bottle of beer and when they tried to get him on his feet he collapsed. I had no choice but to charge him with being unfit for police duty which was confirmed by the Police Surgeon. When he sobered up I took him home and it was apparent that his wife was at the end of her tether with his drunken behaviour. I persuaded her to remain with him pending the outcome of his appearing before the Chief Constable. It was the usual practice for an elected member of the Police Federation to appear with and assist the person charged. He told me in advance that he intended to plead guilty and wanted me to represent him, which I did. When he was sober he was an active and competent policeman and I said so. He was admonished and moved to another Division in order to give him a chance to reform in new surroundings. It was within my knowledge that he kept sober for a long time thereafter but I do not know if it was permanent. It was a sad and unpleasant task.

At Darlington, amongst other duties, I was an Inspector of Drugs under the Drugs and Poisons Acts which authorized access and inspection of Pharmacists' Registers and the security and control of certain poisons. It was an interesting and useful duty. One morning about 11.00 am a local doctor was brought to the police station by two motor patrol officers who had stopped him because of his wayward driving. It was a warm day and he took his jacket off to reveal both arms peppered with syringe marks. He was barely receptive to our questions and the Police Surgeon came to the conclusion he was under the influence of drugs to the extent that he was unable to drive a motorcar. He eventually appeared in Court, pleaded guilty and was fined. My interest was to find out how he had obtained the large amounts of drugs necessary to sustain him in the condition he had reached. A scrutiny of pharmacists revealed he had issued prescriptions to patients who when interviewed said they took the drugs back to the doctor as they were not required. The doctor had asked that they go as far afield from his surgery as possible and to use different pharmacists. The evidence gathered was sent to the BMA and resulted in his being struck off the Medical Register.

I enjoyed three years working at Darlington. It was a busy station but there were many happy memories. Outstanding characters were the people having difficulties coping with life who called regularly and were usually content to go away a little happier after a chat and a cup of tea. One never-to-be-forgotten couple, probably in their sixties, walked about the streets in all weathers. The lady always wore a bright, wide-brimmed hat decorated with flowers and a thin floral dress with lightweight shoes, totally unsuitable for winter wear; the husband wore a dark suit and spats. She made unbelievable claims and complaints and on occasions it was difficult to get her to leave the station. A policeman who was always kind and considerate to them thought she was rambling more than ever so he decided to have a word with the husband who up to that time had never uttered a word. He took him aside and said he thought his wife needed urgent medical attention. The husband went berserk and had to be restrained. It became apparent that his mental condition was just as bad, or worse, than his wife but they were harmless and they continued their visits.

It was not long after the policeman had been dealt with for the breaking offences that I was asked to go and see the Chief Constable. It was obvious he had done his homework on me as he started off by saying he understood I thought it a waste of time filling in and forwarding returns which served no useful purpose. He continued that he wanted me to start work at Headquarters the following week and he gave me a free hand to go through every department and to take whatever action I considered necessary to reduce unnecessary work and reduce waste. I was to remain in the same house at Darlington which pleased me, Lucy and the family. I had, so far in my service been employed on operational duties which I enjoyed. I looked forward to the challenge.

During the few months at Headquarters I took the opportunity to learn as much as possible about the functions and responsibilities of the various departments in the course of sorting out what I considered was unnecessary paperwork and forms. In certain Departments there were stacks of old files which were neatly stored and indexed, but as far as could be ascertained, had never been referred to and appeared to serve no useful purpose, so they were destroyed. The cancellation of requests for returns had to be published and the appropriate instructions amended or cancelled which was quite time-consuming. There were also instances of departments asking for and retaining identical information. It needed a little diplomacy to streamline those sorts of problems but progress was made and the objective realised.

The effect of reducing the flow of paperwork and returns posed the obvious question about staffing levels. The point had now been reached when personalities were concerned about their future; some of them had been in sheltered situations for a long time, and realised changes were likely to come about. The future duties and possible postings were not a matter for me to comment upon. I therefore rounded off my brief, recommending changes to the structure and establishment by reducing the number of sections within departments which would provide a given number of police and civilian staff to be re-deployed elsewhere.

A Tough Assignment

Quite unexpectedly the Chief Constable offered me an appointment to take charge of West Stanley Sub-Division which was part of Consett Territorial Division. He explained that for the time being he would be unable to promote me to the rank of Chief Inspector to which the post was entitled because there was not a vacancy in the authorised establishment, the previous incumbent having been moved sideways, retaining the rank. It was made quite clear to me that if I declined the posting there would be no repercussions. He advised me to think the offer over and in the meantime to see Mr Alf Reay, the Deputy Chief Constable, who would enlighten me on some of the problems likely to be encountered.

Mr Reay was a highly experienced officer with whom I had worked when he was a Detective Chief Superintendent. He gave me a full account, in confidence, of certain personality clashes and other difficulties which had arisen, necessitating his having to give senior officers strong advice. He added that the sub-division was not in good order and required hard work to clean it up. Finally, in a jocular manner he said that if the occasion arose when I gave a certain person a black eye I should ensure there were no witnesses. He probably had a good idea of my tolerance level. The following day, after talking the matter over with Lucy, I informed the Deputy Chief Constable I would accept the posting. He wished me Good Luck.

Within a few days we packed up and moved to West Stanley, about twelve miles north-west of Durham City. The police station had the usual offices, cells, two court rooms and the Chief Inspector's house which was an integral part of the complex. It was an old, solid-looking building with round turrets. The living accommodation consisted of large, high draughty rooms with no central heating. Lucy named the place 'Hatters' Castle'!

The dwelling house door opened on to heavy stone steps and a main road. Immediately opposite was a cinema, the sounds of which could be heard in the bedrooms where the children slept; they used to sing themselves to sleep with the music. Next door was a busy fish and chip shop with the attendant smells and around the corner a coal mine. In windy weather, which was quite regular, as the area was on high ground, coal dust blew everywhere. The road to the right went up a slope and at the top some 500 yards distant there was a large transport depot with several hundred coaches. Until one has lived in a coal-mining area it is not realised that coal miners go to and from work at odd hours throughout the 24 hours of each day.

The traffic of coaches from the depot was something we grew used to but in cold weather when drivers had difficulty in starting their engines or were too lazy to swing the starting handles, they would roll down the hill in neutral and engage the gears right under our bedroom windows. Continuous sleep was impossible in these circumstances and one of my immediate tasks was to see the Depot Superintendent. He was a nice chap and thanked me for complaining, explaining that it would be helpful to him in giving the drivers advice, the reason being that there was a strong Union influence and strikes could be sparked off if he had not good reason for taking action. He told me that he would impress upon them that unless the practice ceased the police would issue summonses to the offenders. Thereafter, except on rare occasions, the practice ceased.

We had difficulty in placing our son in a new school. At Darlington, where he had been, the eleven-plus system was not in operation whereas in Durham County it applied. At the time of our arrival it was too late for him to sit the examination for the local Grammar School which was only a few minutes distant. Appeals fell on stony ground. He was finally accepted at 'The Upper Standards' School Annfield Plain which necessitated his travelling by public transport. Naturally we were disappointed but in fact it was a highly-regarded school where his progress was excellent. Our daughter was younger and there was no problem in her being accepted at the local Junior School. On the day appointed for her to start, Lucy accompanied her and was met at the entrance gate by a teacher and four girls of about similar age. They hoisted Margaret on to their shoulders and marched her off to her classroom. The welcome was typical of the warm and friendly atmosphere readily apparent in coal-mining communities. Our son made friends with Alan Brown at school and although they have lived miles apart for most of their lives, they and their wives are still close friends. Lucy and I were accepted into the community where we had a good social life and the children were happy.

Lucy found it frustrating when even on a fine day the washing on the line was soiled with coal dust. However, the two Court Rooms were centrally heated in the winter and when not otherwise in use she dried the clothes there. The other bonus was that we did not need baby sitters, as there was a connecting door between the living quarters and the main office which was manned 24 hours a day. Living in an operational police station involved and impinged upon the life of the whole family and the conditions then may sound alien compared to the present day. Noisy drunks in the cells frequently disturbed our sleep; stray dogs in the adjoining kennels were at times noisy and we had the responsibility of feeding them and the prisoners.

Margaret, from being a small child, was fond of animals. She had a way of managing them and took the stray dogs out on leads to give them exercise. On one occasion Ronnie Harrison, a policeman working in the front office, rushed into the living quarters in an agitated manner. He had seen from the office window Margaret with a dog which had been brought into the kennels, with difficulty, for attacks on people and was waiting to be destroyed. All hands were mustered to trace her and the dog with instruction not to interfere provided she was safe. She soon appeared with the dog and returned it to the kennels, giving it a parting pat on the head before she left it! She also kept and bred guinea pigs in the yard, and on one occasion caused consternation on a bus when she was taking them to sell at a market. Alex decided to use a cell which had been blocked off from the main quarters, where he did his homework, listened to the radio and built model aircraft. The allowances for feeding prisoners and stray dogs were at workhouse level.

The population of the town was about 50,000 and the sub-division included South Moor, Craghead, Annfield Plain, Dipton, Tantobie, Bloemefontein and Burnopfield, making the total population in the region of 80,000. I understand the population is less now with the closure of the coal mines.

At that time in the 1950s there was a great demand for coal and the miners were reaping a harvest of high wages which was obvious from the large number of clubs and public houses throughout the area. The provision of financing the clubs was done through the Federation Breweries in Newcastle. The clubs, most of them furnished to a high standard, were tied to the brewery for their supplies. It was surprising to find clubs being adjacent to or near public houses. The real beer drinkers explained that the quality of the Federation beers was inferior to that sold in the public bars. They would spend a couple of hours in an evening in the public bars and then adjourn to the clubs which were well-appointed with concert rooms, dance halls, snooker rooms and the opportunity to participate in a variety of games, betting and gambling being popular activities. There was a greyhound track operated near the police station patronised by people from far and near and where frauds were perpetrated. Betting in all its forms is endemic in coal mining communities. However, it would be quite unfair not to mention that within this lively community there were people with strong religious beliefs actively involved with their various places of worship leading quite different lifestyles.

There was a strength of five sergeants, three of whom were in charge of detached sections, two detectives and a variable allocation of about 50 uniformed constables and two civilian clerks. There were no policewomen and when women were arrested there was a wait until a PW from Divisional Headquarters arrived, a situation which was unsatisfactory and embarrassing. I sent a memorandum to my Superintendent pointing out the problem and asking for two policewomen to be posted to the sub-division. I never did get a reply but the Chief Constable, who had a habit of dropping into police stations, arrived one day and I mentioned the problem to him. Within a fortnight two bright young probationer women arrived. There was plenty of work for them, and they were extremely useful in gathering evidence in the clubs under assumed identities. The two of them would go to the clubs accompanied with young constables appearing to be normal couples on a night out. It is surprising how police officers out of uniform look quite different and are not generally recognised. The strength comprised a good balance of experienced officers and probationers and when I got to know them and explained my intentions, they responded with enthusiasm, though naturally there were one or two who needed a push.

The most apparent problems arose from the way the clubs operated. There was no check on whether the people using the facilities were members, or non-members being signed in by members. The outcome was that when it became known there were large sums of money, frequently several thousand pounds, to be won from lotteries and other forms of gambling, there was an influx of coach loads from other towns. If the incomers won, there was disorder and fighting and the situation was equally bad if the locals got the big money. Before boarding their coaches to go home or on the way home, they would show their discontent by wanton damage to property. There was great competition among the clubs to provide the best prizes and entertainment and so the disorderly conduct rotated from club to club. We used undercover officers to gather sufficient evidence to apply for warrants to raid the premises selected. It could be a tricky task and there were instances elsewhere of police officers being identified and badly mauled. We were fortunate and all our officers did wonderful work without being identified.

In organising a raid it was important to have an up-to-date plan of the premises which could be obtained from the Local Authority for a small fee. Despite the raids, Federation Breweries continued to finance premises for new clubs and to refurbish existing buildings. On the opening of new premises there was usually a celebration party and on occasions I was invited and accepted. In the course of the speeches the District Manager for Federation Breweries made appropriate remarks, including the fact that it would save the police money. He handed me new plans of the premises which I accepted with good grace and which brought loud cheers from the assembled company.

In planning raids it was necessary to brief large numbers of police officers and detail them to carry out specific duties as some of the clubs had capacities for up to 2,000 people. Entrance with a raiding party had to be executed quickly and efficiently to enable control to be maintained, otherwise hell could break out. We also tried to arrive when people were seated being entertained as they were easier to control. Most of the officers would be in uniform but a few were in plain clothes and they were slipped in slightly ahead of the raiding party and took up position at the light switches, as otherwise there could be pandemonium in the darkness, with black eyes all round or even worse. I used to lead the uniformed party and quickly get on the stage, taking possession of the microphone and explaining that a police raid was in progress and asking for co-operation which was usually forthcoming. We always had a snatch squad at hand to remove any dissenters. On a particular occasion we entered a club and when I mounted the stage I was mistaken for a local comedian named Jimmy James who used to do a turn dressed as a policeman. There were cheers and applause which carried on for some time... and then groans when I finally managed to address them! The raid was, from a police point of view, a success.

There is a lot of paperwork in preparing raid charges for Court, but it depends upon your objective. I was under no illusions that club life could not be dispensed with and therefore there was no point in applying for the clubs to be struck off the register unless there was very good cause. These clubs were in some sort of affiliation and they retained a solicitor to defend them at Court. He would telephone me after a raid and make all sorts of hints that he was going to fight the cases but what he was really trying to get over was to find out if an application was to be made to strike the club off the register. Once we had reached an understanding that he would plead guilty, provided not too many serious charges were made, the preparation work was less time consuming. He always kept his word. The effect of the raids deterred coach loads from coming into the area and there was an improvement in the behaviour on the streets which was commented upon by members of the law-abiding community. The action cost the clubs a few hundred pounds in fines but they continued to thrive. There did not appear to be any animosity towards police and the Chairman of a club which had been raided sent me a bottle of whisky and Christmas Greetings. I thanked him by letter and returned the bottle.

In the meantime we had not been idle in attending to other matters. Coal miners are strong, fit people and when they get into fights severe injuries and broken bones are inflicted, occasionally resulting in death. At one time there were in the Annfield Plain Section nine people, five of whom had been sentenced to death for murder, reprieved and allowed out on parole after about nine or ten years. The other four had served sentences for manslaughter: all of them were regarded as 'ticket of leave' men and were required to report regularly at a named police station until such time as their sentences expired. Any deviation from normal behaviour could result in their return to prison.

Gambling, drinking and fighting still continued and where there were reports of serious injuries, we had the duty of trying to find the aggressors. Most of the injuries were sustained at weekends and wanted men would lie low until it was time to report for work. On Monday mornings it was common practice for a policeman to be on duty, probably at about 2.00 am when the miners started their shift, and to find the culprits with black eyes, broken jaws and even broken arms and legs being helped by their mates into the cages to go underground. Provided they could get underground for an hour or so, even in great pain, and fake an accident, they were eligible for compensation for injuries at work and it was more difficult to prove previously-committed offences. They could not have escaped detection without the help of their colleagues and quite a number were stopped at the cage entrances and were brought before the Courts charged with criminal offences.

Accidents causing injuries were dealt with promptly and efficiently by skilled first-aid teams at the scene so it was not often necessary for police to go underground. My first trip down a mine was to enable me to understand better the terminology used by the miners. The drop in a cage for several hundred feet until reaching the bottom was a sobering event and just as terrifying as the black-hole ride at Alton Towers many years later. Along the brick-built wall leading to the coal face there were, at prescribed distances, first-aid boxes containing ampoules of morphia for application to the injured; they were known as golden bricks. Now and again there were thefts of the ampoules, not for use to the injured, but for doping greyhounds.

The greyhound track was in regular use and well-attended. The management did their best to stamp out all forms of cheating but the sport attracted criminal elements endeavouring to make money by dishonest means. Greyhounds were entered with false identities; on at least one occasion a greyhound was entered for a race with patches painted on its body to resemble another dog. Drugs, including the stolen morphia, were administered with the intention of upsetting the betting forecasts and making money. Some of the punters were equally devious and brought along well-prepared betting slips ready for presentation if the colours appeared to coincide with the genuine articles. The cashiers were sharp-eyed and usually spotted a fake but at busy times thieves were occasionally paid out as the false slips went unnoticed until the end of the evening when final cashing up took place. Photographs of suspects were displayed in the police station and when identified they were kept under observation. Persons with known previous convictions, if spotted, were not allowed in the stadium.

House-breaking occurred at weekends when workmen's wages were likely to be found. The culprits were a mixture of old hands and teenagers. Those with criminal records had their individual modus operandi which was recognised and led to their arrests. The teenagers were usually local and a good percentage of them were caught. There were shop-breakings and house-breakings on premises containing valuable property which were frequently committed by dedicated criminals who travelled the districts. These were more difficult to trace and we had to form joint teams with personnel from adjacent divisions and other Forces to tackle the outbreaks.

Indecency and sex offences were the subject of regular complaints and absorbed a large proportion of police time, making investigations and also in preventative work. Sergeant Allison who was in charge of one of the toughest sections aptly described what was taking place, or what was likely to. He used to say that at the first trace of spring sunshine Indecent Exposures (his actual works were more expressive) would occur; by the month of May, Indecent Assaults would be the fashion and by mid-June the advice should be, 'Lock up your daughters'. We cleared up a good proportion of the offences but we failed to stop them from happening.

Occasionally an attack would result in a death, hence the number of people previously mentioned on parole. My thinking on the subject was that part of the problem was due to the living conditions in which a large number of families lived. There were streets of terraced houses with rooms, two-up-and-two-down and a scullery-cum-kitchen with toilets in the backyard, and here and there toilets had to be shared with the families of neighbouring houses. The living conditions were the same as we experienced at Tindale Crescent earlier in my service.

There were large families of both sexes born and brought up and still living there after leaving school until they married or left home to work elsewhere. The miners' houses were spotlessly clean, well cared for and great credit must be given to the wives and mothers for managing so well in these conditions. The lack of privacy and space must have had a bearing on the minds of young people and been a hardship for parents. Council houses were being built and there was an on-going programme but there was much to be done.

Fifty years ago, traffic was relatively light but there were many road accidents occurring for varied reasons. One cause was driving whilst unfit through drink or drugs. Dealing with these offences was time-consuming and the results could be disappointing. There were no legal or scientific guide-lines on the amount of alcohol permissible. The chain of events in dealing with suspects was on the following lines. Police would stop a driver because of the irregular or erratic manner in which a vehicle was being driven, or arising from a road accident. The driver would be questioned and if his answers were considered unsatisfactory he would be asked to get out of the vehicle. Abnormal or exaggerated conduct, his being unsteady on his feet, having slurred speech and a strong smell of alcohol were the facts which decided the officer on the road as to whether or not to arrest the suspect.

At the police station the arresting officer would in the presence and hearing of the prisoner relate the reasons for the arrest to a more senior officer. If he decided there was a charge to answer a Police Surgeon would attend and if the suspect failed the medical test he would be charged and bailed to appear at a Magistrates Court at some future date. The Magistrates found guilty a higher proportion of people so charged than those who elected to be tried before a Jury. In those days Juries were notorious for findings of not guilty even when the evidence was exceptionally strong. Those who could afford it employed barristers to fight their cases. The cost of engaging them was much greater than likely fines but retaining driving licences was the objective. I have spent days, along with other witnesses, including doctors, at Quarter Sessions, knowing the results would have little relevance to the weight of the evidence. There was a feeling among the motoring public that they were not really breaking the law. A common comment was, "There but for the Grace of God..."

On a lighter note, the two cinemas in the town were popular and up-to-date films were shown. The manager of the cinema directly opposite the police station called upon me one morning in a considerable state of panic. On opening his post that morning he learned that the Bill Haley film 'Rock around the Clock' was scheduled to be shown at his cinema in about three weeks' time. He was in a dreadful state and I sat down and drank tea with him until he calmed down. He was a nice, kind chap whom I knew quite well. He handed me the correspondence which directed that in view of the history of disturbances in cinemas elsewhere he should make suitable preparations to prevent the audience getting out of hand and causing damage to the furnishings and building; it was not an encouraging document and no help was offered.

The history for his concern was well-founded. In previous weeks there had been reports of audiences taking over cinemas and wrecking them, the music and the scenes having made them get up and imitate the new and unusual type of film. The dancing started in the aisles but developed into unmanageable behaviour, so that damage to the cinemas and injuries to patrons and staff ensued. The unruly conduct spread out on to the streets. The result was that cities and boroughs with legal powers and authority to ban the film being shown did so. Counties had no such powers and the cinema companies were showing the film in places outside the main centres of population, hence the intention to show it in Stanley and similar towns.

The Cinema Manager spent the whole morning with me and he telephoned his area manager, asking if consideration could be given to cancelling the booking; the answer was emphatically no. Between us we made plans: he agreed to doubling the price of the admission tickets, subject to approval from his manager, and that tickets had to be pre-booked. The keeping of good order was very much a joint operation because if disorder broke out inside, the troubles would spill out into the public domain.

My first thoughts were that the local strength of the police would be inadequate without re-enforcements from other areas. But a stubborn streak in me refused to accept the task could not be undertaken by local resources. My Superintendent had never been near the place to my knowledge and appeared to have little interest in the policing of the sub-division. I thought that if I had asked for his help I would have been rebuffed. I will elaborate on that matter later. There were a number of Special Constables whom we had kept up to scratch and who willingly turned up whenever assistance was required. Most of them were Ex-Service NCOs who had seen active service. They would be placed in the cinema at fixed points wearing uniform. Special Constables were unpaid volunteers so I proposed to the manager that on the occasion they were on duty they should each be given two complimentary tickets for their families. A meeting of Special Constables confirmed they were more than happy to assist.

The film, which would be shown twice nightly, lasted longer than the usual showings, making it difficult for patrons to get home at such late hours. The Bus Company manager co-operated when approached and published a temporary time table. The Press kept the public in the picture and were not unhelpful, but the publicity probably resulted in demand for bookings from people living a long way from the cinema. In the light of these demands and the fact the numbers could not be accommodated, it was agreed that the film be booked for a second week. In the event the film continued with a full house for a total of three weeks.

Naturally we were a little apprehensive until things got going. The first night or two, despite the publicity, people turned up wishing to pay at the door. With a few exceptions they accepted the situation and left peacefully. During that first week there were two occasions when attempts were made to start dancing in the aisles, one by a couple, the other by two young men. At the first sign of movement the Special Constables bundled them out on to the street. We knew if that sort of conduct were permitted, serious trouble would develop.

On the first Saturday night there was a gang of about 15-20 young men and women from Gateshead who arrived by public service transport without tickets and there was a hint from them that they would cause trouble, but eventually they dispersed after strong police advice. They returned later, the worse of drink, threatening what they would do. They said they would come back the following night, a Sunday, bringing large numbers of their friends with them. The temptation to lock them up for the night for Conduct Likely to Cause a Breach of The Peace was tempting. Our resources were fully stretched and locking them up would probably have led to physical violence with most of the police personnel being committed to deal with them.

I decided we would hustle them out of town to prevent further disorder. We mustered everyone available and told them that if they did not move away they would be locked up. There were mutterings and they dragged their feet a bit, and by their demeanour it seemed they were in the sort of rebellious drunken state for breaking windows and committing damage of that sort if unsupervised. We could not afford to take policemen away from the cinema which was still operating, so I was driven behind them in a police vehicle fitted with a public address system. The driver kept right on their heels, driving them down the hill on the way to Gateshead some eight or nine miles distant. I addressed them in Sergeant Major like terms of endearment with threats of their being locked up and eventually they broke into a trot. We kept at them in the same manner for about two miles by which time we had reached open country with fields on either side of the road. By then they were quiet and looked a sorry dishevelled bunch. There was no sign of them on the Sunday.

The three weeks showing of the Bill Haley film concluded without any real difficulties. I expect in modern times what I authorised would probably bring me to some sort of Court for Human Rights or some such organisation, very likely for Health and Safety offences. The result pleased the local population: they said so. No one received injuries and there were no convictions recorded against anyone. This was zero tolerance in action and it was successful!

In my early days at Stanley one Saturday night a coach carrying 21 men and a driver stopped outside a very well run public house situated in the main street. It was soon after closing time and the bar was unoccupied with the exception of the licensee and two male staff. All but two of the passengers and the driver entered the bar and demanded to be served. Upon being refused they set about wrecking the place. The police were notified and three of us attended. They were still trashing the place a few minutes after our arrival, chairs and tables being thrown about and bottles of spirits being smashed on the counter. The licensee and his two staff had sensibly kept out of the way but they were able to keep observation and saw everything that was happening. We went inside and closed the door to the street behind us, but it was still a little time before we could make our presence known. We established they were from Gateshead and we escorted them one by one to their coach and asked the driver to take us to the police station where we were met by two other policemen.

It took a bit of persuasion to get them to leave the coach and get them into the police station, with the exception of the driver and the two passengers who had stayed on the coach. It took us virtually the whole of the night to record their particulars, make notes of damaged clothing, scratches and bloodstains on some of them. We also verified their names and addresses with their local police. We took statements from the driver and the two passengers not involved: the three of them confirmed that all those who left and returned to the coach were the only people to have entered the licensed premises. The licensee and his two staff were adamant that each and every intruder had taken part in the damage, shouting and threatening and continuing to demand to be served. There was prima facie evidence for preferring charges under the Riot Damages Act and other offences. However, I did not wish to delay getting rid of them : the cell accommodation and other facilities would have been strained to deal with such numbers, in addition to which we were all ready for bed!

A file was prepared with the evidence and suggested charges, bearing in mind that charges of affray would necessitate briefing a solicitor to have them committed to a higher court. My final request was to ask for the appointment of a solicitor to discuss possible charges. The cost of the damage was considerable which was an important point to be borne in mind. At that stage the brewery manager was content to leave the matter to the police, subject to keeping the company in the picture. All these facts were on the file which was submitted to the Divisional Superintendent. After a time I received a terse note on the file pointing out that there was insufficient evidence to take proceedings as none of the persons involved had been identified and I was instructed to arrange an identification parade. I read and re-read the file and pondered how I could convince the Superintendent that a parade was out of the question. All the participants had been seen by the licensee and his staff committing the damage and their entrance and return to the police station left no doubt that they were the people from the coach.

Initially I wrote a report reiterating the strength of the evidence and pointing out that an identification parade would provide no more evidence, even if such action was required, and that their sober appearance would be quite different from when they were a disorderly gang. However, I had second thoughts. I had met the Superintendent only once and did not know him so I decided I would telephone him and put my point of view in the hope that he might have another look at the file. His reply was brief and I was ordered to comply with his original request. I tried to explain to him that such action was unnecessary and impossible in the circumstances and I was on the point of asking him to get another officer to undertake his orders but I was not given the opportunity to finish the conversation. He said I had disobeyed his instructions.

My next thoughts were that I could avail myself of an item in Standing Orders which allowed any policeman to submit a report to the Chief Constable's Office if they were not content with any matter by a superior officer. After further consideration I came to the conclusion that whatever the outcome of such a disagreement there would be no winners and there was the possibility of being branded a trouble maker. I had to find a way to deal with the situation without appearing to disobey a written and repeated verbal order from my Superintendent. I telephoned the area brewery manager and explained that before any further action it might be helpful for him and the brewery solicitor to review the case. The meeting was arranged there and then and the outcome was that the brewery staked a claim to take proceedings and make substantial claims for the damage caused. I asked if the case could be dealt with quickly, without explaining that I was on the hot seat. Within a short time an Occasional Court was arranged. The charges dealt with conduct causing damage and requesting that substantial damages be awarded to the brewery company. The majority pleaded guilty and all were found guilty. Heavy fines were imposed and orders made for substantial damages to be paid. The sting was in the tail, the magistrates stipulating a date by which the fines and damages had to be settled; failure to comply would result in six months' imprisonment. It was, in my mind, a satisfactory conclusion to a delicate situation. In normal circumstances I would have sent the Superintendent a closing report outlining the penalties and any other relevant information, but not on this occasion as I thought that the least said the soonest mended. I heard no more on the subject.

It was unusual being posted to a new station not to be seen by a senior officer, but even more unusual to have only seen my Superintendent on three or four occasions during two years under his command; the meetings I refer to were not specifically between the two of us, they happened in the company of others. Initially, I was disappointed and could not understand why I was being ignored as we had not previously met and therefore did not know each other.

As time went on I was surprised at some of the memoranda sent me. For example, I applied for a mileage allowance to use my private car for duty purposes to which the post entitled me. The approval note from the Superintendent laid down a number of conditions: one to be strictly adhered to was that I must not use my private car when the sub-divisional vehicle was available. The order did not stop there; it demanded that each month when submitting my claim, the police vehicle log book should be included so that the claims could be verified. The order was compiled with subject to operational requirements which I submitted with explanations but that did not satisfy him. He asked for the log books for the sub-divisional vehicle and my car to be submitted to divisional headquarters at the end of each month and they were retained there for a period of three weeks or more. On enquiring of the reason, I learned that they were in the Superintendent's office whilst he personally compared times and dates of entries, which surprised me as there was a competent civilian finance section quite capable of carrying out the work. It was tedious and time-wasting to have to keep duplicate records and transfer the information into the two log books each month. I submitted a memorandum pointing out that if the time-wasting procedure was to be continued could duplicate log books be issued. There was no written reply to my request but a message was passed by the civilian staff that the practice of the two log books being submitted together was no longer necessary. Apparently the Superintendent had spent much of his service at Headquarters and had the reputation of reducing personal claims by a penny or two.

A few months after taking up my appointment at Stanley, I had to have a surgical operation to repair part of my body, arising from the activities of military service. I was admitted to the local Miners' Hospital at South Moor, a small efficient establishment with a modern operating theatre. It had been provided by the owners of the coal mines and run in conjunction with members of the Miners' Union. The welcome, attention and treatment I received was excellent.

Following an operation I was unable to eat or drink by mouth for a period of ten days: it was an uncomfortable time. However, it was a learning period: the other patients in the ward were all miners. The custom in the mines is for each man to have a 'Marra', that is someone he can rely upon and be given help when necessary. As soon as I arrived the miner in the adjacent bed asked me if he could be my marra, an offer which I gratefully accepted. I was quite incapable of doing anything for myself let alone return the compliment to my new friend. The Miners' Union supplied each patient with a bottle of Newcastle Brown Ale each evening which was consumed there and then by those fit to drink; I believe I was the exception. After my first night in hospital, my Marra expressed his concern that I was unable to drink and said he was going to do something about it. During the course of the day he had been in touch with the local shop steward who arrived that evening with a bottle of brandy for me. I explained that I could not take liquid but it transpired that Matron had been consulted and gave approval provided the brandy was served to me by the night nurse on a teaspoon more or less to moisten my lips. The drop of brandy was duly administered and enjoyed and with a little coaxing and a sharing with the night nurse! I believe my ration was in excess of that approved by the Matron! They were really good-hearted, jolly people to have as companions.

Mr Lee, Assistant Chief Constable, visited hospital and spent some time with me as well as calling upon Lucy to ensure she and the children were managing. They were being very well looked after by the members of my staff and they ensured she could get to the hospital during visiting hours. I assumed the Superintendent had arranged to cover the sub-division during my absence but he and his second in command, a Chief Inspector, just made cursory visits to the station, signed the Occurrence and other books in daily use but gave no indication of wishing to be further involved. I had capable and reliable staff and when a sergeant had a problem they came to hospital and we sorted matters out between us. On discharge from hospital I spent two weeks at the Police Convalescent Home in Harrogate. Lucy and the children were entitled to be conveyed to see me each week which was arranged by Police Headquarters. During the five weeks I was on the sick leave, the Superintendent did not pay me or my family a visit. I was disgusted but said nothing. By this time it was what I had come to expect, as when I was promoted Chief Inspector some months earlier there had been no comment from him.

I had recovered from my spell in hospital when I came across a young constable getting a rough time from three young men in one of those deep shop doorways: he had found them trying to break into the shop and was endeavouring to keep them from breaking free. It was a dark cold night and although he was shouting for help there was no one about until I arrived by chance. We grappled with the three men and in trying to overpower them my right hand became crushed, causing a fracture to my right thumb. My right hand and forearm were in plaster for several weeks and I had to do most things with my left hand; fortunately I had as a child used my left hand to write until prohibited by a teacher. I could have gone off duty but it was winter-time, the children were at school and I would have been bored doing nothing. I submitted details of my injury for the record and continued working. The Superintendent disregarded the incident and never paid the station or me a visit. He must have been reminded of what had occurred because my signature was completely different. On cold days I still get nagging pains as a result of the injuries.

The Chief Constable, the Deputy and the Assistant made occasional drop-in visits, which was their custom: they would talk over current matters and provide opportunities to explain problems. I could have mentioned that I was unhappy to serve under a Superintendent whom I did not know and was unapproachable but I did not do so. On a more formal occasion the Chief Constable gave notice of his forthcoming visit with a request that as many as possible of the staff be made available as he wished to talk to them individually. It was a welcome exercise and at the end of a full day he asked me if there was any matter I wished to discuss. I drew his attention to the fact that although there were a good many people who caused police problems living within the sub-division there were also a high proportion of non-resident trouble makers who came from Gateshead and South of the Tyne, including the adjoining Whickham Police Division, adding that there was a greater affinity between that area than Consett which was the Divisional Headquarters. We looked at the map together and he went on his way. Within a short period of time a reorganisation programme was published showing that my sub-division was transferred complete with personnel to serve under Superintendent James Gibson, Whickham Division. He telephoned me on the day the details were published, welcomed me, visited me at my office and met Lucy. Life was so different and I enjoyed serving under his command. There was no goodbye from the Superintendent!

Within a few months of the boundary changes, Mr Alec Muir, Chief Constable, asked me to consider applying to be a Director of Studies at the Police College, which was at that time based in temporary quarters at Ryton on Dunsmore, Warwickshire. On his recommendation I would be required to attend a three-week course with other candidates and if found suitable would be put on a waiting list to be called as required. Up to this time Directing Staff had been appointed solely on the recommendation of their Chief Constable. I said I was quite happy in the post at West Stanley. He then told me that my Superintendent had asked for me to move to Divisional Headquarters to be his Deputy and he approved, subject to my acceptance of the offer. Alec Muir was the sort of chap one could talk to and I was really playing for time to think and said that I did not consider I would make a good deputy; he agreed with me and the outcome was that I volunteered for the Directing Staff Course.

Upon completion of the course I was listed eligible for a post and informed that it would probably be about a year before I was required. I accepted the post of Deputy to the Superintendent at Whickham which included being in charge of Blaydon Sub-Division. We moved to a new senior officer's house in the police complex at Whickham which of course delighted Lucy. She was more than happy to say goodbye to 'Hatters Castle'! There were other families with children around us and we were very happy.

In many ways I was sad to leave the Stanley Sub-Division and especially the staff who had given me unstinting support. We had become a family: we knew the wives and children and had enjoyed the social activities. Each section held whist drives and dances which were well supported by the community.

We had been at Whickham for only four months when I was offered a secondment to the Police College. It was a difficult decision to make. I had undergone the course on the understanding that I would accept the post when called upon. I have always found it difficult to go back on my word but I had requested that I would require married quarters at the college as I had no intention of leaving Lucy and the children behind. The initial offer was to go as a single person as there were not quarters for a family. On my declining the original conditions, there was an immediate response that married quarters were available! We moved to Ryton on Dunsmore in Warwickshire in March, 1958 and I became Superintendent Grade 1.

College Life

The Police College was formed in 1948 and was housed in temporary buildings which had been built to accommodate workers for the City of Coventry which had been severely damaged by bombing. It was later used to house refugees from Europe. The single-storey buildings were linked and included an administrative block, a limited number of units for staff and married families, with single rooms for the students. We lived in basic accommodation comprising three bedrooms, a living room, bathroom, kitchen and storeroom. On the plus side we got central heating free which was necessary in a single-brick building. Other families lived in similar quarters. There was space to roam for the children on the campus and there was free transport to and from the schools at Leamington Spa. Our son went to Blakedown High School and within a year was Head Boy. Margaret did equally well at the Girls' School. Social life in the camp was good. There was shopping transport which Lucy used occasionally although she preferred to cycle.

Initially, I was responsible for a syndicate with a Chief Inspector as my Deputy; later on I was appointed Deputy to the Department. There were two courses running at the College at this time, one for senior officers of the rank of Superintendent which was small in numbers and of three months' duration. The course of six months in which I was involved was for sergeants qualified for promotion to Inspector and newly-promoted Inspectors assessed with the potential to gain higher rank. The content included lectures with visiting speakers from a variety of educational and business establishments. Tutorials, discussions and projects involving students with operational-type exercises formed a part of the Course. Students also prepared and gave lectures and produced a thesis, which was submitted and subsequently delivered in a lecture to the individual's syndicate. A high proportion of the students were ex-servicemen who were keen to do well and catch up on lost years. Each syndicate spent two weeks covering a wide variety of subjects under the two Liberal Studies staff. The Home Office people, with little knowledge of policemen or policing, advocated greater emphasis on liberal studies as the years went on and got their way which is probably a subject still debated by policemen.

My brief on appointment was to deal with the responsibilities and duties of middle management and to involve students in decision-making exercises in administrative and operational matters. I believe the best benefits derived by the students from the course were increased confidence and a greater awareness of policing at large. Between five and ten percent of the students were from Commonwealth countries. Colour was not a problem but care had to be taken in arranging the composition of syndicates and the seating arrangements in the dining hall. Religious and tribal differences and other customs and beliefs could get in the way of acknowledging and communicating with each other.

Bramshill House, a large Jacobean mansion standing in several hundred acres of parkland near Hartley Wintney in Hampshire, had been acquired to be the permanent home of the Police College. Initially limited use was made of the house whilst lecture rooms, bedroom, a dining hall and other essential buildings were added. Major General (Dick) Jelf, the Commandant, in appointing me second-in-command of the department, asked me to make preparations for the move of the college from Ryton on Dunsmore to Bramshill. The new outdoor exercises were based on the geography of the area which created quite a lot of work. His service background and previous military rank were beneficial in maintaining the progress of the development. When schedules were slipping, he took a firm stance and endeavoured to keep previously-agreed programmes on target.

Establishments such as the college came directly under Home Office for administration and finance for which there was a Secretary and Finance Officer with supporting staff. The secretary could be vulnerable because in effect he was in the unenviable situation of serving two masters. Normally things went smoothly but when additional items were required there were demands from the Home

Office to cut expenditure usually in financial percentage terms. In my work in preparing for the move to Bramshill I worked closely with the Secretary and Finance Officer and with them got along very well. However, there were occasions of incidents of wires being crossed, causing unnecessary problems, two of which I now relate.

At the conclusion of the courses at Ryton on Dunsmore there was a gap of two or three weeks before the courses resumed at Bramshill. The Commandant went on leave for three weeks and the Secretary for two weeks. I was charged with supervising the final stages of the move to Bramshill. To my surprise I came across the two handymen/gardeners, refugees from Europe, known as July and August, loading the old worn-out chairs and desks on to a lorry for delivery to Bramshill. Much of the furniture was riddled with woodworm and a previous firm decision had been agreed that it should be destroyed. The handymen also knew of the decision and said they were surprised with the order from the Secretary immediately before he went on leave. By this time new furniture and fittings to match were being installed at Bramshill by the contractors. The handymen were confused: they were two lovely fellows but they were not too familiar with the English language and accepted they might have got their orders wrong. We stacked the condemned furniture in a pile and the College families had a bonfire with hot dogs.

The Secretary gave my friends July and August a rough time when he returned. I tried to explain that I accepted responsibility but he refused to discuss the matter. On the return of the Commandant I learned that an enquiry had been requested into my conduct. The Commandant sorted things out and gave me a pat on the back for the work covering the move. Apparently at the eleventh hour the Secretary had been pressurised into making savings relating to the move and there were few options, so he decided the condemned furniture should be retained.

Home Office and Treasury Departments could be quite demanding and another example of the sorts of things they did related to the approach road to the garages. The approved plan was to build a row of garages with the doors facing each other with a common road between them. It was not until the garages were built and a common road laid that, in order to save money, it transpired that the garages had been moved closer to each other, narrowing the approach road, the result being that only small and medium-sized cars could be manoeuvred in and out of the garages with difficulty! Any query as to how those sorts of blunders arose just seemed to peter out.

At this time there was a large number of Police Forces in the United Kingdom, some quite small. City and Borough Forces were very much under the control of Watch Committees whose decisions, including promotions, had a tendency to political influences. There were regular vacancies for senior officers as people retired and/or moved on to higher ranks. It was not long before I learned on joining the College staff that there was a sort of restless infection and ambition among them to apply for mostly anything and everything advertised. There was much banter and secrecy on the subject. I had no intention of making any applications. Our children had had more schools than most and I believed I had a loyalty to the College to stay sufficiently long to justify being so selected. My secondment was for two years but in the event I served there for over two-and-a-half years at the request of the Commandant.

Towards the end of my two years, Alec Muir, my Chief Constable, telephoned me and drew to my attention a vacancy for the post of Deputy Chief Constable, Salford, in the rank of Chief Superintendent. He explained that Mr Gray, the Chief Constable, intended retiring in about 15 months and he and the committee hoped, provided the new Deputy Chief Constable fitted the bill, there was an excellent opportunity for him to move up to Chief Constable. I was grateful to my Chief Constable looking after my interest. I applied and was short-listed with five other candidates.

I arrived there on a cold, wet, foggy night in February and was put up in what must have been the worst bed and breakfast accommodation in Salford. The wallpaper was hanging off the wall in places owing to dampness. I wandered out and found the Town Hall where I was due for interview at 10 o'clock the following morning. There was a railway shunting yard virtually overhead which continued in use most of the night. I had already decided Salford held no attractions for me.

The next morning it was still damp and foggy and as I approached the Town Hall, a tall, well-dressed gentleman collapsed on the pavement in front of me. I sat him up and realised he was exceptionally thin, so much so that I picked him up and carried him into the Town Hall. After I had sat him down on a form he seemed incapable of replying to my questions. A young cherub face appeared at a small hatch in reply to my ringing the bell. I suggested an ambulance or doctor be sent for. The cherub looked down at the sick man and promptly disappeared whilst I was still trying to explain what occurred. An older face appeared at the hatch, had a glance at the man and immediately he, the cherub and another man rushed around, picked the man up and disappeared without a word to me. I sat down on a form and waited for some time before I again rang the bell. I was assured that the man was being looked after and the hatch was quickly shut without further comment. Again, I rang the bell and when a mature male appeared I put my hand on the hatch long enough for me to explain that I was there by appointment as a candidate for the post of Deputy Chief Constable! I was aware of considerable consternation in the conduct of the people I had so far seen but I had no idea of the reason. I was early for the appointment but in a short time there were five of us in the waiting room. I knew them; they were or had been on the College Staff. The interviews took place in alphabetical order and after the fourth man, there was a long interval. Those present who had done their homework concluded that the person being interviewed was the local man with the rank of Superintendent.

Eventually I appeared before about nine or ten members of the Watch Committee and had an excellent interview, probably all the better for my being in the mood that I could not care less. The Chairman and Chief Constable informed us that the local man had been appointed and thanked us for attending. They then asked me to join them in a side room. They were both very frank and explained they were disappointed with the appointment, the Chairman adding that politics beat him by one vote. He then went on to explain that the person appointed was in very poor health and that neither he nor the Chief Constable thought he was medically fit for the post. They then asked me if I would consider being put on reserve and in the event of the new Deputy being unable to continue the post it would be offered to me without further interview. I thanked them and agreed to bear the offer in mind. As Mr Gray showed me out, we met the successful candidate and we were introduced. I recognised him immediately as the gentleman I had rescued from the pavement! He did not recognise me.

I wrote to my Chief Constable explaining the situation and thanked him for his interest in my career. In less than three months, I was offered the post at Salford as the new man had retired due to ill health. I declined the offer on the grounds it was not the right time for me and thanked the Chairman for his kind and genuine offer. The brief look I had of Salford put me off taking Lucy and the family to live there; perhaps my comments are unfair to Salford but first impressions lingered. Another important reason was that I had a feeling I would be circumscribed by political practices. The Salford experience was good for me in that I was pleased I had not joined the rat race and the lesson learned was that I would be selective should other opportunities come my way. I had in just under ten years risen from the rank of Constable to Superintendent with the support of my Chief Constable and other supervising officers and had been provided with a broad experience of the police service, with which I was content.

Returning to Durham County

It was a busy time for the family. Our son had made a firm decision to apply for a place at Welbeck College, the Army Public School, which provided a sixth form education, the emphasis being on mathematics and physics with a broad general syllabus. After two years, provided their progress was up to standard, the students were expected to join the Army and become the backbone of the technical services. To be offered a place there he had to undergo a series of written work and verbal interviews and eventually spent several days at an Army Selection Board covering physical exercises, interviews and dining with Generals and other senior officers which he thoroughly enjoyed. The workshops at Welbeck were equipped with a wide variety of up-to-date engineering equipment which he made good use of. At the end of his two years he won the Workshop Prize for building a boat which remained in use for many years. He also achieved good academic results and went from there to Sandhurst for two years. We proudly attended his Passing-out Parade on his being commissioned. His interests and natural ability for every aspect of engineering have remained with him throughout his life.

Our other concern was to find a school for Margaret as we did not know where we were to be housed in Durham County. Eventually we were allocated a standard police house right on the busy A1 road on the outskirts of Durham City. We arrived in the first few days of January and because of the continuous noise of the traffic found it difficult to sleep. Within a couple of weeks of our getting settled there was a severe snow storm: the road was impassable for nearly two weeks and the silence kept us awake! Margaret soon settled into the Girls' Grammar School and made new friends. She was a great mimic and within days was reeling off the Durham City accents which were new to her.

The Chief Constable welcomed me back to the Force but informed me there were a few obstacles to be overcome before he could give me a posting and in the meantime I should kick my heels. I expressed a preference for an operational post but was given no hint as to what he had in mind. I suppose I should have been grateful for the time to myself but uncertainty is a bit wearing. Lucy and I enjoyed the free time together until towards the end of January when I was called to Headquarters. The Chief Constable offered me the post of Chief Clerk in charge of the Force administration. The post carried the rank of Chief Superintendent but there were no vacancies in the rank because of sideway moves. I remarked that this was not the first occasion I had been in a similar situation. He was apologetic but made it quite clear that he wanted me to accept the posting. I saw the Deputy Chief Constable about a take-over date. He gave me a kindly pep talk and said I was being given a wonderful opportunity which with my previous varied experience would fit me for any position in the Police Service. He added that I had been chosen because the Chief Constable did not enjoy Yes men around him. The remark gave me food for thought!

The post had historically and traditionally been filled by officers who had spent much of their service in administrative posts in Headquarters. Mr Muir did not follow any firm pattern but had previously appointed officers whose experience and rank had been achieved mainly on operational work. I fitted the latter category and although I had as an Inspector spent a few months at Headquarters I was regarded as a hard-headed operational policeman which was quite appropriate. I had when on operational work probably been a thorn in the side of some of the traditionalists by suggesting changes which I considered beneficial to police work. Now and again a suggestion was adopted but I knew that it was really a game of chance as to who and which department got their hands on my suggestions, which could be easily filed away and intentionally forgotten. On my taking over the post, my many friends in the Force wished me Good Luck but I was well aware that some regarded me as a square peg in a round hole. The responsibilities of the job and the volume of work kept me far too busy to concern myself with trivial matters.

Durham was in those days one of the larger County Forces and the extent of my work touched upon every aspect of constabulary business. An important role was in preparing and assembling reports for the Chief Constable for consideration by the sub-committees and finally the main Police Authority meetings which took place every quarter. The Authority was made up of elected councillors and nominated magistrates, their duty being to provide the necessary finance to ensure the provision of personnel and equipment to maintain an efficient Force. The responsibility of Chief Constables is for operational matters. Sometimes the division of responsibilities is misunderstood by members of the public at large and also by elected representatives. The Clerk of the Peace, a lawyer for the County Council and the County Treasurer attended the Authority meetings. We had regular contact with the council staff and an excellent relationship existed.

The Treasurer had the unenviable task of finding the money to meet the approved budgets. The Police Authority members took great pride in the Force and the police usually received what was requested. Revenue from the coal mines, heavy Industry, and ICI at Billingham brought in substantial sums of money from the rates and increases made little impact on the domestic rates. On preparing estimates I soon realised the significance of the benefits and could include marginal increases without breaking the bank. This aspect of work was new to me but I had excellent support staff and was much enlightened by attending Police Authority meetings with the Chief Constable. I sat by his elbow passing papers and notes and did not expect or wish to have to say anything; but after I had been with him for some time and there was an item which he had asked me to prepare but probably had not familiarised himself with the details, he would when a question was asked turn to me and say that he had an expert at hand who would be happy to answer any questions.

Mr Muir lived in a large rambling house owned by the Police Authority on the outskirts of Durham City: it was known as West House and had an extensive garden. He was in great demand in the north-east as an after dinner speaker. Included in his humorous talks were items which were controversial and hit the headlines; questions arose and courses of action had to be taken afterwards. I had copies of the local daily newspapers delivered early in the morning and if I thought anything he had said the night before appeared to be of a controversial nature, I did not leave for work to travel to Headquarters at Aycliffe so early in the morning. Invariably my decisions were correct and I would answer the telephone with a brief message to call at West House. On arrival I found him dressed in pyjamas, dressing gown, open sandals and bare feet, summer or winter. We would walk up and down the lawn discussing what needed to be done in the course of the day to clarify and explain questions.

There was one occasion I shall never forget. Mr Muir had been invited as a guest speaker by members of a North-East Trade Organisation to a dinner at Newcastle. The theme of the evening was to improve interest in mounting a Trade Exhibition in Norway with a view to better trading with the north-east of England. The morning after, newspaper headlines varied, but all of them indicated Mr Muir had stolen the show; there were also questions as to his authority for promises made and the question of costs. According to the Press he had given an undertaking that the seven Police Forces comprising the North-East Region would provide policemen in uniform with transport to police the two centres scheduled to accommodate the exhibition, one at Oslo, the other at Bergen. There would also be a British-manned police station at each centre. When I read the news I knew he had made these promises on the spur of the moment after a good dinner in congenial company! If there had been any previous schemes, I would have been involved in the planning and finance. I could foresee all sorts of queries and possibly objections from Police Authorities and Watch Committees.

The call came, "Call at West House" whilst I was still digesting the news. We spent a long time walking up and down the lawn, he in the dress and conditions previously described. We talked to each other on equal terms, the conclusions being decisive. Finally he said he was sure I would come up with some answers by the end of the day. He let me know he would not be in the office and that he would be unavailable on the telephone. On my arrival at Headquarters, the Deputy and the Assistant Chief Constables were waiting for me. I confirmed that the gist of what the papers said had occurred and I had been given the task of trying to sort things out. It was explained that Major Vaux,

Chairman of Vaux Breweries in Sunderland and Chairman of the Police Authority had been asking on the telephone to speak to the Chief Constable, as well as many other callers. The Deputy and the Assistant both informed me they would be visiting territorial divisions in the course of the day and were not to be disturbed. My brain was reeling.

Someone was kind enough to give me a cup of tea in my office where I spent a few minutes by myself. I assembled a team of about 20 personnel from the various departments in Headquarters and asked them to provide some information on the feasibility of acquiring transport, equipment, accommodation and any other items they could think of, including the means of getting it to Norway. There were seven Forces in the north-east region and every quarter the Chief Clerks met, exchanged information and discussed mutual problems. We knew each other very well so I decided the best approach was to speak to them personally and put them as fully in the picture as possible and for them to pass on the information to their respective Chief Constables, hopefully involving their Chairman.

The first helpful call back came from Mr Jackson, Chief Constable in Newcastle. He was a bachelor, kept a good wine cellar and he and Alec Muir were good friends. He asked me to accept his support subject to the agreement of his Watch Committee. I had met Mr Jackson and I asked him if he would consider having a word with his colleagues in the region and later that day I had a call of support from Northumberland Police on the same terms. I also had a few calls from my fellow Chief Clerks, some of an uncomplimentary nature which their Chief Constables had expressed. From time to time I met members of the team and was impressed by their hard work and ingenuity which was showing progress. Then, surprisingly, I had a call from the Head of an industrial organisation. He said he was delighted and thought the police involvement was a good idea. Two other similar calls followed. In talking to them I hinted that the Press might be interested in their views and by late afternoon the evening papers contained a few references which were less critical than the morning issues.

Things were looking brighter: we had offers of more vehicles and equipment than required and at no cost. Included was an offer from the Durham Carpet Company to cover the floors of the two exhibition centres with their top-quality carpets. A shipping company offered to take whatever we required to and from Norway, free of charge. The last outstanding item was accommodation for the officers engaged in policing the exhibition. The members of the Norwegian Police made a most generous offer to take the policemen into their homes as guests. The net result was that any costs incurred would be negligible. Therefore, apart from finalising details, the outline plans were complete. My team had drifted off home and I was putting the final touches to my notes for the Chief Constable when he walked in. I briefed him over a drink in his office and went home, by which time it was after eight o'clock. It had been a hard but satisfactory day, drinking gallons of tea and the occasional bite out of a sandwich – not to be recommended. There were other occasions when the morning papers alerted me to mark time and await a call from the West House but they were insignificant compared to the Norwegian outing!

The Durham Miners' Gala in its heyday was an impressive sight with the influx of thousands of miners from throughout the county and neighbouring coal-mining areas. They were led by brass bands, flags and banners with the families of the individual mining communities marching behind. It was a political occasion which had become the miners' fun day and was held annually in July when the weather was usually fine. Vehicular traffic was excluded from the city from the very early hours of the morning until late in the day. The shopkeepers and those with premises facing the streets turned out the protective equipment which they kept stored from year to year and bolted it to their premises. The public houses were open throughout the day so there were occasional problems from over-indulgence of alcohol but considering the number of people and the crowding together in the streets the general conduct was good. Political and religious speakers were everywhere and when controversial statements were made they could find their platforms and tenting overturned.

The leading politicians, the President of the National Miners' Union and the Bishop of Durham made their speeches from the balcony of the County Hotel which was encompassed with metal railings facing a busy part of the city. When a Labour Government was in power, the Prime Minister and other senior members of Parliament would spend quite a lot of time talking from the balcony, trying to answer questions, a policy which was not very successful because of the noisy crowds processing to and fro. Apparently, but not in my time, the then Bishop of Durham upset people with his speeches and on running for his life jumped in the river from which he was rescued by police!

In the meantime the public houses were bulging with people. Families and children would be enjoying themselves on the adjacent race course with the many amusements and stalls which were everywhere. There were cheap jacks and con-men using every trick known to man to part the people from their money. Police were brought in from every part of the county to police the event with a good measure of humour and tolerance.

I had spent one day on duty when a uniformed constable and on a second occasion as a uniformed Inspector in charge of a sector in the city centre. We used the technique of asking the miners and their families to take people the worse of drink into their care. The response was usually highly successful and a good means of maintaining law and order in these particular conditions. The people were generally friendly to police and we endeavoured to make their day a happy memory. The Chief Constable was always about on these occasions and to the surprise of most police officers and members of the public alike he appeared in uniform in the street when the bands and supporters were beginning to march off in the afternoon. It was a warm sunny day. He was in shirt sleeves with his uniform cap when he took his place behind a band and marched the length of the street. He was given generous space which made him outstanding on his own. He was cheered and cheered all the way and although there were critics of his action the event was long discussed and admired by many.

In my post as Chief Clerk it fell to me to arrange the catering for the large number of police required to police the Gala. Most officers performed at least twelve hours' duty on the day. They were brought from all over the county, some leaving home very early in the morning and others not arriving back home until late evening. My memory cannot now recall the numbers involved in policing the event but it would be about 2,000. Provision had to be made for each officer to be provided with two well-cooked substantial meals during the course of the day. Each officer, under his Supervising Officer, was issued with tickets to eat at pre-arranged times and it was essential for the smooth running of the operation that timing was adhered to.

We rented the Market Hall in the city centre where most of the meals were supplied, and the Masonic Hall, with a lesser capacity, catered for people operating slightly off the city centre. Both places had adequate and up-to-date facilities available for cooking and seating. Private caterers tendered for the provision and service of meals: we accepted what we considered was the best food, not necessarily the cheapest. Full breakfasts were supplied up to about 11.00 am, then lunches until mid-afternoon and evening meals were served until about 8.00 pm. There were two choices. At lunch time the demand was for roast beef, fresh vegetables, roast potatoes and Yorkshire pudding; the other choice which now escapes me was not in demand. The evening meal was also substantial with a choice. There was always a sweet and plenty of tea. The Durham Miners' Union made provision with Newcastle Breweries for each officer attending lunch and supper to have a pint bottle of Newcastle Brown Ale as a gift. There were soft drinks available for the rare number of abstainers. Each batch was allowed a total of 40 minutes sitting at trestle tables and was served individually. We closed down the dining facilities about 10.00 pm.

My team had done a great job with much praise from the people we were looking after. Some of them had a long way to go to get home. I had in the meantime moved to a senior officer's house with a clear view overlooking the Cathedral. I walked home up a hilly winding path. I was tired but satisfied that things had gone well. The following year was more or less a repeat performance but with less tension.

Routine work kept the department busy but it was rare to have what might be termed a routine day. Each week a General Order was published and distributed throughout the Force for action and record purposes. It contained the particulars of personnel joining the Force, promotions, transfers, sickness, retirements, pensions and any other matters relating to individual entitlements, courses, new legislation and the details of firms wishing to employ pensioners. A requirement was for me to sign the pay sheets for members of the Force.

Every three months there was a recruiting day which was held at Headquarters, the candidates being interviewed by a board of Chief Officers. Those surviving the interviews were examined by Mr Ritson, Police Surgeon, who also examined those with long illnesses and gave advice where appropriate. He was for a long time Chairman of Sunderland Football Club and when Sunderland was playing at Newcastle he would walk all the way to Newcastle and back when he was still getting on in years. He was a man who took special interest in the health of the members of the Force.

The Clothing Contract came around each year and the firm securing the work went to the main police stations by arrangement where officers were measured. When the uniforms were ready, there were fitting-on parades by the suppliers. A varied range of uniforms were maintained in the clothing stores for fitting out recruits, and when people got too fat (or too thin!), the alteration was done by three fully-qualified civilian tailors working full-time, it being considered important that the personnel looked smart in uniform.

Almost daily there were demands from the territorial divisions to post officers to fill gaps brought about by promotion and resignations. There were always emergencies creating demands for special equipment, clothing and catering arrangements to be dealt with at short notice.

Much to my surprise I learned within a day or two of taking post that I was responsible for the administration of the Mounted Branch, as well as the Dog Section and the Dog Breeding Centre. One section of the Mounted Branch was stabled at Stockton and another section at Harpley Hall near Bishop Auckland, which was the Force residential training establishment. The police dogs were housed and trained there and became based on divisions when ready for operational work. The dog-breeding kennels were also at Harpley. The cost of feeding horses and dogs with their special needs and paying veterinary fees was quite costly. The horses carried out standard patrol duty but their real purpose was in controlling unruly people during demonstrations and strikes when they really earned their keep. The use of dogs for police work was still in its infancy in this country but they and the handlers learned a lot from experience and much useful work was done even in those early days. There were quite capable people in charge of these specialist duties but there were aspects of provisions for the animals and their deployment which were discussed with me. In fact I quite enjoyed a half day at one or other of units now and again which refreshed me for the office work; I used to feel I had escaped and was free for a few hours.

After a few months in post I decided to set up a typing pool as I found that the volume of work was not equally shared. Each little section had a typist, for which there was no justification, although they might well have done other work. Other units were fully employed and when pressures of work arose there was a backlog. The Chief Constable smilingly approved the idea and wished me luck in winkling out possible resisters. The civilian employees belonged to unions and although they took a bit of convincing, final agreement was reached. On the appointed day for the commencement of the project I was unable to be at the office. When I returned it appeared there had been objections mainly from departmental heads of sections who had lost their typists... and in some cases their tea-makers! It took a little time for the unit to settle down but the nett result was that the work was better shared, and the quality of letters and correspondence improved under the supervision of a well-qualified bright young lady in charge of the pool. In course of time I gradually reduced the number of staff which went nearly unnoticed owing to the high turnover of young ladies and I believe they were happier in a group as some had previously been tucked away in small offices.

The original home of Durham County Police was Durham City, but the premises were old and inadequate and after the war the Headquarters were established at Newton Aycliffe, on a temporary basis until such times as a new building could be erected at Durham. Because of the regular clamp-down on spending by successive governments, the final move back to Durham did not take place until the sixties. Whilst the Headquarters was at Durham most of the staff lived in and around the city and met socially at the Police Club. They knew each other and initially transport was provided to take them to and from the temporary Headquarters. As time went on and new staff were engaged, they came from different areas nearer Newton Aycliffe which was the first new town to be built in the county after the war and was still expanding.

On getting to know the staff I realised that there were no arrangements for their meeting socially. There was a club at Headquarters operated under a Certificate of Exemption by the Home Secretary, for which I was responsible. There was a billiard room used by a few at lunch times but the bar was only open on special occasions. As my first winter in post approached, I floated the idea of having a weekly club evening with wives, husbands, staff and their friends. The response was good, and the attendance developed. Whist, dominoes, darts and other games were played; birthdays and other events were celebrated and enjoyed. A family atmosphere was readily apparent at work simply because people got to know each other better. Lucy and I regularly attended and the Chief was known to pop in for a pint now and again.

Mr Muir was a great innovator and would pass out lists of brief notes for my attention. He had a profound memory and now and again he would ask how an idea was progressing, frequently asking if I considered it was another daft idea by the Chief Constable which would finish up in the waste-paper basket. Invariably, I waited for his approach rather than submitting prepared work direct to his desk, as discussion was more productive by going over the work together. The first thing I did was to run through the items, explaining my reasoning for non-action. He rarely disagreed with my judgement, but he did enjoy the banter during our discussions. Having got the non-event material out of the way, I would produce papers which we would go through together and he decided what further action to take if any. By this means, adjustments, new methods and experiments were tried out, many of them becoming permanent features.

One item which he listed was the possibility of the use of helicopters. I produced a paper with an order of costs which he took for discussion to an ACPO District Conference with a view to establishing a service in the region, the costs to be shared between the seven Forces. This was the early sixties and apparently not one of the six Chief Constables showed the slightest interest. He was disappointed but he had no intention of giving up. I was asked to prepare a paper for the Police Authority, explaining that the 'eye in the sky' would give another dimension to police work in conjunction with patrol cars in pursuing and searching for criminals and assisting in other ways. A costing was included and there was a hint there would probably be a saving in the event of operations being concluded in less time. The costs which I had to find would not require increases of estimates. Therefore it would not necessitate seeking specific Home Office approval.

The Police Authority approved a six-month experiment with a ceiling on the expenditure. A two-seater Brantly was hired and used in a variety of roles. Unfortunately neither the public nor some senior police officers had the foresight to pursue the experiment and despite Press briefings there were suggestions that it might be seen as a gimmick. The Home Office were also less than helpful. Durham was the first Force in the country to try such an experiment which I believe was worthwhile but it was years ahead of its time.

Another subject he wanted me to look at was the development of computers and I was dispatched to spend a few days in a hotel at Southampton, where IBM were holding a business conference; I was the only policeman present. Computers were still very much at the development stage and the machines envisaged weighed tons and took up a lot of space in rooms with specially-regulated temperatures; but my visit was not a waste of time. There was a need for more up-to-date equipment for centralising certain records and I learned a great deal which eventually was useful in filling in the gap. Throughout the remainder of my service I endeavoured to keep abreast of the rapid development of computers.

Mr Muir did a great deal for charities, especially Boys' Clubs and for young people generally. Well-known entertainers of the day were invited to boost publicity for the various funds; we had them for lunch and they gave freely of their time. One I remember was Frankie Vaughan whose song 'Green Door' was popular at that time. One idea hatched between Alex Dickson, later Sir Alex, and Alec Muir was to send young people for a period of two years to contribute to the life of third-world countries. The scheme was VSO and two of the Durham Police Cadets were the first to participate. One of them, David Blakey, became Chief Constable at West Mercia, while the other, whose name escapes me, also rose to high rank in the service.

There were of course instances when pronouncements were at odds with those in authority and with the public when the media would have a field day. Mr Muir's unconventional and independent actions did not always endear him to the Home Office and Treasury officials and might have been a reason why he was not knighted, an honour to which many people thought he was entitled. He had the happy knack of getting the best out of his staff and he helped those who wished to avail themselves of the opportunities provided. He enjoyed retirement for a number of years and there was a Memorial Service in Durham Cathedral after his death, well-attended by police and the public at large. It was hard work but fun working for him and I benefited enormously from the experience.

A Move to Shropshire

I had been in post for two years when I was given a nudge that it was time to seek higher office. At that time there were about 127 Police Forces in the United Kingdom. A Deputy Chief Constable was required in Shropshire where I had spent a few weeks at the Shropshire Light Infantry depot in wartime. I liked the countryside and was familiar with North Wales having spent time climbing Snowdon. It would not be a big step forward but ambition was not a driving force and we thought we would like to live there. The new town of Telford was scheduled for development which was a challenge and I had experience of policing the new town of Newton Aycliffe in Durham and in the preparations for the Peterlee development.

My application was successful and as I mentioned earlier I am not sure to this day if my success had any bearing on the fact that the Chairman of the Shropshire Police Committee, then a Colonel in the Yeomanry Territorials, was showing his appreciation for a face-saving action from the Press in which I was involved.

We moved to Shrewsbury in April, 1963, leaving Margaret to complete her term at Durham. We were planning to bring her home when she rode in on her 50cc lightweight motor-cycle having worked out the route. She was suitably clothed for the journey but on arrival had difficulty in controlling herself, arising from the vibrations experienced from the long journey. Although provision had been made for her to continue her education at The Girls' Grammar School, Shrewsbury, she rejected the offer. Shropshire educational facilities were very good and during the holidays she sought out what she wanted and was accepted at the Shrewsbury Technical College where she took up Business Studies. One of the reasons she gave for not going to the Girls' School was that because she was very tall she would look damn silly in the boater the girls wore! Alex, was by this time well on his way at Sandhurst.

We were provided with a substantial house in a pleasant part of the town. It was in need of a good clean up and re-decoration which I requested at police expense, this being the normal procedure, but the request was rejected on the grounds that no money had been included in the estimates to cover the costs.

After a couple of days Miss Carver, Secretary to the Chief Constable, brought a document to me. She asked me to sign it and said she would take a copy back with her. A glance showed a full-length sheet of foolscap paper numbered and itemised in the form of an order covering the duties I had to execute and for which I was to be responsible. I declined to sign, sending my apologies, because I wished to have time to digest and study the content. Time and again I read and re-read the instruction and could not bring to mind any other duties within the Force that were not included. I took the document home, where Lucy and I went through it together and were somewhat nonplussed. A day or so later there was a message that I return the document duly signed. Instead of signing the paper, I went to see the Chief Constable and suggested we have a discussion as I was not convinced the order was the best way of maintaining harmony in the Force. I begged him to talk the matter over, but to no avail. His response was that he had learned to keep a foot on dry land. I signed and that was how the management of the Force operated.

The population of Shropshire at that time was around 306,000 and the establishment of the Force was 429. Shrewsbury Borough was the largest centre of population, and secondly Wellington; there were lesser centres of population at Oswestry and Ludlow. The county stretched from the Cheshire boundary in the north to Herefordshire in the south with the Welsh border on the west. One of the features of the county were the many miles of public roads, more than any other county in England and Wales which of course created work and problems for police. The new town of Telford was taking shape around Wellington, eventually absorbing much of that part of the county. I was invited to be a member of the planning meeting of the New Town which was most helpful in building up and preparing the Force to deal with increased traffic and population. We were warmly welcomed by the police and civilian members of the Force and invited to join them in their social activities and in doing so soon got to know members of the public. It was apparent that the Force was well regarded and 40 years later on there are those with whom I then served who are still my friends.

It is the practice for government and local authorities to settle their budgets ready for the financial year commencing in April and to review and re-adjust them in the autumn. As finance was my responsibility I began work for the autumn review to find that the police estimates were decided by the County Treasurer. Nevertheless I began a thorough examination and understanding of the money allocated for police purposes and concluded that, bearing in mind the need to prepare for the expansion of police responsibilities with the Telford development, more money was required. In my scrutiny of expenditure I found there were items being charged to the police which were the responsibilities of other departments of the County Council. The importance of correction was to ensure that the money provided for police purposes was used solely in accordance with the government grant which in percentage was higher than most other council functions. I also made savings by eliminating certain police practices which were outdated. The savings from the two sources reduced the extra money now required.

What I had done was not popular in some quarters and initially the advice was not to rock the boat. I pointed out that knowingly misusing police funds could lead to serious consequences. The pressure ceased and I prepared a minute for the Police Authority asking for a modest increase in the budget, which was approved. The members of the committee were honourable people and would not have wished to break the rules. Thereafter I prepared the estimates in accordance with police needs in conjunction with members of the Treasurer's staff.

I was still finding my way around when an allegation of rape was reported at Wellington. Genuine rape is an abhorrent crime the investigation of which is taken very seriously. About 8.30 pm on the day of the occurrence, I drove the short distance from my home to Wellington Police Station to get first-hand knowledge of any progress. A bright young woman sergeant brought me up-to-date with the rape case, having taken a leading part in the enquiry, which resulted in the alleged offender being locked up.

She had completed her work and I asked if she would care to have a drink in the Police Club. She thanked me and informed me that ladies were only allowed in the club by invitation on special occasions. I encouraged her to accompany me to the club room where she was barred from entry by a man who was obviously not a policeman. The Superintendent invited me to have a drink with him which I declined and asked him to accompany me to his office. I asked for an explanation of why a woman police officer was not allowed in the Police Club on police premises which had been provided by the Police Authority and the Home Office for the benefit of police officers and their families. The majority of the committee were civilians and in full charge of all activities. I ordered him to turn everyone out of the club, to secure the premises and to report personally to my office for 9.00 o'clock the following morning bringing the books covering the Constitution, the Rules of the Club and any other relevant documents. He said he believed that as President he was entitled to run the club as it was. I found difficulty in believing he was that naïve and instructed him to clear all items of property from the premises which was to remain closed. In due course, when another Superintendent took over the division, a club was re-established and conducted in a proper manner.

Considering the number of estate and mansion houses in the county containing valuable property, the number of crimes against property was relatively low. There were however pockets of families in several places where there were regular outbreaks of disorderly conduct resulting in personal injuries and damage to property. There were also complaints of assaults of a sexual nature against women and under-age sex.

During my first year in office, a spinster lady of mature years who had lived alone in a farm cottage at Tern Hill was murdered. The Detective Superintendent was an experienced and capable detective with an excellent knowledge of the people and their way of life in rural Shropshire. The local policemen knew most people scattered about in this lightly-occupied part of the county. It was confirmed that a portable radio was stolen and other items and it was believed a sum of money was missing. The radio and other missing items, but no money, were recovered behind a hedge nearby and were sent to the forensic laboratory. The immediate suspect was a local man who lived mainly on unemployment or sickness benefit. He was well-known to police for his uncouth manner and violent temper leading to assaults when he did not get his own way. He had been arrested several times and had served time in prison for non-payment of wife maintenance and bastardy arrears. When questioned or challenged he would leer at people, including police, making derogatory remarks and outbursts of filthy language including threats. He was never known to admit to anything wrong and would deny his identity even when he was known. He was normally dressed in scruffy dirty clothes in which he was known to sleep out.

On the day after the murder he was wearing a complete set of new clothing, including shoes and had had his hair cut close to the skin. The places of purchase were traced where he had paid cash, but he took his old clothing with him and despite extensive searching it was never found. He had a clean up at the public baths, all of which he paid for in cash at a time when he owed money to the court. We did not close our minds on the matter and also continued other enquiries. We decided no useful purpose would be served in arresting the suspect until we had the laboratory reports. We kept the Chief Constable up to date with developments, and he did at one point express the opinion that it should not be difficult to get the truth out of what he referred to as a simple country lay-about. We had reached this point within three days of the finding of the body.

The following morning I was aware that the Detective Superintendent had been in the Chief Constable's office for over an hour, after which he came into my office. He was absolutely devastated and trembling. I got him a cup of tea and when he had settled down he said he had been verbally taken apart without the opportunity to respond and during the whole time he had been kept standing. He was informed that the assistance of Scotland Yard had been requested and that neither he nor I were to take any further part in relation to the murder enquiry. He had been asked to inform me accordingly. The Superintendent was very upset and I suggested getting him a doctor, which he declined, but I insisted he should go home and stay there until he felt better.

I went to the Chief Constable's office and expressed my displeasure at his conduct in distressing the Superintendent and for not having the courage personally to give me an order. My visit was brief; he was speechless. The Chief Constable was perfectly entitled to call in Scotland Yard but I would have expected he would have informed us before doing so. The calling-in of Scotland Yard was usually done by small Forces in complicated or difficult cases because of lack of experience, manpower or facilities. There is also a financial benefit to the Force from a central fund which covers the cost of Scotland Yard detectives.

Two days later the Scotland Yard team of a Superintendent and a Sergeant had not arrived but the laboratory confirmed our suspect's handling of the portable radio. This evidence was not conclusive that he had been in the house as they were found outside but that information coupled with other evidence and strong circumstantial evidence was sufficient for a positive arrest and charge; the situation was frustrating. Eventually a Chief Superintendent and a sergeant arrived and booked into a hotel at Market Drayton and all the information was made available to them. They spent many hours in the Chief Constable's office. Some considerable time passed before they interviewed the suspect and in keeping with his character he publicly boasted his innocence to all and sundry. In his arrogance he took it upon himself to call at the police station, sometimes more than once a day, offering himself for interview, followed by scenes to attract attention. The adverse publicity arising from his attitude and conduct and the lack of official information resulted in a poor image of police and the public at large were asking questions. I was in an invidious situation and knew no more about the continuing enquiry than the man in the street.

In about the fourth week of the presence of the Scotland Yard officers, I decided to discuss the matter with my Chief Constable. He did not welcome my intrusion but I planted myself in his office and calmly told him that I believed it was my duty to be informed of what was taking place. I assured him of my loyalty but made it clear I was prepared to take independent action if I thought necessary. With some reluctance he admitted there was no new evidence to hand since the Scotland Yard officers took over but he felt they would get an admission from the suspect. I told him it was apparent that the suspect had got the upper hand and that something had to be done before the situation became more farcical. I was making little if any progress so I told him that I was prepared to arrest and charge the suspect with or without his blessing or authority. He did agree that the evidence was sufficiently strong to warrant arrest and charge, and eventually this acceptance led to his promising he would think matters over. He was still less than enthusiastic about my proposition to override his authority but I stood firm and informed him that if there was no action within 24 hours I would do so.

The following day the Scotland Yard officers arrested and charged the suspect. He appeared at Shrewsbury Assize Court in due course. At the trial much play was made of the fact that time and again the accused had voluntarily presented himself at the police station which Defence suggested was hardly the action of a guilty party. The Judge, an Old Boy of Shrewsbury School, made no secret of the fact that he had never missed the cricket match played on Anniversary Day and it was known he was planning to attend on this occasion. The case commenced two days before the anniversary. The legal profession, the Court officials and the police expected an adjournment for half a day. However, on the morning of the re-union he arranged for his private car, which was normally parked in the police yard whilst he lived nearby in the Judges' Lodgings, to be taken to the school in preparation for his going to his home in Wales. Therefore he had intended finishing the case by 12.00 noon on the third day. It was a not-guilty plea and even in the simplest of cases the time allowed was totally inadequate. To the surprise of most people he stopped the case before noon on the third day of the trial, informed the Jury there was no case to answer and discharged the prisoner. He left the Court for his 12.00 noon appointment. He was an old man and retired soon afterwards. There are some decisions hard to swallow and this was one of them.

Within a year of the Tern Hill trial it was on the news that a man in Cheshire living adjacent to the Shropshire border had met his death in suspicious circumstances. I immediately recognised the surname of a woman with whom the Tern Hill suspect had been associating. I spoke to the Cheshire Detective Chief Superintendent and learned from him that the man who died had been cycling down a rough country lane towards his home in darkness when a wire, which had been stretched across the road, caught his neck and tumbled him into a large round tank full of slurry where he died and was found to have a broken neck. I informed the detective of the background of the suspect of the Tern Hill murder and sent him the relevant paperwork. Within a day he returned my call and informed me that the widow of the murdered man had made a statement to the effect that she had paid our suspect a small amount of money to kill her husband and her knowledge of the use of the wire across the path of her husband. They made an immediate arrest. He denied all knowledge and pleaded not guilty at court but was found guilty and sentenced to life imprisonment. Justice had finally caught up with this unscrupulous beast of a man. It was satisfying news.

Shropshire had a good record for road accident preventative work but like all rural areas the number of accidents and casualties was high. During daylight in fine weather a solo motorcyclist was killed on the A5 road near Nescliffe by an army vehicle which was being driven by a territorial learner driver under the supervision of an NCO instructor. The legal responsibilities of driving instructors were at that time imprecise and proceedings against them were usually unsuccessful. The evidence against the instructor was quite strong and in consultation with Mr Bolfield, a solicitor, it was decided to charge the learner and the supervisor with motoring offences. The learner driver was convicted but the charge against the instructor was, not unexpectedly, dismissed. An appeal was lodged to the High Court in the name of Geoff Woolham, Superintendent, Oswestry Division. The High Court allowed the appeal and the case was sent back to the Magistrates' Court for re-hearing. A conviction ensued. Thereafter driving instructors were liable to prosecution and conviction, provided of course there was sufficient evidence. The change in the law brought about considerable publicity nationally and locally.

After the motoring appeal case, BBC Radio approached me to join a series of six weekly broadcasts with a small panel of well-known people from different walks of life. The programme went out live and dealt with questions on motoring and road safety sent in by listeners. My Chief Constable did his best to discourage me from participating.

I took the view that it would be good for Shropshire to be so involved and pointed out to him that road safety was one of my responsibilities. It was good fun and sharpened the brain on the subject. Members of the Police Authority made complimentary remarks and quite unexpectedly my annual pay increment was increased by two years instead of one year which was my entitlement. It was much appreciated.

Preparations continued to strengthen the Force to deal with the Telford development now well underway. There was a programme of new houses being built but there were still a number of officers and their families living in appalling conditions. Finding sites, obtaining planning authority and approval of finance absorbed much time and energy. Prior to my joining the Force, approval had been given to build a new Force Headquarters but nothing positive had been done to get things moving. When I had a spare hour I worked on the project and finally completed scale plans and explanations suitable for presentation to the Police Authority, but a site could not be agreed.

One of the things which caused me continuing concern was the conditions in which the police vehicles were serviced. There were two lock-up garages and in cold weather the doors had to be closed, which placed the mechanics in possible danger when using welding equipment and blow lamps. There was no space for expansion on the site and it took a long time to solve the problem. Finally the work and the staff were transferred to new council workshops and suitable financial arrangements agreed.

In the early sixties illegal use of drugs was not commonplace but young people, in this rural county, were being approached by dealers and some were indulging in the practice. One of the difficulties, which was apparent when talking to Parent-Teacher groups, was the belief among them that drug use was confined to the run-down areas in large towns and cities. What they did not realise was that dealers were seeking out youngsters from good homes with money to spend and they found the information unbelievable. Some parents were offended when it was suggested they have a friendly talk with their teenage sons and daughters on the subject. Quite a few were surprised when they learned the truth. Being a parent can be difficult! Police officers and their families do a great deal of voluntary work with youth organisations and find it disappointing that some parents have no knowledge of how their young people spend their free time. Of course it is not easy to get teenagers interested in what is available as not all of them are interested in joining youth clubs or playing games. When involved it is a never-ending mental exercise thinking up new ways and new interests.

One idea we tried in Shrewsbury was with the generous help of an Italian restaurateur who made his dining room available one night a week when otherwise it would have been closed. A menu much discounted was provided, and a talk was given by the restaurateur on all aspects of the social graces expected when taking a lady out for the evening, including the use of the table cutlery. Places were set for 20 people and a requirement was that they brought a member of the opposite sex. Lucy joined me in helping out and welcoming them. The girls, dressed in their best, ensured that the boys were well turned out. What started out as an experiment went well and brought confidence and enjoyment to these young people. Some things are truly worthwhile.

The Amalgamation Announcement

In August 1966, Lucy and I were enjoying the sun and sea in the Adriatic. Lucy could swim for hours at a time and enjoy every minute of it; I was not in her class and while she was in the water I bought a 'Daily Telegraph', some two or three days out of date. What I read and re-read was difficult to digest. Roy Jenkins, Home Secretary, had published a list of the intended amalgamation of Police Forces in England and Wales, reducing their number from about 127 to 43. Shropshire, Herefordshire, Worcester City and Worcester County were to become a single Force. There had been no consultation with police and no indication as to the future of senior officers. The number of Chief Constables would be reduced by over 80 as would Deputies. The fate of the Assistants was unknown; other ranks might be affected but their continued service was guaranteed. We talked and talked about nothing else and felt so out of things as we had no one with similar interests with whom we could have a discussion. We both agreed that if we have been financially comfortable we would have stayed in Italy! We had a son at Sandhurst and a daughter at college, both to support, so when our holiday ended we set off home not knowing what to expect.

I was greeted with the information that the new Shropshire Force Headquarters had been cancelled. The Chairman had left a note thanking me for producing what he called a monumental piece of work. The information was the least of my concerns but I appreciated his thanks. The shock, mixed feelings and anger at the major decision being forced upon the police service had probably diminished a little by the time we arrived home.

The Home Office followed up with a directive from the Home Secretary which included specific details of the future of senior ranks.

In the case of the four Forces with which I was involved, any one of the four Chief Constables would be eligible, subject to selection by the Police Authority, to fill the top post. All Chief Constables were able to retire on an enhanced pension if they so wished and were also eligible to continue in the new Force at a lower rank. Deputies and Assistants were not eligible for enhanced benefits if they chose to resign but they were to be retained in whatever posts were available. My Chief Constable wanted to object to the inclusion of Shropshire in the amalgamation and he informed me that a number of the members of the Police Authority were of the same mind. He wanted me to prepare a paper for discussion. Although I considered the size and shape of the proposed Forces was a bit unwieldy and the grouping of the Forces could have been different, I was of the opinion that for financial reasons and the changing needs and mobility of the population, small Forces were becoming out of date. Therefore I decided not to accede to his request; pressure did not make me change my mind.

The next step was a meeting of the six members of The Association of Chief Police Officers (ACPO) at Hindlip Hall, Headquarters of Worcester County. The four Chief Constables were in an invidious position. One of them would be appointed Chief Constable of the new Force. There was understandably a gentlemanly reluctance for any one of them to take the lead lest they might be thought to be presumptuous. Tom Gaylor, Deputy, Worcestershire, said he was thinking of retiring and might be unable to complete the task, but he continued to serve as an Assistant in the new Force for many years. I was the younger so the job fell to me of re-organising the new Force and I would have a free hand in inviting officers and civilian staff of whatever ranks from the four Forces to make up working groups. The six ACPO members met fortnightly and I would present the reports of the various working groups.

From my point of view the plan worked well and I cannot recall an occasion when the recommendations were altered or rejected. However, there were instances when my Chief Constable and Bob McCartney, Chief Constable Hereford, approached me after the meetings and on occasions made strong representations for their ideas to be included in future plans. There came a time when I had to remind them that the place to raise matters for discussion was at the main fortnightly meetings. After each meeting action was taken to arrange the implementation of the decisions reached by each of the four Forces so that on vesting day, which was still unknown, the change would go smoothly.

For the next eight months I worked long hours and travelled extensively over the three counties. The people I was working with were not all happy about their future prospects and of where they were likely to serve. The small working groups, changed regularly, were usually limited to one person per Force, and at first meetings the task of explaining the inevitable had to be overcome before the real business for which we met could be considered. There was understandably pride in their Forces and in their methods of working which were varied and we had to find a common approach to each aspect of the work. They took away tasks to prepare for the next meeting and as we got to know each other, different points of view were accepted and progress was made. We usually finished up with new forms, for recording matters and for dealing with different aspects of police work and it was good for those involved to feel they had made contributions to the running of the new Force. My aim was to keep paperwork to a minimum which resulted in discarding unnecessary procedures.

The name of the Force had been chosen from suggestions made by members. West Mercia was a fitting choice. In the Spring of 1968 John (Sandy) Willison, later Sir John, Chief Constable of Worcester County, was nominated Chief Constable of West Mercia which was a popular and deserving choice. We then spent a day together writing new divisional boundaries which reduced the number of territorial divisions from thirteen to seven. The intention was, as far as practicable, to blur the boundaries of the four original Forces and mix the personnel to enable them to get to know each other better by working together. It was a pleasure to work with Sandy Willison but it was the last occasion I did so for the next two years.

Called to the Police College

In March 1967 I was surprised to receive a personal telephone call from Mr John Gaskain, the Commandant of the Police College and formerly Chief Constable of Gloucestershire, whom I'd never met, inviting Lucy and me to spend a day or two at the College with a view to a possible secondment. We were made very welcome by Mr Gaskain and his wife, and Lucy was looked after and introduced to other ladies living on the campus while we were talking business. It was explained that a recent meeting of the Board of Governors decided to appoint a new officer to be Director of the Senior (and) Intermediate Courses, whose additional duty would include preparing a new syllabus for the Senior Command Course. Their wish was to have the course more operationally oriented and for the students to be more involved in decision-making exercises and projects and dispensing with some of the lectures which had become a feature of the course. I was fully aware from my previous service as a student and on the staff that there would be many obstacles to overcome to achieve the desired objective. There were Chief Constables and Home Office officials, who with the best intentions expected to be given space on the timetable to address and impose their contributions on the course which were probably of interest but did not always fit in with pre-arranged timetables.

I discussed my reservations with the Commandant and asked him how he came to invite me for consideration for the appointment. He informed me that Col. Eric St Johnstone, later Sir Eric, then Chief Inspector of Constabulary and formerly Chief Constable of Durham prior to Alec Muir, both of whom knew me well, had made the suggestion. In years past I had criticised some of the content of the College courses and my remarks were now overtaking me. The

Commandant promised that once a new syllabus was approved by the Board of Governors I would have his blessing and support to be free to implement pre-arranged plans. We thanked the Gaskain family for their hospitality and kindness and I promised to speak to him within two days. He told me no one else had been approached about the post.

Lucy and I discussed the offer on the way home and took into consideration a great many things. Lucy thought she would like to live at Bramshill and enjoy the social life with the wives of other staff. She would also be able to get about in our motorcar as I would rarely need it. I would have been quite happy to serve under Sandy Willison at Hindlip but there were still three spare Chief Constables and a Deputy in addition to me on the strength. Mr Fenwick, my Chief Constable, had been nominated Deputy of the new Force which did not alter the situation. I could foresee possible difficulties in the allocation and sharing of areas of responsibility between officers who had experienced their own commands. Another thought was that arising from the drastic reduction of Chief Constables' posts throughout the country, prospects of advancement in the service were unlikely to occur in the foreseeable future. It appeared the post offered would give me a degree of independence which I might not otherwise have and that by the end of the secondment I would have completed over 30 years' service and could retire if I so wished.

I put my thoughts to Sandy Willison who was most understanding. He was unable to predict and make specific plans about future senior posts as the date of the amalgamation was not scheduled until the end of September 1967. He warmly thanked me for work done in preparation for the amalgamation, wished me well and said he looked forward to my returning to the new Force in due course. To this day I do not know whether or not my decision was good or bad but I had had enough of the method of command in the few years in Shropshire and needed a change.

On confirmation of my decision, we moved into a small flat at Bramshill and left most of our furniture in the police house at Shrewsbury until we were allocated a new house on the site a few months later.

There were two courses for which I was responsible. The Intermediate Command Course was of three months' duration and catered for middle management officers of the ranks of Inspector and Chief Inspector with the experience and potential to attain higher ranks. It was a well-balanced course and appeared to fit the purpose for which it was designed. The Senior Command Course was of six months duration: the students were mainly of Chief Superintendent rank, with one or two newly-appointed Assistant Chief Constables and experienced senior police officers from various parts of the Commonwealth. The object of the course was to prepare officers for the most senior ranks in the service. The courses rotated so that there was only one course at a time. Two experienced Chief Superintendents on secondment assisted me.

An interesting and useful training exercise was carried out in conjunction with the Royal Ulster Constabulary and the Secretary of State for Northern Ireland. It was no secret that members of the Irish Republican Army were planning to create disorder on a large scale in the Province. It was normal practice for members of the Senior Command course to be attached in small groups for a week or so to UK Forces and be allocated specific tasks to research. On this occasion the RUC was chosen and the Chief Constable readily accepted the proposal. The final arrangements were for the whole of the course to spend two weeks with the RUC, in groups of three each from different Forces, to form working parties and be given a single task to research. There were nine groups to cover every department and section of the Force, thus the whole of the Force would be subject to scrutiny. Each group was required to complete a paper with their findings.

It was clearly understood by the RUC Officers and the members of the Senior Command Force that this was solely a training exercise and it was accepted that whatever views or recommendations were expressed there was no requirement for the RUC to take action. The members of the RUC welcomed us and went out of their way to explain and answer questions. Back in college, a day was set aside for each group to present their papers, and to explain and discuss their findings with the other groups.

The Secretary of State for Northern Ireland and senior officers accepted our invitation to listen to the presentations and join in the discussions. Afterwards the Secretary of State invited me to join him and members of the Authority at Storment to present the findings of the groups. There was genuine interest and enthusiasm with meaningful discussions. One of the recurring observations made by most groups was that the RUC was very much under strength and needed expanding in readiness to meet the challenge of the IRA. I took a message of appreciation back to the members of the Senior Command Course and was warmly thanked. Within weeks approval was given for a substantial increase in the RUC establishment. The RUC and the mainland Forces have a long history of good relations; the exercise resulted in renewed friendships and new friends.

It was a busy life. There were numerous visitors from different backgrounds, many from overseas, interested in the work of the College. We enjoyed discussions and exchanging information. When there were spare moments I got on with the job of preparing a new syllabus. There were of course a number of outstanding lecturers whose services would be retained, but I felt there were places for experienced people from business and industry to come and talk and have discussions which would provide a better balanced course. Suitable people were approached and were willing to give their services. It was not a popular decision reducing the number of existing visiting senior officers and academics from the lecture list and in course of time there were a few questions posed. An endeavour was made to answer then as diplomatically as possible. There were a great many alterations to be made with the intention for more active participation by the students.

Eventually a detailed and comprehensive paper was completed. The Commandant recommended it as presented to him for consideration by the Board of Governors. He informed me that the paper had been well-received and approved. It was as if a load had been removed from my back and the profuse thanks from the Commandant made me feel the work had been well worthwhile.

We had only been at Bramshill a short time and living in a cramped flat when our son, Alex, by this time an Army Lieutenant, decided to marry Jill Barber, the daughter of an Army Officer. The lack of living space limited some of the things we wished we could have done for this very special occasion. Now, this year as I write, they have celebrated their Ruby Wedding with their son and daughter grown up and married, and with six grandchildren.

The next family marriage was that of our daughter. As a teenager Margaret had many friends of her age and they did things in groups. She was a competent cartoonist and was in great demand to produce items for social occasions and now and again showed the tutors in a different light. When she was about 19 years of age she timidly asked if she could bring a young man home for lunch. It was the first time she had brought a boyfriend home. She did so again soon afterwards when Rob talked about joining his parents in Rhodesia where his father had a dental practice. Some time after he left, Margaret informed us he would be returning at the end of the year when they were to be married. It took us a little time to digest the news but the preparations for the wedding commenced and on 16th December, 1967 they were married from the College at Eversley Parish Church in Hampshire. He had secured a post as a teacher in Rhodesia and off they went. There are two sons and one daughter of the marriage, all settled in Australia with five children between them. There were occasions when we had reservations about moving our children from school to school and the effect it would have upon their education. It is a question to which there is not a definitive answer. They chose what they wanted to do in life and developed into cheerful, self-reliant, confident people acceptable in any company, and even though we are far apart we are still a close family.

Social life at the College was good. Although students were free at weekends, there were a number from overseas and others unable to get home. A regular custom for those staying was to gravitate to the bar on Saturday evenings with resident staff and their ladies. Students would be invited to our homes and there were occasions when the lounge floor was covered with them sitting drinking coffee and putting the world right until the wee small hours. They were from different countries of different colours and customs. It was fun and we made good friends. Lucy enjoyed life at the College: she was a good driver, and was in demand as an unofficial driving instructor by some of the ladies who had difficulties in passing the test.

My original secondment was for the period of a year but the Commandant asked me to continue for a second year. During the first year my salary was in accordance with my post in Shropshire, plus a non-pensionable allowance which all seconded personnel were paid. In the meantime the Shropshire Force no longer existed and on my agreeing to serve another year at the College it was on the understanding that my salary would be in accordance with the West Mercia rates which were an improvement on the Shropshire salary and of course the non-pensionable allowance. The salary I was granted after being in post for some weeks was unrelated to and lower than the West Mercia rate for Assistant Chief Constables. I appealed, with the support of the Commandant, without success. Unfortunately, he took ill and had to resign and sadly died soon afterwards. I believe he would have continued the appeals if he had remained in good health. Lest the reader think I am a doddering old man and do not know what I am saying or that I am prejudiced against the Home Office, I have in my possession the letter of confirmation. I decided there and then not to accept Home Office decisions in future unless in writing and signed. The year was 1968. Now in 2008 the police pay agreement has caused more problems than the few pounds saved. What is new?

The College had a spell without a Commandant and the post of Deputy Commandant was vacant. I was the senior police officer on the staff and for some weeks dealt with all essential matters requiring attention. The Home Office was unsympathetic so I telephoned Col. Eric St Johnstone, and within a few days Peter White, Chief Constable of Gloucestershire, took over the Commandant's duties on a temporary basis. A new Deputy Commandant was appointed but he had neither a police nor a college background and it took him a long time to grasp what was required. A few weeks before the end of my secondment, a new Commandant was appointed which made life much easier and I was more able to concentrate on the work for which I was responsible.

There were no examinations or grades but a confidential report signed by the Commandant was sent to each student's Chief Constable. The last two weeks of the course were busy with tutorials, final interviews and report writing. Students were informed in general terms of the content and any points of ambiguity discussed. With the majority there were not problems, but there were always one or two who questioned the assessments even though the matters in contention had been referred to and discussed previously during the course. Some of the Senior Course members had been my students in earlier years and it was gratifying to see them again making good progress. In later years a good proportion of them became Chief Constables.

Decision time had come. Offers of employment other than police work were made to me at salaries which were a considerable improvement on what I was getting. However, police work which had been my life and which I enjoyed would be missed and I was doubtful if I would get the same satisfaction in business or industry. Sandy Willison was keen for me to join him and I knew I would be happy under his command which is what I decided to do. I have had no regrets.

Assistant Chief Constable West Mercia

In April 1969, on returning from the College, we moved into a standard police house at Hindlip, Headquarters of the Force: it was a pleasant site with a view towards the city of Worcester. The new Force had continued to develop, but a limiting factor was the shortage of manpower. Pay rates were low, experienced officers were leaving before being eligible for their pensions and officers in their early years of service were also finding better paid situations elsewhere.

Initially, my responsibility was Force Administration which kept me busy. Financial matters were an important part of the job but equally important was career development and getting the right people in place to make the best use of their talents to provide a good service to the public. West Mercia being the largest inland Force in the country made it inevitable that police officers had to be moved about and houses found for them within reasonable distance of their place of work. Few officers were financially placed to buy their own houses and travelling was too expensive and time-consuming because of the length of journeys. In Cities and Borough Forces, changes of duties and promotions can usually be achieved without the need to move houses.

When preparing to move people, account had to be taken of their domestic circumstances: they might have children at school taking important examinations, or their spouse might be working. In such cases a note would be made when a suitable date was appropriate so that in the event of a vacancy arising they were not overlooked for promotion. Therefore approaches had on occasions to be made to more than one eligible person to fill a post. In my experience it was never a problem as plenty of officers were keen to have a varied experience to enhance their career prospects. There are of course excellent officers doing a good job and not interested in promotion; in so many ways they are the backbone of the service and provided they are happy where they are the best course is to leave them but not to forget them. Now and again for different reasons officers are moved in their own interests, and the interests of the Force, irrespective of their wishes.

After a few months I was given charge of Operations bringing me back to the sharp end of police work, which I really enjoyed. There was still a proportion of time taken up with paperwork and planning but there was a measure of freedom and independence. Getting about the Force area, getting to know people better, discussing the best way to tackle problems, visiting scenes of serious incidents and being readily available for consultation was the main function. Sometimes it meant long days and night-time calls which were an acceptable part of the job. When police officers get involved in serious crime enquiries there is a tendency for them to become so dedicated to finding solutions that they work day and night without proper meals or sleep. In such instances it is necessary to insist, despite protestations, that they have a break and a rest.

On 8th October 1969, a few days after my being in the Operations post, there was a Senior Officers' Mess night at Hindlip. We were in Mess kit and relaxing with our guests after a good dinner when a message was received from Worcester City of a particularly vicious disturbance. With other Worcester Division officers I hurried to Worcester. We learned there was a history of friction between youths from Worcester and Birmingham. Two nights previously, two Birmingham youths sustained knife wounds. Four Worcester youths were arrested and charged and one might have thought justice was being done but reprisals were planned by the Birmingham youths. A gang of about 40 youths from Birmingham entered the Swan Inn at Worcester, and without provocation attacked the patrons who had no connection with the previous incident. A sword stick, knives, iron bars, hammers and truncheons were used in a particularly vicious manner. Fittings and furniture were wrecked in the process and a state of extreme terror was created. On leaving the premises the gang smashed windows of adjoining property. Of the many injured, 13 attended hospital for treatment and one was detained for nearly two weeks suffering from a serious stab wound to the back; another required 20 stitches to the head.

The immediate police action was to set up road blocks and within an hour 18 youths were arrested; a 19th was arrested later. All were charged with causing Affray. Of the 19 accused, 18 were sentenced to three years' imprisonment and the other, the youngest, to Borstal Training. The Police Surgeon attended the police station and provided treatment and advice. The work of dealing with the large number of truculent youths in the limited space in the old City Police Station was a mammoth task. Obtaining their personal particulars was time-consuming because of their attitude and reluctance to co-operate. Therefore the preparation of charge sheets, one for each prisoner, agreeing that the property and money listed was correct and finally obtaining their signatures, was a trying exercise. Everyone mucked in and by about 7.00 am the immediate tasks were completed. Those of us arriving from Hindlip were still in our Mess kit and onlookers seeing us on our way home might have been forgiven if they put the wrong interpretation on how we had passed the night! The initial action and the co-operation with the Communication Branch in co-ordinating the exercise was a piece of good professional police work.

In 1971, the Pakistani Cricket Team came to Worcester for the opening match of the tour and attracted a great deal of publicity as demonstrations against the team by supporters of Bangladesh intended to stop play. In anticipation of the likely disorder a large number of police were drafted to Worcester from other parts of the Force. The numbers expected did not materialise; there were noisy demonstrations but no violence, no doubt owing to the well organised police presence. The match went ahead without interruption.

Attack on Building Workers

When knowledge of public disorder is anticipated at specified events, police can be in place ahead of the potential trouble. Unfortunately, there are occasions when the police have no indication of where and when public disorder is likely to occur. There was such an incident at Telford in 1972. For a number of years ring leaders of strikes purporting to represent building workers had made repeated raids on building sites and had brought developments to a standstill. Initially the attacks were concentrated in the London area but eventually they spread to the provinces. A large number of building workers were employed at the new town of Telford, where there had been no labour disagreements or threats of strikes. However, quite unexpectedly a group led by the usual troublemakers swept through building sites at Telford assaulting workers, knocking men off ladders and causing injury and damage. A number of workers received serious injuries and one man was never physically fit enough to continue heavy work. The surprise attack lasted a matter of minutes: the criminals moved off swiftly, shouting threats and abuse alleging the workers were blacklegs. The police were thin on the ground and by the time they were alerted the offenders were leaving the scene.

The history of these attacks was well known and there had been incidents in neighbouring Forces where injuries and damage had been caused, some on quite a large scale, but there had not been any prosecutions.

I visited Telford after the attack and talked to the workmen, some of whom were most concerned there would be further disorder. They just wanted to work in peace. It was a sad situation: they were hard working, decent citizens, and I felt strongly that the perpetrators of the crimes should be brought to justice. I made an approach to my opposite numbers in the neighbouring Forces where there had been attacks suggesting we form combined teams to trace the offenders. Regrettably, my overtures were rejected. I decided to form a team within the force to concentrate on the Telford incident.

The late Fred Hodges, then a Chief Superintendent, later to become an Assistant Chief Constable and the late Colin Glover, then a Detective Chief Inspector later to become a Chief Superintendent, headed the team which I co-ordinated. It took many months of hard work but eventually the ring leaders were traced and sufficient evidence for prosecution assembled. The Editor and staff of the 'Shropshire Star' newspaper were a tremendous help as were the building workers and many others. Twenty people were charged with a variety of serious offences and in 1973 were dealt with at Shrewsbury Assize Court.

The persons charged received a great deal of publicity from the media. Their theme was that they were merely peacefully picketing building sites in an endeavour to improve the pay and conditions of their Union members. During the weeks leading up to the trial, the increased propaganda stirred up strong feelings against the police action. Other Unions supported them and time and again statements were made to the effect that the trial would be disrupted to the extent it would have to be abandoned. Our information-gathering services did a wonderful job of infiltration and we had virtually a day-to-day update of the intentions and plans being formulated. Special trains were hired by the South Wales Miners' Union, fleets of coaches were hired by the Liverpool Dockers and many other organisations made firm arrangements to be at Shrewsbury on the opening day of the trial. It was apparent that thousands of demonstrators were planning to disrupt the proceedings. The Shire Hall and the Assize Court combined building is situated on the other side of the road from the Lord Hill monument at the rear of open ground.

On the opening day of the trial, a police assembly point was selected nearby out of sight of the monument. There was a communications control centre and police remained out of view until such time as they were required. Portable interlocking barriers with a height of about four feet were erected for a distance of over 200 yards. All normal traffic was diverted and the demonstrators' vehicles were not to be allowed within half a mile of the monument. It was a good decision as the beer-bellied leaders of the various contingents struggled with the effect of marching and their voices were muted with their exertions. It was a mile from the railway station which also took its toll and instead of their arriving with the appearance of a robust and organised party there were stragglers. Their plan was to be in place in strength by 10.00 am and a large number were there but not as many as expected. The trains were late and traffic diversions and police checks caused delays. Coaches from Liverpool were stopped as they entered the county at Whitchurch and an inspection of the work tickets, a legal requirement, showed the passengers were on the way to Ludlow Races. We had pre-knowledge of this ploy and the drivers were escorted by police motorcyclists on diversionary routes far from Shrewsbury. Therefore large numbers never reached the intended place. The leaders were annoyed and frustrated at the non-appearance of the Liverpool coaches as they were depending upon the occupants, mostly dockers, to take a leading part in the disruption. Nevertheless, by about midday there were several thousands present, shouting through megaphones, encouraging the demonstrators to be ready for action.

When the first contingents of demonstrators were seen approaching, a column of police officers marched from the other direction and stood shoulder to shoulder facing the monument from behind the portable barriers with instructions to stop anyone getting past them. In the event of anyone doing so they must not break the police line. On higher ground behind the cordon there were an adequate number of well-trained, young fit officers, with experience of judo and self-defence, with orders to arrest and take the prisoners to the court cells nearby. They were under the command of Jan Mead, whose expertise had trained them specifically for the task. I think that there was some disappointment that on this occasion there was no opportunity to put their special skills to the test. The officers on reserve nearby were marched into position as required. In all there were about 1500 officers involved in the operation, including those on diversionary duties. 700 were provided on request from neighbouring Forces in accordance with the 'mutual aid' arrangement between Forces.

When police contingents were being brought forward they were marched military style: their turn out was immaculate and the impression conveyed to the demonstrators was that they meant business, indicated by a lull in the shouting. Nevertheless, the leader standing on the plinth of the monument using a megaphone raised the noise level and ordered the demonstrators to be ready. He did not specify exactly what he expected of them but he was stirring them up and there was a feeling that disorder was likely to break out. We knew the name of the leader with the microphone and I asked two of my officers to go to him, address him as Mr Xxxxx and inform him that I would be pleased if he would join me on the roadway for a chat. Apparently he was upset when the officers addressed him by his surname, which was intended to make him aware of what we knew about him. After a short time he and two others joined me. I allowed him to let off steam by trying to convince me that he was an elected leader of a Trade Union branch and was merely carrying out the wishes of his members by peaceful picketing to improve their pay and conditions. I knew he was a docker and asked him to explain why he was involved with the Building Workers' Union. He huffed and puffed and became less aggressive in tone and finally asked me what I wanted to speak to him about.

As he was speaking he took an empty cigarette packet from his pocket, threw it on the road and asked one of his colleagues for a cigarette. I formed the idea that he had convinced himself that with the large numbers in support he had the upper hand and he made no secret of the fact that having made many promises he was not going to be deterred from his purpose. He refused to listen to reason and I had to find a way in which to discredit him in front of his followers. My duty was to prevent disorder.

Whilst he was still with me, he started to destroy the empty cigarette packet with his feet which gave me an idea. I pointed out that he had committed an offence by throwing litter on the roadway and I asked him to pick it up. He replied by using strong language and making scornful remarks about my request. I quickly added that unless he did so he would be arrested immediately, charged with Conduct Likely to Cause a Breach of the Peace and also for using indecent and foul language in a public place, adding that I would ensure he remained in custody until the conclusion of the court hearings. He looked towards his two companions for support. They told him to do as he was asked, advising him that they thought I meant what I said. He picked up the litter with a great effort. He was aged about 40, with a pot belly, and went on his way back to the Monument where he sat down. The noise from the supporters diminished and they gradually drifted away. He had lost credibility and was a broken man. I was fortunate in taking a chance which might have had the opposite effect, leading to disorder, injuries and damage. The day ended without injury, damage or arrests and the court proceedings were uninterrupted. The provisional arrangements for mutual aid for the following day from the neighbouring Forces were cancelled. During the remainder of the trials, we policed the area with a moderately strong force as a precautionary measure.

The Shire Hall staff whose offices overlooked the scene and the people living in neighbouring houses came out all smiles and congratulated us for ending the day without disorder. The only people showing disappointment were the Press and especially so the representatives of the television companies. They had spent hours and hours filming and forecasting all sorts of outcomes and their tone turned to remarks such as a 'Non Event' to which I countered by expressing satisfaction that it had been a most successful day. Twenty people were found guilty as charged and sentences of up to three years' imprisonment were imposed. The main ringleader has for some years starred in a television soap and appears to have done well since his term of imprisonment; now and again he makes public statements complaining about his conviction and the conduct of the police.

On 1st July 1973, on the retirement on pension of Eric Abbott, Deputy Chief Constable of Worcester City, I was appointed Deputy Chief Constable which was very much appreciated. My duties included standing in for the Chief Constable in his absence, and supervision of all aspects of the work of the Force which took me out and about checking records, meeting and talking to all ranks and civilian staff which I enjoyed. Discipline and complaints were also my responsibility.

In the years since amalgamation progress was hampered by the shortage of manpower and additional work. The Force had taken over the policing of the M5/M6 motorway link, and the population of Telford and Redditch was increasing. A disruption which we could well have done without was the re-fashioning of police boundaries to coincide with the new West Midlands Local Authority. The Sub-Division of Stourbridge and a large part of Halesowen Sub-Division involving 141 officers (132 men and 9 women) was transferred to the West Midlands Force. The proposed changes led to a great deal of uncertainty for the officers affected. They were given the right to opt to stay with West Mercia Police and remain where they were. The situation was bad for morale. Many questions were posed and the only advice we could give was that they had to make a personal decision. It would have been quite improper to have influenced their choices.

Appointed Chief Constable

Sir John (Sandy) Willison decided to retire on 31st December 1974 and gave due notice. The vacancy was advertised and candidates approved by the Home Office were interviewed by a sub-committee of the Authority. I considered I was extremely fortunate to be selected for the post. By this time I was 57, and no doubt would have been disappointed if I had been passed over, but the thought of being that age was in my mind and might have been a barrier. I was physically fit, not too confident and when informed of the decision was inwardly bubbling over. Forty years earlier I had been a farm servant in Aberdeenshire sleeping in a loft above horses and getting up at 5.00 am to groom and feed them before beginning the day's work. The appointment was a prize beyond my wildest dreams. The Police Authority was generous and put me on a starting increment above the beginning line which was gratifying.

Sandy Willison was a popular figure and in the few weeks up to his retirement the various divisions and departments wanted to show their appreciation to him and Lady Willison. I was approached and informed of their intentions, being asked to advise on suitable ways of giving them a really good send off. They wished Lucy and me to attend the various functions but I considered our presence would have been an intrusion and would distract from the purpose of the occasion which Sandy and Jess fully deserved. We decided to spend three weeks in Rhodesia, now Zimbabwe, with our daughter, husband and two grandchildren and to arrive back in time to have a final party for Sandy and Jess and send them off in good order on the last day of the year.

We had a wonderful time in Rhodesia with our daughter and family. We visited Victoria Falls and stayed in the magnificent Victoria Falls

Hotel, sailed on the Zambezi with the crocodiles under the boat and spent time in the game parks observing the wild animals at close quarters. The Rhodesian Police had picked up our presence on the passenger list when doing security checks and we were inundated with invitations from senior officers from the Police College days. We had to turn down a lot of them simply because there were too many but we did attend a formal lunch in the Senior Officers' Mess specially arranged for us. We were also pressed into making visits to a few homes of both black and white officers.

I asked about one particular chap who had been promoted Commander after his College course. He was black, well over six feet tall and always immaculate in uniform, a bright officer with a good sense of humour whom we both remembered. We learned he had retired and was now Headman of his village and we were taken to see him. We found a figure asleep in the open in the sun with a long straggly beard, with beer tins, a pipe and tobacco by his side. The officer who took us there awakened him by kicking him lightly on the bare sole of his feet. He stood up erect, saluted us and gave us a very warm welcome. In conversation we talked about his life in the police and his reason for retiring. He said he had enjoyed being a policeman but had realised the whole of his life that as he was the eldest of the family it would be his duty to take over as Headman of the village on the death of his father and he was therefore obliged to retire when his father died. His wife who had paid a visit to England when he was a college student joined us and it was pleasing to meet her again. She was a happy smiling lady and explained that when her husband was in the police service he was allowed to have only one wife. He interjected and said that it was the only thing that he did not like when he was a policeman! It transpired he now had three more wives. We met them and there was a gathering of many young people and children all of whom were very happy. His duty as Headman was to rule the village, deal with complaints and meet out justice in accordance with tribal laws. It was an enlightening experience which Lucy and I enjoyed.

When it was time to take the air journey back home, we were escorted into an office by security men without much explanation except to inform us that they were so instructed. The passengers were boarding the plane and time for take-off was approaching when an ex-Deputy

Chief Constable of Rhodesia appeared with profuse apologies for not having learned earlier that we were in the country. He had been one of my students and had spent time drinking coffee with us but was now retired on pension and was Chief Security Officer for South African Airways. On scrutinising the passenger list the previous evening he saw our names and in the morning took the first flight from Johannesburg to Salisbury to meet us. We had only a brief time together but the reunion was warm and genuine. We were the last passengers on the plane and as we stepped out of the office with him a pipe band, which had been out of our view, started playing. That short walk was memorable as we heard the tune, 'We are nae awa tae bide awa'. The tears were running down my cheeks. We were introduced to the captain and the crew with special instructions to the Chief Steward to look after us. We were taken to first-class seats and treated like Royalty. The first-class accommodation, the best brandy and specially-prepared meals were a bonus to our holiday. We did return to Rhodesia but political changes had soured the country and there was apprehension as to the future.

My appointment as Chief Constable West Mercia was made in the autumn of 1974, a few weeks before my parents' Diamond Wedding. My two brothers, two sisters and families decided we would arrange a celebration in a hotel in Aberdeen to which the extended families and friends would be invited. I had written to the Palace and HM The Queen acknowledged the occasion with a personal telegram, which is now in my possession together with messages from the Queen on the occasion of the Diamond Wedding of Lucy and myself and of our 65th Wedding Anniversary, together with colour photographs.

The occasion in Aberdeen was attended by a great many people and at a late hour of a long day and evening of celebrations I accompanied my parents in a taxi to their home in Balgownie Road, Aberdeen and saw them safely home. Father was not a demonstrative man and as I was growing up I regarded him as rather stern but with a good sense of humour. He heaped praise upon me for doing so well and said how proud they both were of my achievements. We had always been on good terms and we enjoyed visits and in latter years long telephone conversations. Two nights before his peaceful death in bed, we had chatted and although he was not in the best of health his mind and memory were as good as ever. On parting after the Diamond Wedding Celebrations, Mother squeezed my arm and added how proud she was. Mother and I had an easy relationship whilst I was growing up and this continued throughout her life. We had a lot in common: she was a prolific letter writer and reader and kept up-to-date with world affairs. On my first birthday away from home, which was my 21st, she sent me a fine pocket-sized leather-bound Holy Bible. Thereafter, except during the war years when I was not available, she would send me an up-to-date book on my birthdays until her failing eyesight at about the age of 90 limited her actions. Father was 83 and Mother 93 when they died.

Diamond Wedding Anniversary of Charles and Susan Rennie

My sister Betty and I are the only survivors of the family – she lives in Aberdeen. We speak to each other regularly and get the news of major family events. It is good that families keep together. In my early days away from home that is what kept me going. I suppose I was at times homesick.

On 1st January 1975, I took occupancy of the Chief Constable's Office in the fine old mansion house known as Hindlip Hall, Worcester, with a pleasant view of the countryside. Sir John (Sandy) Willison my predecessor had since the formation of the Force on 1st October, 1967 shaped it into a viable organisation with a fine reputation. I considered myself exceptionally fortunate to succeed him. Having a hand in the administration and structure of the Force, which had altered little in the meantime, together with my time as an Assistant and Deputy, the take-over went smoothly. Lucy had also got to know the area and many members of the Force and their families by attending social and sporting functions.

A Crime of the Century

On 14th January 1975, exactly 14 days after my taking over my new post, Lesley Whittle, aged 17 years, was reported kidnapped from her home at Highley, Bridgnorth, Shropshire. The unique crime may go down in history as one of the longest police enquiries mounted in Britain, covering a long period of terror created by a ruthless killer. Bob Booth, Detective Chief Superintendent and a large supporting team worked from an Incident Room established at Bridgenorth and throughout 1975 a substantial number of the Force were employed on the enquiry.

On more that one occasion ransom money of £50,000 was demanded and for a variety of reasons aborted. We learned from these operations that we were dealing with a clever elusive criminal who had gone to great lengths to prepare and execute the crime and to escape captivity without leaving evidence which would help us to lead to his identity or place of abode. However, a dymo tape recovered after one of the abortive ransom demands gave a strong indication of his modis operandi which led to the possibility that he had attempted to murder Gerald Arthur Smith by shooting at Dudley in the West Midlands on 15th January 1975.

We compared crimes committed as far back as five years earlier in 1970 at Dewsbury in Yorkshire when premises were burgled and a number of firearms stolen and a large quantity of ammunition. A similar type burglary was carried out at Cheadle Hume, Cheshire in 1971 when again a large number of firearms and ammunition was stolen. It then became apparent that three murders had been committed by the same person when burgling Sub-Post Offices. One was at Harrogate in Yorkshire in 1974. It was deduced from the three murders committed in the course of burglaries that if there was a possibility of the burglar being recognised, he shot them. The confirmation of the same person having committed the crimes mentioned took police no nearer to forming a description of him as there were no witnesses. The burden was shared with the other Forces involved and a continuous exchange of information and liaison resulted.

The West Mercia team was instrumental in tracing the body of Lesley Whittle to a complex underground drainage system in Bathpool Park Kidsgrove, Staffordshire on 7th March, eight weeks after the kidnapping. Many items of evidential value were recovered from the scene of the murder but none of assistance in identifying the culprit. Arthur Rees, Chief Constable of Staffordshire, called in Scotland Yard and Commander John Morrison and a colleague took over at Bathpool Park and dealt with gathering evidence from the scene. The personnel in the other Forces and West Mercia continued as before and shared any grain of information which came to light. We agreed that there was a need to inform the public at large to take precautions and not to intervene in the event of seeing anyone in suspicious circumstances and to inform police.

The kidnapping was being publicised by the Press and television but much of what was publicised was speculative and as the media had dubbed the culprit 'The Black Panther', members of the public were querying police about a black man being wanted. We were of a mind that police on patrol at night were equally or perhaps more so in danger and could well be murdered by shooting if they questioned him. It was agreed by the majority of Forces involved that a BBC radio broadcast be made and it fell to my lot to do so. The emphasis was on the fact that the wanted person was liable to commit crime anywhere in the country. We had no idea what he looked like or from where he came but stressed that everyone should be alert, especially during the hours of darkness.

On 11th December 1975, five years after the commencement of the burglaries, and eleven months after the kidnapping and murder of Lesley Whittle, Donald Neilson was arrested at Mansfield in Nottingham by two alert and brave constables; they were Tony White and Mac MacKenzie. Their suspicions were aroused when they saw a man late one evening carrying a holdall. When questioned he tried to bluff them. They were not satisfied with his answers and in the process of arrest the man fired a shot within a panda car which wounded PC White on the head and on one hand. Fortunately the wounds were not serious. They grappled and overpowered him after a struggle. At the police station his identity was difficult to establish but eventually his correct particulars were obtained and verified. He lived in Leeds Road, Bradford. He was charged with the murders and other serious crimes and was dealt with at Oxford Assize Court and given a number of life sentences which should keep him in custody for the remainder of his life.

We suffered criticism from some sections of the Press, including inaccurate reporting, quoting things said by individual officers out of context and frequently giving the public a completely false impression of police action or lack of action. I think part of the problem was that the Press expected us to report progress or they thought we were keeping information from them. The truth of the matter was that for months there were no developments and therefore no real news to give. The free-lance reporters were completely unreliable and I barred one from entering any of our police stations. Long gone were the days when police could take reporters into their confidence and they adhered to their promises. The local Press throughout the three counties policed by West Mercia were as helpful as ever. It had been a custom to hold a monthly conference open to the Press at Hindlip which had to be cancelled during the Whittle enquiry.

At the conclusion of the trial there was discussion with other officers about whether or not a complaint about the conduct of the Press should be made to the Press Council. At that time the best that could be expected even with the complaint upheld was a brief entry in the newspaper with possibly an apology. I took the view that a formal complaint was not worth the hassle.

After sentence was passed I arranged an open invitation to all Press and television reporters to attend a conference at Hindlip Hall. A large number turned up complete with television cameras and the meeting lasted no more than five minutes. I told them, cap fitting, of how disgusted the police were with their behaviour during the past year and that they ought to be ashamed of themselves. Furthermore, as they could not be trusted there would be no more monthly conferences. I thanked, without mentioning names, those who had been fair-minded. Mr Lewis, then a young television reporter and two other people stood up and upbraided their colleagues, supporting my action. I received one letter of apology from an author for including in his book something I had not said and later I had telephone calls from two different editors with apologies, both thanking me for not making the complaints public. Press relations improved and for the remainder of my service relationship with them was good.

The usual practice in murder cases is to retain the papers and exhibits for unlimited periods of time. In this instance case papers and other materials were spread about in other Forces. In West Mercia we had a cell half full, kept doubly locked, containing thousands of statements and other documents gathered in the course of enquiries. Over the years I had been pressed by journalists, authors and others, including police officers, to give them access to the material, no doubt to write and, hopefully, make money. Some of the information was of a sensitive and highly-confidential nature which was given by people on the promise that it would remain so. I was concerned that on my retirement the information might in course of time reach the public domain. I had been responsible for the assurance of secrecy given so I decided the honourable course was to destroy the material.

The heroes were constables Tony White and Mac Mackenzie of the Nottingham Force. They were invited to a CID Annual Dinner at West Mercia where they were warmly welcomed, applauded and suitably entertained.

Upon amalgamation of the four Forces which was imposed upon the public and the police without reference or consultation, there was much publicity and serious doubts expressed as to the feasibility of the project. One of the worries by members of the public and police was that they might be neglected because of the remoteness arising from the extent of the area, which extended to about 832,690 acres and a distance of over 100 miles from the Cheshire boundary in the north to the Gloucestershire border in the south. Although measures had been introduced to mix personnel to work together and to get to know each other better through social and sporting events, the remoteness and distances slowed the progress a little. Understandably there were some lingering doubts. They were good hardworking officers whose lives had been interrupted, creating uncertainty as to their future.

When the kidnapping occurred the Force was not yet eight years old and was still developing. The enormity of the crime was a challenge. The members of the Force, police officers and civilian staff rose to the occasion, willingly working long hours when the burden was heavy, displaying a determination to deal with the task ahead of them. Personnel from all departments were involved. We would meet at all times of the day and night and we soon got to know each other so much better. Organisations provided us with material help and members of the public were equally supportive, which was good for morale. We could probably have done things differently but I very much doubt if any other course of action would have brought about an earlier result. Hindsight is a wonderful degree to award to the critics. What it did for the West Mercia personnel was noticeable. There was a closing of ranks which united us into a very fine Force.

Increasing the Strength

The next few years took a considerable amount of time and energy in trying, with the full support of the Authority, to get Home Office approval for a realistic establishment of police officers. The ratio of police to members of the public was the lowest in the country and the population was growing by approximately 11,000 per year with the building of the new towns of Telford and Redditch. The workload had also increased with the extension of motorways, necessitating taking officers off beats to man patrol cars. There were restrictions on spending imposed by the Home Office because of the national economic situation. A standard reply, received months after the applications were made, was that the money for the increases had to be found from savings on goods and services. The savings requested were achieved and an application for 49 officers was applied for in 1976. After months and months of protracted negotiations only 20 of the 49 asked for were approved.

The Authority had the money available and a further request was made. I had visits from one of HM Inspectors of Constabulary and regular communication with the Home Office but to no avail except for one additional Superintendent to fill a special post. Eventually the Home Office responded to our application that the balance would not be approved until a review of the Force establishment had taken place. The late Tony Mullett, Assistant Chief Constable, later Chief Constable of the Force, formed a Working Party including members of the Superintendents' Association and representatives of the federated ranks. A Sub-Committee of the Authority considered the review report which recommended an increase of 330 officers, taking the establishment to 2,000 over a period of four years. The report was sent to the Home Office for approval with a request that an immediate increase of 84 be approved. After the usual months of protracted negotiating, approval was refused on the ground that consideration had to be given to the number of divisions and sub-divisions being reduced. To say the members of the Police Authority were annoyed is an understatement.

The refusal was considered by a Sub-Committee of the Authority and it was concluded that the successive conditions were merely a delaying tactic. It was agreed that a deputation including the Chairman, two other members and myself should go to the Home Office and put the case as strongly as possible. In due course we got there and were welcomed by Mr Robert Armstrong CB, CVO Under-Secretary of State of the Police Department at the Home Office. His name was well-publicised years later in connection with the publishing of a book by a former Government employee when it was alleged he had been economical with the truth. Of course it is not unusual for people in public life to be accused of all sorts of things without justification. I know: I have had my share of unfair allegations.

The meeting went on for hours and hours. We kept being served with tea for which we were grateful. We were informed in a number of different ways that the points we were making, which I left very much to the members, were noted and after consideration replies would be sent. We were immovable and there were indications of frustration and irritation from the other side. They had from time to time passed notes to each other and finally the Chairman, directing his words at me, said there was no possibility of my being able to recruit the numbers requested in the current financial year. I made no reply and he then said the request for the 84 officers would be granted for implementation in the current year and the balance of 79 the following financial year. There was a shaking of hands and we left quite happily, well knowing we had overstayed our visit.

I was well aware of the difficulty of recruiting and retaining officers because of the years of low rates of pay. There had been a slight slow down in resignations probably in part owing to the poor economic situation in the country and the imminent publication of a report chaired by The Right Honourable Lord Edmund-Davies, looking into negotiation machinery and police pay, to which the police service was looking forward with great expectations. The low strength of police was a general problem but West Mercia had a high proportion of young officers who required supervision. My concern, in addition to the shortage of manpower, was that many of the supervising officers who had joined the service after the Second World War were now retiring on pension and that although we had good officers in the Force they were not ready in sufficient numbers to replace the wastage and the additional supervisory ranks now approved.

Immediately after returning from the Home Office I explained to my Deputy and Assistants that I intended advertising for supervisory ranks up to the rank of Superintendent. They were good chaps and were doing their best to give me good advice and be helpful by gently advising me that it was a risk which, if effective, would solve lots of problems, but there was the morale of existing personnel to be considered. I had already made up my mind to meet the Superintendents and the representative of the federated ranks and be completely open and honest about my plans. The meetings with those parties went very well and I then as a matter of courtesy informed the Chairman of the Police Authority. He was a businessman: he knew the risks I was taking and he wished me well.

The advertising brought more applications than expected and after enquiries and the usual reference checks with copies of the personal files of those selected for interview, the selections process began. The final result was the recruitment and transfer of 60 officers each on promotion to one rank higher than held in their previous Force and 13 Constables wishing a straightforward transfer. The increase in ranks was five Superintendents, 19 Inspectors and 36 Sergeants making a total of 73. There were also promotions for West Mercia officers who were eligible for promotion and made applications to be considered. One might have expected criticism and reluctance on the part of the original West Mercia officers to embrace the newcomers. Their reception was generous and included the welcoming of families for which I gave my thanks at the time. They settled well, made good progress and they and their families integrated well and became West Mercians. The strategy paid off to the benefit of the people served by West Mercia Police but the Home Office officials were less that impressed.

In the midst of the establishment saga, Sir James Haughton, Chief Inspector of Constabulary whom I knew very well, having served with him on the Police College Staff when we were both Superintendents, came to see me. He had been despatched by the Home Office in an endeavour to persuade me to accept a much lower number of officers than requested. We had a friendly chat and nothing changed. I also had a visit from the Right Honourable Merlyn Rees, MP, Secretary of State. I really owed him an apology for speaking to him the way I did at a police and family occasion when we were meeting Her Majesty The Queen. He was following the Queen, after introductions, and as he was approaching his usual address was something of the order of being happy in the service. I could not resist saying that a lot of things needed to be done to improve the situation and make us happier. He asked me questions and said he would look into the matter. I should have apologised for my ungentlemanly conduct in raising the subject in the wrong place and on such an occasion, but I was too slow and the moment passed.

When he came to Hindlip by himself, it was my intention to make a belated apology but he stopped me and explained that he had the greatest difficulty in getting to know what was happening in the Service. We spent several hours together. He asked many questions and displayed a genuine interest in the work of the Force. On parting he thanked me for bringing the problems to his attention and expressed satisfaction with the way the Force was managed. His final remarks were that he was sympathetic and would do his best to help, but added that he had very little influence as the Treasury had the last word. He was most understanding and from time to time when we met I enjoyed his company.

The policy in West Mercia was that Traffic Patrol officers dealt with all aspects of police work, and in 1977/78 the department made 1,400 arrests for a whole variety of crimes and offences. The fleet at that time was well above 400 vehicles, 99 of them being on road patrol work. Most of them were supplied by the Longbridge Plant, Birmingham. Patrol cars have to carry heavy loads made up of radios, batteries, emergency lighting, road signs and that sort of equipment. The problem was that the vehicles were not built to carry heavy equipment and on average gear boxes or half-shafts gave way at about

12,000 miles. Continued representation to Longbridge resulted in the replacement parts being supplied free of charge but that was not a solution. We had to employ additional mechanics to cope with the extra maintenance work and to have a large reserve of vehicles, which was costly. The worst feature was that on some occasions the vehicle broke down when they were on a pursuit task which was most embarrassing.

Motor manufacturers were keen to let us have vehicles for unlimited periods on trial. Finally the most suitable and reliable car at that time was a BMW, which was kept on patrol virtually full-time for six months and stood up to the hard work better than any of the others we put through their paces. A strict check on the running costs compared to the vehicles we were using showed savings of one penny per mile on running costs. Longbridge had been kept abreast of the trial and pleaded with us to continue to purchase from that source but declined to guarantee improvements. I realised that the purchase of non-British vehicles would create a great deal of adverse publicity and took the precaution of advising Mr Harry Purcell CBE, Chairman of the Police Authority, of my intentions.

The custom had been for the Chief Constable to choose the make of vehicles for use by the Force, this being regarded as an operational decision. He thanked me for reminding him, which was just as well because when the news broke he and other members of the Authority were inundated with questions and criticism. The news media had a field day and wanted to know the costs involved which were kept confidential for a meeting of the Authority. The BMW Company were keen to sell cars to the police. No other forces in the country had, so far, purchased their vehicles. It was apparent we would get a good deal and eventually I negotiated with the representative in charge of the United Kingdom sales organisation. The stage was reached that if the price was acceptable I would place an order forthwith for the supply of 27 patrol cars for delivery as and when required during that current financial year. It was obvious that the size of the order was beyond his expectations and he said he would speak to me as soon as he had consulted BMW in Germany. The final price reached was much better than I had anticipated.

The conditions were that the vehicles would be delivered on transporters with zero mileage and fully-equipped for police work with pre-use servicing completed. The contract was honoured to the letter and the service engineers arrived by helicopter, unloaded the cars and checked them before handing them over. The vehicles stood up to the hard work without a problem. For some considerable time, my postbag was overflowing, mainly from trade union people, alleging among other things that I was a traitor and should be sacked for purchasing foreign cars. My drawing attention to the fact that we were now Europeans was glossed over and it was frequently pointed out that I had made a grave mistake. I survived.

The savings made enabled the number of patrol cars to be reduced, the communications system to be updated and other technical requirements installed. A few more policemen were added to the strength and over a number of years the savings to the public was substantial. There came a time when I got a pat or two on the back!

In negotiating for approval of finance with the Home Office there were occasions when it was implied that because we were a largely rural area there was not a lot for police to do! What was not acknowledged was that being the largest land-locked Force in the country we were subject to criminal attacks from all sides. There were a large number of estate and mansion-type dwellings containing high-value belongings which were a continual target for small highly organised gangs and also raids on business premises.

A typical example of one of these was a raid on the main sorting office of the Worcester City Post Office, for which we were well-prepared. Armed police were secreted in the building, one of whom received injuries from a firearm from one of the raiders. Fortunately he was not seriously wounded. Five of the six criminals, all the way from Liverpool, were arrested at the scene and a record of their actions made on video. The sixth man, the lookout on the outside, got away on the night but was known to the police.

There were also burglaries and breakings by criminals living within the area. There were frequent cases of violence. Juvenile crime was increasing and the misuse of drugs was taking place even in country villages. The extensive mileage was time-consuming and costly and road accidents were high.

During my six years in office, there were 37 formal Royal visits and two Maundy Money ceremonies, one at Worcester Cathedral and the other at Hereford Cathedral. A lot of unseen work went into planning and preparations for Royal visits, ensuring adequate safety measures were taken. There were always people wanting publicity or with a grudge, and one or two prepared physically to attack and injure members of Royalty. They had to be identified ahead of the timing of events, sometimes at the last moments, as they could be very determined and turn up in all sorts of disguises. There was never an occasion when the proceedings were interrupted by their presence or any of the Royal Party being exposed to personal danger. Our policy in dealing with them was perhaps a little unorthodox: our plain clothes staff would pick them up quietly and they would be taken to the nearest police station and asked innumerable questions, probably quite irrelevant, to keep them there until the conclusion of the Royal visit. They were usually very much annoyed as they would have preferred to be charged with offences, however minor, as their intention was to seek publicity for their believed causes. We had plenty of work and at times were stretched to the limit.

Getting Out and About

I tried to get out and about in the Force area, driving myself and paying informal visits to police stations as much as time would allow. The operational books and records in the front offices were readily available and I would have a look at them, but my equally important objective was to get to know the cadets, the civilian staff and officers on the front line. A lot can be learned by talking to people and providing the opportunity for them to make suggestions for improving procedures. The visits were useful in assessing if people were reasonably happy with their lot and capable of giving of their best. Now and again action had to be taken if there were round pegs in square holes, and in the event of neglect of matters, strong and immediate action taken. Supervisory duties cannot be smiles all the time!

On the whole the visits were pleasant and re-assuring. I can recall a Welshman, a constable who had quite a lot of service and because of a permanent injury was given charge of the front office, responsible for dealing with callers, prisoners' care and recording accurate entries in the various documents provided. Any time I called he was smiling and would immediately produce the records and challenge me with opening them up at any place I wished, assuring me that I would be unable to find any faults. He was a wonderful policeman with the personality and charm to deal with people who needed help and to put troublemakers in their place.

I would be in civilian clothes on these visits and quietly slip into a Magistrates' Court and take a seat alongside the public and listen to a constable giving evidence or an Inspector prosecuting a case. I believed I learned a great deal more than I would with formal inspections for which people would have been specially briefed for the occasion. I also took the opportunity to call upon the many Magistrates' Clerks spread about the extensive area and other people in public life. It was much easier knowing them to find solutions to minor problems and misunderstandings. It can be a lonely place out on sites in charge of serious crime investigations and paying visits and discussing all aspects of cases was welcomed and eased the pressures a little.

One resolution I kept was not to be office-bound. The volume of paperwork, reading reports, interviewing officers and dealing with members of the public was never-ending. Fortunately I could deal with these matters fairly quickly, which gave me more time to concentrate on recruiting and promotion boards. The service stands or falls by the quality of the personnel and therefore the selection of recruits and the promotion of personnel was high on my list of responsibilities.

There was of course a flow of persistent letter-writers who wanted to see me and others who expected me to call upon them at their bidding. Here is an example of a solicitor who lost the appeal against a decision I made to revoke a firearms licence. He was refused on appeal at court at which I gave evidence. He thought that the court should have insisted on my being represented and that I had been favoured because I was the Chief Constable. His complaints went on for over two years with different suggestions and variations in an endeavour to have the Firearms Certificate renewed. I acknowledged all his letters, writing politely and briefly. Eventually he submitted a large volume of paperwork in the form of a review with his usual pleas for me to change my mind. My reply placed centrally on a large letter form simply read 'NOTED'. His reply was 'VERY WELL' which was the last I heard from him.

Another difficult chap was a newly-elected Local Authority councillor. Having made repeated promises in his electioneering addresses that he would get five more policemen on the beat in this quite small town, he called the following morning and demanded that the local Sub-Divisional Inspector put the five promised policemen on the beat forthwith. Eventually the problem was diverted to Headquarters and he made demands for me to visit him at a time and place he stipulated. Stella, my secretary, experienced in dealing with difficult people, eventually got through to him that if he wished to see me it would be by appointment at a mutually-convenient time and date.

The day arrived. I was in uniform and I asked him to explain why he wanted to see me. He commenced full flow that he was a councillor and was entitled to have the five additional police officers as promised and he also produced the names and addresses of several local people against whom he alleged the police were taking proceedings or had arrested. I explained it was impossible to accede to his requests and I showed him the Act and Section of the Police Act which laid down my responsibilities. There was no appeasing him and he finally asked what information I was prepared to give him, saying that if I did not do so he was going to write to the Home Secretary. Time was passing; he had no intention of leaving, explaining that he would lose face in the community if his promises were not fulfilled. I finally explained to him that he was not entitled to any more information than the chap who swept the roadway outside my house, adding that he and I were friends and often had a chat. He disappeared out of my office more quickly than he had arrived, vowing all sorts of vengeance.

Some time later I was at a cocktail party on an occasion the late Queen Mother was meeting Senior Police Officers. The late Willie Whitelaw MP, a delightful chap, was present and said something to the effect, "Alex, it is good to know you have some bright road sweepers to look after you." We had a laugh and I heard no more from the councillor!

Keeping the Peace

Refresher courses are essential to keep police officers up-to-date with new legislation and changing procedures. I believe it equally important now and again to draw attention to the solemn and sincere declaration which all officers are required to make on being appointed to the office of constable. The Declaration is as follows:

> "I do solemnly and sincerely declare and affirm that I will well and truly serve our Sovereign Lady the Queen in the Office of Constable, without fear or affectation, malice or ill will, that I will to the best of my power cause the peace to be kept and preserved and prevent all offences against the persons and properties of Her Majesty's subjects, and that while I continue to hold the said office I will to the best of my skill and knowledge discharge all the duties thereof faithfully according to law."

Keeping the peace involves having to deal with a wide range of incidents and on occasion a great deal of preparatory work behind the scenes. The two items to which I now refer are examples of the more unusual type of incident which arise from time to time.

For a number of years there was considerable disruption to life and damage to property by politically-dissatisfied people in Wales. One of the actions alleged to have been committed by them was in putting out of use with explosives the main water supply from Wales to

Birmingham. The explosion was within the Birmingham City boundary but the supply piping runs through many miles of Shropshire and Worcestershire, the policing of which is the responsibility of West Mercia Police. The timing coincided with planning for the Investiture of Prince Charles to be the 21st Prince of Wales, at Carnaervon Castle on 1st July 1969. Army Air Corps helicopters with police observers based in Shropshire patrolled the length of the pipe line, including Carnaervon, 24 hours a day up to and for some time after the Investiture. Fortunately there were no problems.

Another unusual duty, classified top secret, West Mercia performed in conjunction with the SAS was to provide a rapid response to deal with the threats of attacks from terrorists occurring anywhere in the country. A contingent of the SAS, based at Hereford, was put on stand-by and in the event of a call out, a West Mercia patrol car would lead the way at high speed to the scene of the incident. Police officers taught the SAS drivers high-speed driving and exercises were practised, usually at night time. At least one patrol car with a crew of two had to be permanently within a few minutes' call of Hereford.

Occasionally during these exercises, West Mercia received calls from other police areas demanding to know why speed limits and other traffic signs were not being observed. Every force had a code word which should have explained the purpose of the exercises but because of the emphasis on the secrecy of the plan, they were not always made available to operational control staff. Most senior police officers were of the opinion that the high level of secrecy was unnecessary but the Cabinet Office was adamant on the matter, believing the knowledge if made public would create panic in the community. After a number of years of these exercises continuing all was revealed when the Metropolitan Police in conjunction with the SAS dealt effectively with the siege at the Iranian Embassy in London. Of course there was no panic by members of the public who I believe would have been surprised if preparations were not in hand to deal with such eventualities.

The most distasteful duty I had to perform was dealing formally with officers on disciplinary charges. Provided the breaches of duty were not of a serious nature my preference was for good strong advice and if there was a repetition there was no place for them in the organisation. Serving officers were well aware that any misconduct involving any form of dishonesty would lead to the sack and, on the rare occasions those situations arose, resignations were usually submitted in advance of hearings. There was a saying in Aberdeenshire where I grew up that if someone did you a dishonest or unjust turn you blamed that person. If he repeated the deed, you blamed yourself.

The policy to which I had been accustomed throughout my service was that every supervising officer had the responsibility, from the rank of sergeant and upwards, of taking care of those under their command, including the families. Officers in day-to-day touch with each other were quick to realise if things were going wrong and could take immediate action to remedy situations or to pass the problem up the line and if needs be use specialist people to help. In the case of those suffering regular bouts of sickness the Police Surgeon would if necessary call in a specialist and deal with the problem, improving the life of long-term sufferers.

All sickness reports were recorded at Headquarters and I personally scrutinised the returns on a weekly basis. In the case of those terminally-ill I would consult the medical people looking after them and call upon them at their home or in hospital. It was in the best interests of the families that I got to know them well and to establish complete trust with them. It takes time and patience to lead up to the point when you have to advise a dying man to submit his resignation, the purpose of which is to provide his wife and family with an improved pension.

There were two such cases during my time as a Chief Constable. One young man, cheerful to the end, still clung on hopefully to life and after spending a whole final evening with him at his home I had to virtually push a pen in his hand to get him to sign his resignation which I had brought with me. It was late when I arrived home. On getting to the office in the morning I learned that he had died soon after midnight. I had accepted his resignation by timing, dating and endorsing the document about a couple of hours before he died. The other case I dealt with was less prolonged: the officer was in constant severe pain and wished to die.

The Home Office via HM Inspectors of Constabulary was pedalling the idea that all Forces should establish a civilian welfare department, in the belief that the volume of early resignations might be reduced. We did not have a welfare department as such but we did record the reasons for officers resigning. With rare exceptions the reasons were that they could earn more money in other occupations. Research and liaison with other Forces indicated the trend was for welfare departments to maintain confidentiality to the extent that supervising officers were excluded from personal problems. I believe that there should be complete trust between officers and their supervisors and rejected the suggestion of a formal department on the grounds that we were adequately organised to deal with the sickness and material needs.

We also catered for the development and fitness of our cadets by arranging Outward Bound Courses from our base at Bishops Castle, with highly-qualified instructors and we included apprentices and other young people from outside the Force to join in the courses thus providing mind-broadening experience. A full-time qualified physical training instructor, with combined duties of Sports Officer, raised the fitness level during residential courses and encouraged sporting activities at which the Force excelled.

Throughout the area officers, usually in their own time, helped to run Youth Clubs. We took this a step further when we invited twelve boys and twelve girls aged 12-14 years from Northern Ireland at the height of the IRA activities. The arrangements were made with the Royal Ulster Constabulary and the 24 included twelve Roman Catholics and twelve Protestants. They were assembled at our Outward Bound base at Bishops Castle where they spent two weeks. The officers looking after them gave of their time free and others contributed to the cost. One might have thought that there would be some show of gratitude for the manner in which they were fed, clothed and trained, but the obstacle was the religious barrier and the close imaginary walls made integration and complete freedom for enjoyment difficult. We hoped the experience might be helpful to them in later life.

During 1980 considerable time was spent on advisory work in an endeavour to prevent children and young people running away from home. It was therefore disappointing that there was a high rise in the numbers during that year. The trend caused me concern and I included the following item in my Annual Report.

"A disturbing feature is the increase in the number of persons missing from home, an increase over the previous year of 973 to a total of 2,856. When persons are reported missing from home it causes the police considerable concern and involves a tremendous amount of work. It also causes anguish within families, especially when the missing persons are of a tender age. In course of time the majority are traced or turn up of their own accord. Some, however, become the victims of crime and many become involved in crime, especially the young. This situation reflects a sad state of affairs in society. Crime and kindred offences by young people are on the increase leading to demands for police to take on additional responsibilities in the education and training of young people. There is a limit to police involvement in preventing youngsters getting into trouble. What is readily apparent is that in many instances where children and young people go missing, or have to be dealt with by police, there has been a breakdown in the relationship within the family unit. If society wishes to make progress in halting this trend there is a need for parents to make sacrifices by spending more time with their younger children, by talking to them and joining in their activities. No outside agency is competent to provide the advice, guidance and activities essential to the development of a healthy society. This, in my view, can only be achieved by caring and responsible parents."

A Family Force

West Mercia had developed into very much a family Force. Each of the territorial divisions, sub-divisions, sections and departments arranged dinner dances, concerts, whist drives and a whole variety of events, including an active Police Choir. They were wonderful occasions for the families to get to know each other and members of the public. The Christmas parties for children and families were long remembered. On such occasions the wide variety of the background of policemen came to the fore and brought out entertainment and talent which was enjoyed. There was an Officers' Mess for the ranks of Inspector and above. We met occasionally for dinners and entertained a few guests. Hogmanay Parties at Hindlip for senior officers and their ladies were well patronised. The high-quality catering was in the capable hands of Gwen Parkes, the Records Office and helpers, whilst Geoff Parkes, Superintendent, worked hard and did a first class job of organising. Each division had a club where billiards and games were played and alcoholic drinks were available. They were popular places to celebrate retirements, promotions and a host of other events.

It was my custom to meet Barrie Florentine, the Deputy, and Tony Mullett and Alan Vickers, the two Assistants, on Monday mornings for coffee, if not otherwise engaged, and get updated on anything that had happened over the weekend as well as dealing with the known forthcoming events for the week. My door was always open and some weeks we would see quite a lot of each other, but the intention was for the four of us to have the freedom to get on with our specific responsibilities. Late on Friday afternoon we would meet again in my office and clear up any outstanding matters and deal with plans to cover the weekend activities. During our discussions we would finish off the week's work with one glass of gin and bitter lemon, or a glass of whisky with a little water. It was a simple system which worked well.

Lucy contributed as much to the social side of life as I did and it was rare for us to have to decline invitations to dinner dances and other functions. We enjoyed the friendliness: we would dance half the night, having travelled long journeys with a driver to and from the functions which I regarded as an important part of my duties.

For Royal visits, Lord Lieutenants of whichever of the three counties involved would make the detailed arrangements with the police and the reception party would include the Lord Lieutenant and his Lady, supported by one or two selected gentlemen with their ladies and Lucy and myself in accordance with Royal protocol. On occasions when the member of the Royalty was likely to be accosted and addressed outside of the formal arrangements, the reception party was useful in forming a screen and unobtrusively discouraging interruptions. There were now and again persistent busy-bodies who were taken care of without fuss by the plain-clothes officers hovering in the background. We had the privilege of meeting, dining and attending functions as part of the Royal Party.

The Lord Lieutenant, his Lady, Lucy and I were present to see Royalty leaving and on the point of departure we were thanked with a little chat for our services. HRH the Duke of Edinburgh would jokingly have a dig at me for using foreign cars. I would defend myself replying that BMW cars were European. On an occasion when he was met after a helicopter flight we used a British Leyland car to convey him. A half-shaft broke and he had to be hurriedly placed into a BMW car which was on reserve. He sought me out and said I had proved my point and we had a laugh. HRH Princess Anne, of whom we saw quite a lot, and her father obviously discussed cars and she told me she tried to use the half-shaft incident to allow her to use a car from an overseas country, but without success.

HRH Princess Anne
It was always a pleasure escorting Royalty.

In my sixth year at Hindlip, I began to realise that Lucy's health was deteriorating. We had come a long way together and I had no hesitation in deciding to retire on pension. The Chairman and Members of the Authority pressed me to stay on and it was suggested as the Force was in good shape they would be quite happy for me to take life easier. It was a kind and generous offer which was appreciated but it was not for me. I had been a workaholic all my life and knew I could not change my ways.

Among other things upon my retirement, it was written in the Force Magazine:

"An indomitable and fearless fighter on behalf of the Force, Mr Rennie has managed to achieve more for West Mercia in six short years as Chief Constable than many a lesser man could achieve in a lifetime. His personal courage and insistence upon the highest of professional standards have been a lesson to us all, whilst his loyalty to those he commanded, police and civilian staff alike, will ensure for him the measure of respect and affection he deserves. He and his charming wife, Lucy, will continue to live in Droitwich and we hope they will enjoy together a long and happy retirement."

With Alex and Lucy at the Palace to receive my CBE in 1980

In the days leading up to my retirement on 23rd January 1981 we were invited to a series of police function throughout the area. We were overwhelmed by the warmth of our welcomes and the special arrangements made to entertain us in a manner to match our individual personalities. We were made to feel part of a large family, long to be remembered.

Upon retirement I received a pleasing invitation from the Scottish National Portrait Gallery, Edinburgh, to provide a portrait or photograph from life to place in the archives of distinguished Scots from about 1560 to the present day. I feel proud to have been included in such august company.

Preparation for Retirement

By the time I was Chief Constable we had lived in over 20 dwellings of varying standards, most tied to the job. We had a good idea of the sort of places we did not wish to live in and after much thought decided on a bungalow. There were none on the market to our liking in Droitwich where we wanted to live and we eventually purchased a half-acre site with planning permission to build a four-bedroomed bungalow. The contract included the services of an architect, but as his experience was limited to erecting factories, his services were dispensed with.

We set about planning it ourselves and with a ball of string and pegs began the lay-out on the lawn at Tibberton where we lived. In summer evenings, much to the amusement and interest of our good neighbours, we adjusted and re-adjusted the pegs and twine until we were satisfied with the result. The next step was to transpose the measurements into detailed plans. I borrowed technical books from the library, from which I learned to write the comprehensive specifications. A reputable builder accepted the contract and it was agreed there was no need to employ a clerk of work or an architect.

Building work commenced: the foundations were partly laid in accordance with the approved plans and confirmed by the local authority building inspector who was most helpful. At this stage the tree preservation officer came on the scene and ordered the pouring of concrete to be stopped. He wanted the foundations to be re-sited because of a large old lime tree. The building inspector argued that the original approved plans had been complied with but he was overruled. The amended site actually brought the foundations closer to the lime tree and made passage to one side of the double garage difficult to access. Because of the possibility of the lime tree roots under-mining the building, the amended foundations stipulated re-enforced concrete.

The lime tree was shedding leaves and light branches and as I believed the tree was dying I appealed to the Wychaven Council to have it felled. The application was refused. I then engaged two independent tree specialists, both of whom provided comprehensive reports recommending the tree be felled because of its dangerous condition. A further appeal was refused.

A bit of light relief away from the building hassles

In the meantime the bungalow was completed and we were in occupation. One evening we arrived home to find a substantial 30-foot limb had fallen from the tree across the drive. According to the law I was required to fell the tree forthwith because it was now indisputably a danger. I advised the local authority what had occurred and engaged a tree surgeon to cut the tree down. The tree preservation officer wanted me to have the rotten limbs removed rather than have the tree felled but I refused to comply with his request. My action, though perfectly legal, was unpopular and almost immediately we were served with an order under penalty, to plant a replacement mature tree on the identical site of the old tree. I was convinced that a new tree would not survive on the identical site and informed the local authority of my opinion, coupled with an offer to supply and plant up to five saplings in a public place of their choice. The peace offering was not even acknowledged.

My final appeal was to the Secretary of State whose officers over-ruled the local authority in a scathing report. During the years of dispute with the local authority we had many letters of support and sympathy from people who knew the true situation and who had similar problems. We also had criticism from people obsessed with tree preservation irrespective of the condition of the tree and when invited to the site ignored the invitations. There was regular Press coverage which culminated on 17th June 1982 with the headline, 'APPEAL ENDS TREE SAGA'.

The reader might think we had been singled out by the local authority for special treatment but the late Gwylam Rhys, Chief Planning Officer, who lived nearby, was not immune from the indiscriminate policy of tree preservation. Shortly after our appeal was allowed, a large dying tree situated in an unoccupied site, adjacent to where Mr Rhys lived and was under a preservation order, fell and damaged his garden fence, wrecking a family car.

In the meantime we had many messages of thanks for our endeavours. Apparently a measure of common sense was applied, applications being decided on their merits, rather than the policy of blanket enforcement. Although we were being credited with having some influence on the changed policy, the problems experienced by Mr Rhys were probably taken into account. When pressure of this kind arises it is good to be thankful for living in a democracy.

The farewell by the Police Authority was held at the conclusion of a full Authority meeting at Hindlip Hall. It was the practice for the members to have lunch after the meetings. On this occasion Lucy, my Deputy, the two Assistants and their ladies were invited. The Members presented us with a gift which was provided by them as private individuals. There were the usual speeches and in the distance I heard the sound of the bagpipes approaching. In marched a piper in full Highland Dress! We drank each others' health with the correct spirit, and on resuming piping, he marched off. It was a thoughtful surprise which brought tears to my eyes. In past years when moving from one situation to another, I had been bidden farewell in a whole variety of ways. This occasion was different: it was my last place of work and unforgettable.

Nearly 45 years had passed since I looked after working horses, as well as doing other farm work, during which time never in my wildest dreams had I expected to reach one of the 43 top police posts in the country. I was not ambitious but I liked things to be in order. I was fortunate in being given the opportunities to serve in every department in the police service by the senior officers it was my privilege to serve. Equally I wish to thank the many officers for whom I was responsible for their support and loyalty: without that, advancement would have been impossible. The final prize, West Mercia Constabulary, was worth the study and work involved.

THANK YOU ALL!

Alex A Rennie CBE, OStJ, QPM, MiD

What Next?

It was unthinkable to do nothing. Lucy was a keen swimmer and when at home went to the baths in the mornings with friends. Over the years I had played a little golf when time permitted but was far from proficient at the game. Others on retirement were very much in the same situation and we met regularly and had fun. Lucy and I had always enjoyed hill walking so we spent time on the Malvern Hills and the Long Mynd in Shropshire. A few hours of walking in the fresh air followed by a pub lunch was good for us.

I was invited by a newly-formed Probus Club, the first in Droitwich, named The Probus Club of Droitwich Spa, to become a member. The task of arranging outings and lunches fell to me and we used to reconnoitre for suitable venues. Lucy checked the toilets, we ate different meals and if we found the place to our taste we would negotiate substantial discounts for coach loads of members and their ladies. I gave talks to Probus and other clubs, making new friends.

We also spent a lot of time on holidays in most European countries, the United States of America and Canada. We stayed in Belize, where our son was in charge of an army unit and where we explored the country as well as spending time in Mexico. We visited Rhodesia and later South Africa. One trip was by Royal Mail Ship, *St Helena*, which was part goods and part passengers, with a swimming pool. We stopped at the Ascension Island and St Helene where we spent about ten days enjoying the place and the hospitality of the people during which time the ship took passengers and goods to other islands. On return we sailed for Cape Town where we met our daughter and subsequently travelled to her home at Pietermaritzburg in the province of Natal.

Lucy's 80th Birthday – Droitwich 1996
Standing: Philip Arnold, Jill and Alex Rennie,
Andrew and Faiza Rennie with their daughter Murrium, Lester, Sue and Cimmie.
Sitting: Claire Arnold and son Daniel, Lucy, Alex and Margaret.

Keeping busy was not only interesting and enjoyable but was intended and, I believe, helpful to Lucy in slowing down the onset of Alzheimers Disease from which she had been suffering for several years. Gradually the time came when I was fully occupied in looking after her and eventually the only course was for her was to go into a care home. Her general health is good and she is not suffering. She still knows me and I visit regularly but feel helpless as there is not much I can do for her to improve her quality of life. When it was apparent there was no possibility of her returning to our home to live, I sold the bungalow and bought a flat in Droitwich. It is one of about 30. The House Manager does a first-class job in keeping the place going. I look after myself, doing the cooking, the laundry and personal chores. The company is good: we have a communal lounge where we meet and arrange social functions. My minor contribution to the house is to arrange an occasional fish and chip night!

During the first year I was on my own I felt rather lost and spent too much time alone but I gradually realised it was not good for me and I had to be more outgoing and active. I was encouraged by my many friends in the Probus Club and especially the positive actions by my ex-police colleagues. They take me out; all former ranks are involved – we have lunches together and I attend functions which they arrange. We have fun and at present I am trying to teach two of them how to enjoy malt whisky! Barrie Florentine spends an afternoon with me most weeks and we enjoy a gin and tonic together. I have become the unofficial travel agent for friends at Rowan Court. We get about on coach holidays: we have visited various places in England and Scotland with a brief trip to France and we are currently looking forward to going to Eire. Now and again I get chastised for referring to other flat dwellers as 'inmates'.

None of my family lives near me but I have regular telephone calls from those living overseas as well as those living in the United Kingdom and also see them now and again. There are eleven great-grandchildren and I am kept up to date on the progress of them all. I have been fortunate to have been born with a strong constitution and profound memory and to have so far knocked hell out of a police pension for over 27 years.

Throughout my life I have been a celiac, bringing with it moments of discomfort and embarrassment, and it was not until I was 60 years of age that the condition was diagnosed. There is no cure but the diet prescribed, if adhered to, provides relief. The medical people on learning of my background informed me that in the 1930s it was a condition which would have debarred me from becoming a policeman and from military service!

We need a bit of luck in life. My share has been generous. I still find life, most times, rewarding, with lots of fun and interest.

Cheers!
Author with Eric Beaver in 2007

Appendix
Family Album

Alex

Margaret

Policewoman Claire Arnold with honours from her Passing Out Parade April 1990. Pictured with her father Alex, grandmother Lucy, husband Philip, mother Jill and grandfather Alex.

Claire and Philip with Daniel, Natty and Ben

Andrew and Faiza with Murrium, Zaina and Henna

The Australian Contingent
Paul, Lester and Cimmie

Tobie, Brooke, Kiernan, Clio and Chloe